Journey to Truth

by
Denie Hiestand

Journey to Truth
ISBN # 0-9684928-0-0

By Denie Hiestand
Copyright 1999 All rights reserved.
Printed in Canada.
Cover Art by Alex Grey
Design and Printing by Scribe Graphics Inc. (250) 480-4000

First Edition published as **Back to Life**, ISBN #1-57901-019-9
by Promotion Publishing 1997. Sold out, March 1999.
Revised, updated, reformatted, recovered and republished in June
1999 as:

Journey to Truth

by ShellDen Publishing,
101-1001, W Broadway #341,
Vancouver B.C. V6H 4E4 Canada.
and
ShellDen Publishing, PMB 654,
15600 NE 8th St. B1,
Bellevue WA. 98008. U.S.A.

Warning - Disclaimer

The author, endorsers, distributors, retailers, or anyone else associated with this book shall have neither liability nor responsibility to anyone with respect to loss or damage caused, or alleged to be caused, directly or indirectly, by the information or practices contained in this book. Please consult your physician, trained medical personnel or health practitioner regarding any of the activities or healing methods described in this book.

DEDICATION

To my three wonderful children:
Mark, Craig and Karen and their incredible,
wonderful mother, Denise.
You walked the path with me, sometimes
hurting, sometimes laughing, but always loving
and trying to understand.
I thank you all for choosing to share that part of
your lives with me.
I am loving you always.

ACKNOWLEDGMENTS

To all those wonderfully loving women who shared their hearts with me, so that I could find mine and allowing me to grow and mature into my present beingness. Thank you.

To Margaret Pinyan in Sedona, Arizona, for encouraging me to start writing and agreeing to edit the first draft, even before pen went to paper. Margaret, a friend like you makes life worth living. Thank you from the depths of my heart.

To Robert Shapiro, channel, outer-worlds communicator extraordinaire and friend. I agree Robert, why words, when it only slows down the conversation.

To Cile Menaugh, who deciphered my longhand and typed up the early chapters in Collingwood, Arizona.

To my daughter Karen, who loaded the first few chapters into my little Compaq Aero back in New Zealand and at the same time persevered in teaching me to use it. Thank you Karen, I have finally become friends with baby Compaq and am now almost computer literate.

To Dr. Kim Kimball, whose help, faith and encouragement enabled this to be printed.

Throughout this story I will at times change names and certain details, but the essence of the experience will always remain.

Any inference or reference to any person, living or dead, other than my immediate family, is purely coincidental and unintentional.

TABLE OF CONTENTS

INTRODUCTION

This is a story of transformation - my transformation from childhood on a New Zealand dairy farm through all the inner struggles, rejections, denial, anger, pain and hurt to my acceptance, at last, of myself and my life. My struggle with life and living has at times been almost too much to handle. Yet always, at the most critical emotional time, I was pulled back from the brink as if some overlord could sense that I could not take any more.

Each time I broke through that emotional brick wall, I gained a new and increased understanding of life and myself. I can now at last laugh at myself for putting up such an incredible resistance to the changes that occurred. Yes, God, You really had a tough one in me. Thank You for not giving up.

Being a male, it was more difficult, I think, to accept that feelings are more important than thinking when it comes to looking at yourself. Many men have incredible difficulty in even recognizing their feelings, let alone following them. This Western society we live in has become so cerebral, so mind-dominant, that it is difficult indeed to break away and be free to feel, to come from the heart, to grow as a divine being, to realize that we all have a God-given right to be free within ourselves and not be trapped by our emotions, the need for money and possessions, or even, life itself.

If, as a result of my story, just one person is able to break out of the shackles of inner struggle and realize and rejoice in their divine beingness, then all the effort will have been worthwhile.

CHAPTER 1
JUST ME

Winging my way northeast across the Pacific on a big United jumbo into a clear summer night, I remember thinking, when would the next weird thing happen? If only I had known how soon, I probably would not have gotten on that plane.

Our tour party was due to land at Hawaii and spend a week with Joan Ocean swimming with the dolphins. As I had never been there, I was looking forward to the stop.

Letting my thoughts drift on toward Hawaii as I tried to sleep after dinner had been served, an urge came over me to get up and move to the smoking section at the back of the plane. Finding an empty seat next to the aisle, I sat down.

Next to me was a young man, no more than sixteen or seventeen, part Maori, well-built and appearing to look fit and strong. I remember thinking that I used to be that fit once.

We acknowledged each other and I said that I had come back for a quick smoke. Reaching into his shirt pocket, he produced a packet and offered me one. Drawing hard and long on the Marlborough, I felt the nicotine do its thing and relaxed into the seat. Thanking him, I went on to ask him the usual, like where was he going etc., and for the next half hour or so we passed the time in small talk.

Slowly drawing on a second cigarette with my thoughts to myself, I became aware of what sounded like soft sobbing. Turning to look at my new friend, I found to my surprise that he was indeed crying. The young man had told me he was a sheep shearer on his way to the U.S. with a contract shearing gang. Young, fit, tough, macho "real men" usually typifies shearers and, as we all know, "real men" do not cry. Well this one sure was, and it was for real.

Taken aback, it took me a moment or two to collect myself. Leaning close to him, in a half whisper I asked if he was all right.

"It's terrible," he whispered, "so much pain."

"Are you in pain?" I asked.

"No, no," he answered, "the Earth, our mother."

Now that got my attention. Either this guy was nuts or he was able to tune into the Earth's energies. So I asked him what he meant, what was he feeling. Had this happened before?

What happened next was astonishing. He proceeded to tell me that nothing like this had ever happened before and he apologized for crying. I told him to not to worry about it and that I had also experienced this sort of thing. I went on to tell him he should tell me everything, because it was okay and I would understand. (Well, I hoped I would, anyhow.)

I must have made him feel a bit better and more at ease, because he stopped crying and appeared more in control as he went on to tell me that when I came down and sat next to him he was feeling fine. Sometime during our second smoke, he was overwhelmed with sadness and grief, and all of a sudden he felt the presence of his ancestors (being of Maori blood, the spiritual/ancestral connection would have been a part of his upbringing).

"The old ones, the ancestors, started to talk to me in my head," he said.

"They want me to say things to you that I don't understand. I'm scared, I don't know what to do."

I told him it was okay to feel like that. Most people do the first time the spirit world talks to them.

"You know all about this?" he asked, a surprised expression magnifying his face.

"Yes, sure," I said, "but carry on, tell me what they say. You don't have to know what they are talking about. It's me who needs to understand what they are saying to you. You just say what they tell you without trying to make sense out of it. Just speak it as it comes."

"Okay," he said, "I'll try."

My young friend relaxed into his seat, paused, then leaned closer and slowly started to talk in a hushed whisper.

"Our Mother (Earth) is hurting. You are being asked to help. You have been guided to be here at this time because this is what you have been trained for. You have answered the call to help mankind. You are the chosen one. Do not be afraid, you can do what is about to be asked of you, we will be with you at all times. This is only a start; your life will take many different turns, to many different places. Just trust in your heart and follow the prompting, your intuition. Do not worry about your life, everything will be given to you for you to do this work. We are loving you, you are held in the highest regard from this, our reality.

You are going to the Big Island (I was on my way to the island of Hawaii, often referred to as the "Big Island," but I had not mentioned this to my young friend), and we ask of you to help Mother balance a large buildup of negative energy. Be open to your intuition and we will guide you.

It is most important that this work is done at this time, because the buildup of energy in the Mother's skin (the crust of the earth) will cause many severe movements and violent releases [volcanic eruptions?]. Many of your fellow humankind have asked through their prayers and meditations that the Mother be helped to release this negative energy in the least destructive way. This may not always be possible, but for now it is possible with your help. We honor and bless you. You will be protected."

There was a long period of silence before I realized that he had finished giving me the message from his ancestors. I just sat there in stunned silence, oblivious to the other three hundred or so people on the plane. I did not know what to do or say to my friend. I was almost afraid to look at him.

I do not remember doing it, but a short time later I realized that I had my arm around his shoulder and he had moved closer to me and was overcome with emotion.

Turning my head slightly, I could see tears streaming down his face. Emotion welled up in me and I was filled with the most intense feeling of humility. Something very special had happened that night, and once again deep within I had a knowing, but no logical rational understanding of the implication of what had happened. So I just sat there holding my friend while he came to terms with what he had experienced.

At 37,000 feet, the 747 eased its way through the rarefied atmosphere and deep within its aluminum belly two very quiet farm boys struggled to face up to the night's events. I think it was my young friend who broke the silence first by fumbling around for another cigarette.

"Blimey," he said, "that was weird. I hope you know what that was all about."

"I think so," I answered. "How do you feel now?"

"Okay, I think," his voice trailed off.

I picked up the conversation and told him not to worry too much about it, that he had been used by the spirit world to get a message to me. I went on to tell him a little bit about the reality of speaking with the "other side" and how many people call it channeling, but that was only a new name for what people had been doing since the beginning of time. And that in all the old cultures it was a very normal and accepted occurrence.

He told me that when he was a kid his great aunt used to speak to the ancestors at every family gathering, and in fact she was quite well-known and highly respected in the Maori community for this. He said that he had always been fascinated and drawn to be near her in his childhood, but as he got older he did not want to be ridiculed, so he kept well away from all the "weird stuff."

"And now this!" he said as he rolled he eyes and shook his head. "This is too much."

I laughed and said that would teach him not to run away

from the weird stuff, and that maybe he could take over for his great aunt one day.

"No way," he said, with a big smile on his face. Then becoming very serious, he told me how honored he felt that he had met me and how he could feel the honor that the ancestors held me in.

"You must be real important," he said, "because there were so many ancestors around you when they were talking to us."

I just let that one slide on by, as I felt I did not want to get in too deep discussing me and I needed to think over the night's events. I wanted to be alone with my thoughts.

We sat for a while longer, each of us with our own thoughts, until sleep brought silence to our minds.

Wakened by the cabin crew as they moved down the aisles serving breakfast, I saw the first rays of the dawning day make the sky dance in tones of red and orange in the faraway east. As breakfast finished, the crew readied the plane for landing.

Our eyes met in a short, uncomfortable pause, then we embraced each other. Not a word was spoken and none was needed. At some deep level, we both knew that we had given and received exactly what was required of us. I got up and slowly walked back to my own seat. To this day, I have never seen that young man again, and we never even exchanged our names.

Clearing customs in Honolulu, the group I was with caught our short flight to the Big Island and landed at Keahola Airport in mid-afternoon. By the time we had settled into our hotel in Kailua, it was early evening and I turned down an invitation to explore the town with the rest of the group. Instead, I just lay down in my room.

I was not thinking about the events that had taken place on the flight across the Pacific, my mind was just floating around with no particular place to go - fairly normal state of affairs for me - when suddenly I had a really strong urge to focus on one of the island's volcanoes.

As soon as I became aware of my focus, an energy surge went through my body. I felt my awareness lift out of my body and there below me I could see the broken cone of the volcano. There was no fear or any other emotion that I can recall, other than a feeling of total commitment. My body was still lying on the hotel bed, but the I that was my awareness was being drawn down into the volcano itself.

It was a feeling of being stretched out like a long piece of elastic. Down, down into the volcano went my awareness. I can remember the tremendous heat, not from the volcano but from the energy that was coming into and through my awareness or energy body. The downward movement seemed to go on forever, and I can remember thinking that it felt like I was 30 miles down into the Earth.

As my awareness came to a stop, a tremendous, overpowering focus became my reality. It was like my whole beingness had become this great funnel reaching down into the volcano, and there was I at the small end inside the mountain while all the energy from the cosmos was pouring in. I was totally and completely focused on the end of the funnel, I *was* the funnel, I could not move. I was transfixed to this spot deep inside the volcano.

At that point things started to get a bit hairy. I could feel myself, I mean all of me, not just my concentrated awareness, start to slide down into the funnel. I can remember feeling a bit of terror at this point, because in all the weird things that had happened to me so far, I had always been able to maintain some awareness of the "real world" as I was going through them. But this time, I could feel myself losing all contact with everything.

As the rest of the world disappeared, I became conscious of only a concentrated point of awareness. This point of awareness that was me had no reality other than an unbelievably powerful, vibrating point of energy.

If you can imagine being the arc of an electric welder and nothing else, but an arc that is about two feet around, you have some idea of what I was feeling. There is no other way I can describe it. I was aware of just the pulsing, jarring, stabbing, all-powerful energy, and I knew that I had to hold this awareness. I knew I had to be the energy, and that letting the concentration or awareness go would be disastrous.

Time had no meaning; there were no reference points. I had no knowledge of anything other than the energy and my focus on it. Strangely, I can recall myself thinking, "How much longer? Can't take much more of this."

Then I slowly regained awareness of my surroundings. I guess I was on my way out of the volcano when I started to think again. I opened my eyes, yes, I was still in the hotel on my bed. I was alive, I think, but whoa, hold on a minute, something was not right! Shit, I had peed myself - no, but everything was wet.

Darn, I tried to sit up, but my body just did not have the strength, so I felt around with my hands. The bed was saturated. I mean, I could flap my hand up and down on the bed beside me and it sounded almost like splashing. My mind was struggling to focus and I felt all light and flowery, sort of floaty, but incredibly fatigued and dying for a drink.

I do not know how long I laid there, ten minutes or so maybe, before I finally sat up. The glow of the outside lights shining through the undraped windows helped me to stagger over to turn on the lights. Straining to get my eyes to focus on the face of my watch, I was shocked to see the time - it was a little past midnight. Bloody hell, I thought, I have been out of it for about six hours.

I drank about a dozen glasses of water, pulled the wet sheets off and laid out all the dry towels on the bed, pulled the damp blankets up over me and told the Earth that if it needed anymore healing that night, it had better find someone else, because I had just resigned and was going to go and die for a few hours, like twenty or so.

Awakened by loud knocking on my door, I rolled over, and to my surprise the clock on the radio said it was 10 a.m. I had slept for ten hours. Making some lame excuse for not going with the others on the tour for the day, I lay back on my very smelly bed and went over the events of the night before, trying to put some logical perspective on it from the beginning of the flight until now.

It did not matter which way I tried to look at it, there was no way I could divorce the occurrences. What had happened last night was exactly what the ancestors had foretold. Okay, I told myself, that was fine. I did what I was asked to do, and it does not matter if I understood the rhyme or reason of it. That was not my concern.

Leaving it at that, I got up, showered and generally cleaned myself up. Having called up room service, I was about to demolish a much-needed breakfast when I had an urge to turn on the radio. A forkful of hash browns were frozen in space between the plate and my mouth as I heard the announcer and somebody from a university discussing details of an earthquake that had taken place early that morning.

They were saying how unusual it was because of the total absence of aftershocks. They went on to discuss that the quake was very mild, about 3.2 I think, and that the seismologist had been expecting a much bigger one due to the recent activity that their machines had monitored.

I was stunned. This was just too much of a coincidence - the message on the plane, what happened last night and now the small earthquake. I could accept that the three events took place, but I was in real trouble when my logic tried to bring me into the picture.

Yet, from somewhere deep inside, I could feel as if my knowingness was saying, yes, we did it, we did it. Try as I might, I could not stop that feeling. The rest of the day, I just walked around town and sat for endless hours staring out over the ocean, my brain refusing to function. The following day, I rejoined the tour group, and, aside from my emotions being totally whacked and out of control, life carried on.

Working through the emotional upheaval that followed, I came to the conclusion that the tremendous amount of energy that my body obviously had handled, for whatever reason, had caused some major malfunctions in my body's energy system, in particular, the endocrine system, which controls the chemical and hormone balance and thus the emotions.

I have seen similar emotional problems in people I have worked with over the years, caused by many experiences, but it is the damage to their electrical system that always causes the emotional problems. When that is put right, reconnected and realigned, the emotions smooth out.

To put somebody else's electrical system back together again is real easy for me, but I had one hell of a time getting myself right after that little meltdown. The rest of the week passed without any other strange happenings, and in fact I had a very memorable two days visiting with Joan Ocean and swimming with the dolphins.

Leaving the Hawaiian Islands, our next stop was L.A. and the Whole Life Expo in Pasadena. What an eye opener that was for this farm boy! The sheer size and number of exhibits and the endless people, thousands and thousands of them, was mind-boggling.

The Expo ran for four days, and it was on the third day, when I was exploring a section I had missed earlier, that the next chapter in my odyssey of experience unfolded. My mind was floating away as the soaring notes of Hilary Stagg's harp come through the loud speakers and I was slowly being carried down an aisle in a throng of people, between stands of every different kind of natural and some not-so-natural health products and practitioners.

Suddenly, I was stopped by a large, firm hand folding itself over I my shoulder. Turning my head, I shrank back in a moment of fear as I realized that the hand that was gripping my shoulder belonged to a very large Native American dressed in full-feathered headgear. The guy nearly scared the shit out of me.

"You," he said without waiting for me to say anything, "I want to talk to you. Come back to my stand just before closing." He then gave me his stand number, turned and left me standing speechless, with knees that were only just holding my legs together.

Finding his stand later that day, I approached it with some trepidation, but I should not have worried because he recognized me as soon as he saw me. Since he was talking to another person, he beckoned to me to take a seat at the back of his stand and wait. It was only a matter of minutes before he was finished and came over and sat down beside me.

"Welcome," he said, "you have come a long way."

What was this guy, I thought, some super-psychic or something? How did he know that I had come from a long way away, from the other side of the world, in fact?

"Maybe," I answered, still not sure of his motives and unsure that I wanted to find out. He must have felt my uneasiness, because his face softened into a big smile. He must have been in his late fifties at least, very large but not grossly overweight, clean-shaven with long silver hair. He was adorned with heavy silver rings and bracelets, and around his neck he wore this amazing silver and turquoise necklace. It was massive, covering half of his chest.

There was an uneasy silence as we sat looking at each other. Is he going to say anything, I thought as he just looked at me with an intensity that very few people ever have. Finally my twisted humor got the better of me and I said to him,

"I thought all you guys got knocked off in the cowboy and Indian wars back in the wild west days."

A slight smile forced its way through his intensity, and with a chuckle he answered,

"Nah, the pale face stopped shooting before we were all gone."

"Yeah, I guess everybody makes mistakes sometimes," I cheekily answered.

That did it. He broke his concentration on me and a great rumbling chuckle reverberated through his body.

"You know," he said, "there is only one thing more obnoxious than a smart-ass Indian."

"What's that?" I asked as I cracked up with laughter, knowing full well what was coming next.

"A smart-ass Paleface," we said in perfect harmony as we cracked up laughing like a couple of school kids. Recovering my composure, I thought I had better find out what he wanted with me, so I asked him if he made a habit of coming up behind complete strangers and scaring the shit out of them.

"It was worth it just to see your face," he said, intermingled with more chuckles. "You looked as if the devil himself had caught up with you."

"Ha bloody ha," I said, "it wasn't so funny from my end."

"But you are here now, and that's all that matters."

"Okay, so why me? Hell, there must be tens of thousands here this week."

He nodded his head with slow meaningful movements.

"Yes," he said, "but only one paleface medicine man." He paused, then went on.

"Many do-gooders, many seekers, many wanting to buy something, something from outside of themselves, nobody with the courage to find their power, to be their power, to become one with everything, to go inside, really go inside past all the pain, past all the hurt, and then have the courage to let go and be who they are and be able to make a difference to what's happening on this Earth, our Mother."

"But," I protested, "I haven't got much courage. I'm frightened as all hell most of the time. I don't even know why I'm here."

He put up his hand and shook his head as if he did not want me to speak.

"Courage is not a feeling," he said, "fear is a feeling. Courage is a doing despite the fear. Courage is following the will of the Great Spirit, of following your heart." He paused.

"You," he said, looking at me with the most intense brown eyes I have ever seen, "you have been called, you have been trained."

Then, as if to answer my unasked question, "No, no, not this life. Many, many lives that have gone, many with the great ones, much learning, much preparing. You have been with us many times and now you come back a paleface. We have no power now, nobody listens, nobody cares about what we say, but you, a paleface, you have the power. It is the turn of the paleface, but your paleface brothers don't listen to the old ones, they don't let the Great Spirit talk to them, to guide them. But you, you can talk to your paleface brothers and they will listen."

"Hang on a minute," I interrupted. "Who will listen to me? Hell, I don't even listen to myself half the time, and when I do I don't believe myself anyhow."

He stopped me with an impatient gesture and went on.

"Just a boy yet, still learning, much understanding to come."

Yeah, I could accept the understanding bit - but just a boy? The cheeky sod. Hell, I had three kids and was thirty something. A boy, indeed. My thoughts were interrupted as he spoke again.

"Many of my people don't approve of what I am doing, but I am listening to the old ones. They tell me to give to the paleface the old ceremony, the old knowledge, but not to just any paleface, only the ones who understand, who have been with us before, who have the power, who *are* powerful medicine.

I was told to leave my home and put myself in a position where those who would use the medicine with honor could be shown to me by the old ones. The old ones tell me there is not much time left and that you are one who is powerful medicine. That is why I asked you to come and talk with me and that is also why you came even with your little bit of fear."

Well, that was true enough. I had been trying to make excuses to myself all day for not coming to see him, but deep within there was a compelling urge I could not resist. Yes, it was happening to me again. I was in a position I did not plan, had very little control over, being told things that made very little sense and had no logic based on normal (or so-called normal) life.

But by now I was getting used to this sort of thing, and since I had always wanted to spend time with a real Indian, I readily agreed when he asked me to come dine and spend the remainder of the evening with him. There was no way I could have known then that a single evening would turn into three incredible days.

Finishing dinner about 11:00pm, my new friend, who said his name was Bill, myself, and three other members of his party all went back to their hotel suite. After pleasantries had been exchanged, the others excused themselves and left Bill and me alone.

I was still a bit intrigued about how he had singled me out of the throng of people earlier that day, so I asked him how he really did pick me.

Sitting down and making himself comfortable, he closed his eyes and started to talk.

"I am Navaho, I am fifth-generation medicine man. My training started at 18 months, when I was taken from my home and sent to live with the old ladies and some wise ones in the mountains. I stayed there until I was seven years old, learning all about the Great Spirit, ceremony and medicine. (In this sense "medicine" means power or energy and is not confined to a narrow healing perception.) I was taught many things that our people used to know, how to be one with the wind, the animals, the earth, the sky; many, many things that our people have lost. Only the old wise ones who live in the mountains remember.

I was one of three selected from a large area, and we were given the knowledge so that it would not be lost. One of the things we were taught was to be aware of other peoples' energy and to know who they are by their energy. We were also shown how to talk to the Great Spirit and how to allow the Great Spirit to talk to us.

This is how I was told to ask you to come and talk with me. Your energy is very different from others, very easy to see to those who know. Also, those who walk with you, the unseen ones, are very great spirits. They do not walk with everybody, so it was easy to find you."

My request that Bill tell me more about his training, especially the period after the first seven years, was met with a shake of his head and a wave of his hand in an impatient manner.

"No, no, not me," he said.

"You, you are the one who is to learn now, learn the old ways, the ceremony, the medicine, there is no time to talk about me anymore."

And that was it. I never did find out any more about Bill's earlier life.

The rest of the night was spent with Bill going over my body and energy fields, getting me ready, he said. It was interesting in that I could recognize many of the points he used as what would be regarded as matching classic Chinese acupuncture, and many of the movements his hands took were along the meridian lines.

Even though he was using a very old cleansing and aligning technique that had been used for thousands of years, I could understand the process, what he was doing and what part of my energy system he was working on thanks to the modern training I had received over the last ten or so years. I was aware of energy moving about my body as he worked and sort of chanted or talked to the spirits that were with us.

This guy was real powerful and obviously had lots of spirit friends who were helping because I have seldom felt the presence of so many so powerfully. It was near 3:30 a.m. by the time Bill was finished with me. He said the spirits had readied me for the next night, when I was to come back, and he would show me things that very few white men had ever seen or done. This would have the effect of preparing me for the work that I would be doing in the years ahead.

Arriving back at my hotel, sleep came easily, as I felt so centered and calm. The next morning I hurried to the Expo and spent as much time with Bill as I could, discussing lots of Indian ceremony, watching the energy frequency change as Bill worked with the people who came to him and listening to them discussing the energy changes with him.

This guy was good; here was a man using centuries-old healing methods that were as relevant and effective as anything I had seen. To somebody who did not understand or comprehend the basis of energy work, it could very easily seem to be mumbo-jumbo, but as I could discern, feel and be aware of the energy changes, I could see what was going on - and believe me, there was no mumbo-jumbo about it. In fact, this man was leaving people with a far better chance for their bodies to be able to regain health than most drug jockeys do when they operate under the camouflage of the so-called medical profession.

Spending the day at his stand certainly allowed me to gain a lot of confidence in my own abilities. Even though we were coming from different angles - Bill from a culture steeped in ceremony and me from a modern understanding of energy, electricity and chemistry - there were times when we worked on the same client using energy healing techniques with which we were both familiar.

Bill would use very different words to describe what he was doing, but from an energy sense it was easy for me to understand, and I was able to relate the processes he was using to my knowledge of the body's electrical system, and at that point, we had a common denominator.

Having helped Bill and his crew pack up after the last night of the Expo, I headed off with them for a bite to eat, feeling some trepidation because I had a hunch I was going to experience something really different that night. Bill had said to me earlier that afternoon that I was ready to be shown some real medicine, so I had a burning impatience to find out what "real medicine" was.

Of course dinner seemed to drag on forever, but finally we all arrived back at the hotel and, as if by some secret signal, all the others left the room. I was not aware that Bill had said anything to them; they just seemed to be able to communicate with each other without talking.

Once we were alone Bill got out his Indian things and went through a short ceremony. Then, turning to me, he did a ceremony over me. At its completion he bent down and from his bag of ceremonial things he selected a large feather, placing it on one shoulder, then the other, then in my hands. The exact ceremony that took place I cannot share, but I will describe the results as I perceived them.

Telling me to hold the feather in my right hand, Bill had me lie down face up on the bed. He proceeded to work on various points on my body. Almost immediately I was able to feel energy start to move, first just a slight tingling on the palms of my hands. But as Bill moved to different points it felt like he was turning on circuits in a sort of circular fashion.

My body responded by heating up from the middle out. At about this stage he stopped holding points on me and looked deeply into my eyes, paused for what seemed to be forever, then said.

"You now have a choice. I can stop now or go on. If I go on there is no stopping. Your body will be charged to a point that if you are not ready, severe damage can and most probably will occur. But all the signs indicate that you are ready, and this decision on your part is also an important part of the ceremony because you must have faith in your ability to hold yourself together and become one with the Great Spirit.

The power that you will become has for thousands of years been given only to very honored chiefs. This is their power; this is how they held our people together and how battles were won. This power brings with it the responsibility of the great ones. If you ever use it without wisdom and honor, you and you alone will have to face that dishonor. The old ones here with us now have much honor for you. They wish you well and hope that you will join with them in ceremony."

Lying there looking up into that old Indian face that was radiating power, feeling and honor, I could almost go beyond his physical features and look at the old ones themselves. They were so much a part of Bill's beingness that it was almost impossible to distinguish any separation between their energies. The raw power and love that I was feeling was so pure and honorable that I knew I wanted to be like that.

"Yes," I said, "I am ready. I accept the responsibility."

Bill started to gently massage very specific points on my body, moving from one to another in a controlled rotation that had the effect of building up a sort of vortex of energy in me. Slowly at first, then with increasing intensity the heat in my body turned to a tingling and then the tingling turned to a burning. It was very different from anything I had previously experienced.

There was no pain, but the burning sensation was incredible. You know the energy shimmer you can see on a hot day above a road? Well, it felt like my entire body was shimmering like that. The vibratory rate of my cells must have been tremendous, because it felt like I was on fire. I was fully conscious, and had full awareness of where I was and what was happening.

Finally Bill stepped back from me and beckoned me to get off the bed.

This I did very gingerly, because every movement felt strange, as if I were moving a great shaft of energy instead of my limbs. He then told me to hold my palms out and walk towards a chair that was about five or six feet away from me.

As soon as I started to move toward the chair, it slid backwards away from me. I stopped dead and looked at Bill as I let out a "bloody hell!" I looked back at the chair and moved forward again, and again the chair moved away from me.

The look on my face must have been one of total shock and amazement, because when I turned to Bill he was grinning from ear to ear and nodding his head in approval.

"Shit," I said, "this is awesome, out of this world."

I just stood there, bewildered and shit-scared of what might happen next.

Bill came to the rescue by pointing to a box of books on the floor near the door about two yards from me.

As I brought my focus to the box, I sort of just leaned toward it, and lo and behold, the box immediately went wham, hard up against the door.

I jumped back in fright, looked around at Bill and said, "Did I do that?"

He nodded and said, "Powerful medicine."

With my body shaking I nodded my head and repeated, "Real powerful medicine."

Bill then told me to sit down at the table, which I did very slowly for fear that everything might fly away from me. He then walked to the refrigerator, filled a large glass with ice and placed it in front of me.

"Now," he said, "how do you feel?"

"Okay, I think," I said. "My hands still feel like they are on fire and are going to explode."

"Good. Now put your hands about three inches away from the glass on each side and start counting."

I placed my hands where he indicated and started to count - one - two - three - four. I could not believe my eyes; the ice was melting, just disappearing almost instantly. By the time I had counted out eight seconds, there was not a solid bit of ice in the glass. I was speechless.

I looked up at Bill with my mouth hanging open, too shocked for words. There was no way my logic could get around that one.

Bill indicated the glass with a movement of his head, and as I looked back at it I shot backwards out of my chair, sending it flying and throwing my arms open wide in panic.

The water was now steaming! It could not have been more than fifteen to twenty seconds since I had put my hands around a glass full of ice, and now the water was hot.

That was enough for me. I ran into the bathroom, what for, I did not know, but at least I was alone with my fear. Looking into the mirror, I could see the shock and terror on my face.

To be confronted with the reality of this much power and ability would take some getting used to, that was for sure.

Bill came in to see if I was all right. "That's bloody powerful stuff." I said to him. "My hands are still on fire." I didn't know what else to say. What else *was* there to say? I think Bill put his arm around me and led me out of the bathroom, sat me down and gave me a glass of cold water to drink.

I think I was in a state of shock, trying to comprehend where this power had come from. Many of the experiences I'd had when working on people were pretty powerful, but this was something else.

During a healing I can always feel the energy come in through my energy system as if I am plugged into a higher source, like a cosmic three-pin plug, but this time there was nothing like that. It felt as if a hidden energy source had been uncovered and released in me. The whole process had taken place within my own body.

I was familiar with the kundalini experience, and in fact was very aware of that entire energy-activation process, but this was not a normal kundalini experience. A kundalini energy, when activated on its own, moves up your spine before it moves out to energize the rest of the body, and if one does not have very good training and has not learned to control the entire process, it can be downright dangerous.

I could accept that the experience I'd had with Bill had a component of kundalini activation, but there was another component that allowed the manifested energy to be used in a way that was more powerful and transmittable than anything I had learned about up to that time.

Was what I had experienced a small part of an ancient knowledge that religion had judged to be too powerful for the masses, making it secret? That "sacred knowledge," which down through the ages had become entangled in so much dogma and distortion that only those with the greatest power (or greatest seclusion) within the world's religions and secret societies knew about.

Was this the power that those at the highest levels of international commerce (the Illuminati) know about; the vast potential power that humans have. Was the control of this knowledge the real reason that since the time of Christ the white Aryan races have tried to wipe out indigenous peoples who used this knowledge on a day-to-day basis?

If genocide did not work completely, then the white conquerors enslaved, ridiculed, belittled and generally disempowered the remaining natives until any semblance of their former knowledge and power was destroyed or scattered far and wide. Was Bill one of the few souls left in the Red race who had been given fragments of that knowledge and the guidance to pass it on in a final attempt to free mankind from the destructive path we are on?

If so, and it sure seemed like it, then I needed to get as much as I could from Bill while I had the chance.

After my body began to feel somewhat normal again (what is normal?), Bill shared more about the old ways. He showed me many ways to use the energy and how to protect myself from others whose intentions might not be in my best interests. We talked and worked right through the night and when morning came we took time out for breakfast.

I was learning things and understanding other realities that had previously been confined to fantasy and science fiction, and I was quickly coming to the conclusion that the old cultures knew more about the human body, its energy system and the cosmos that is a part of us all than most people had ever given them credit for. In fact, the information Bill was sharing with me would make much of the so-called modern medical knowledge and processes look like crude cut and burn butchery.

Time and again it was brought to my attention just how important the connection is between our material world and the much bigger and more powerful unseen world. Of course, it is only unseen and unacceptable to those who are blinded by the dogmas we have been taught and the ignorance that has been fostered in us.

To accept that others may know far more than we do can be frightening to start with, and rather than face and move beyond our ignorance, people often do their best to discredit or destroy those perceived as different or as having, god forbid, secret powers. Sometimes they are even killed. Perhaps humanity deserves the bloody mess we are in now.

As tired as we were, Bill never let up. The rest of the day was spent in intense teacher-student mode. I was almost force-fed information that unceasingly poured out of him, information that to this day is etched with total clarity on my consciousness.

There is much that I have never used during my healing work, and some techniques are so powerful that I have been scared to even use them on myself. But the tremendous gain in knowledge and confidence has allowed me to move on with much more clarity and purpose.

At the time I had no idea why I was receiving all this knowledge and information, but I came to the conclusion that I had better take it all in for the day when I would be required to use it or teach it.

How and when that would be I did not know, but there were too many synchronicities involved in the manner and regularity this information was coming to me for me to deny its importance. I had no choice other than to go with the flow and see where my life would take me. The ride had begun to get exciting.

In a moment of quiet reflection, I took my mind back to wondering how on earth I got to this point in my life.

CHAPTER 2
FARM BOY FROM DOWN UNDER

Born fifth in a family of seven on June 8, 1949, I had three older brothers, one older sister, and two sisters who arrived after me. We lived in a rural, farming environment in New Zealand.

My earliest memories are happy ones of swimming in the river, fishing for eels and summer hay making. How I relish even now the sweet, sweet smell of fresh hay. Back then in the early fifties, Dad still made hay with horse and sweep and built a haystack in the paddock where the hay was cut. All the neighbors came to help and Mum would cook for hours and drive the family car (a big old black American Pontiac straight six) out to the working men with enormous amounts of food and hot tea.

To feel the essence of fresh hay as we kids romped and played in it and the memory of climbing onto the haystack and holding handfuls up to the big draught horses to eat will always bring joy to my heart.

I remember my great excitement when Dad loaded us kids into the old Ponty and drove us to another farm where I saw my first hay baler, a McCormick International.

What a monster! And how it could devour that hay! It made such an impression on me that I fell in love with machinery then and there.

Even though Dad had horses on the farm (he was share-farming at this time), the owner had tractors as well.

How proud I felt when I was allowed to hold the steering wheel of one of the big tractors.

I remember, during one summer, my older brother raking the hay with one of the tractors, a Minneapolis Moline (M-M), and I pestered him to let me have a drive on my own.

I, of course, did not think it was going fast enough because big brother had put it in low gear for me. Well, the M-M had a hand clutch, so smart-ass little me pushed forward the clutch and grabbed the gear lever, which was longer than I was high, and tugged it.

Out of low gear and unbeknown to me, into top gear it went! I then kicked the hand clutch with my foot (which was the only way I could engage it), and the big old M-M took off.

You have never seen a sight like it. That darn Moline could do about 30 mph and the paddock (field) was no golf course! It was rough as all hell, actually. My feet could not reach the foot plate, so as the tractor gained speed, I was thrown out of the seat since I did not have much to brace myself with.

There I was, feet dangling backward over the seat, hands gripping the steering wheel for dear life and this bloody great tractor going hell for leather across the field, which was rapidly getting smaller as the end fence approached. Fear, terror, panic - yep, I had a real early introduction to a whole range of emotions that day.

Now remember, that darn tractor had a hand-operated clutch, and to disengage it I had to let go of the steering wheel. But that steering wheel was the only thing between me and eternity, and there was no way I was going to let it go!

To this day I do not know how I got the courage to let go of the wheel and grab that clutch to disengage it.

The tractor stopped about ten yards short of the fence. The hay rake had dislodged itself from the tractor tow hitch and was lying about 100 yards back on the paddock.

My brother was racing down toward me, arms going in all directions, so I did the only thing little brothers do in situations like that: I got the hell out of there, pronto! I remember I never stopped running until I hit my bed back at the house, and I swear I never left that bed for the rest of the day. God, I was scared!

Yep, those were the good old days down on the farm.

Growing up in a large family in a rural environment certainly gives one a chance to experience lots of feelings. Like having to swim in the river in your sister's underpants because Mum had not the time (or the money) to get into town to buy swimming togs.

Now, those underpants things were called bloomers - and for good reason, I felt. They were great big, baggy and black or navy blue. When I got into the water, the air would get trapped in them and they would inflate around my middle. My older brothers would tease the heck out of me - how I hated to swim in those ghastly things!

We kids did all the things country kids do: built huts in the trees, pushed trolleys (carts) made out of old apple boxes, got into Dad's tools and were right nasty to each other. Trying to be accepted by my older brothers was probably the hardest thing for me. I remember once when I wanted to play with them and they said I could, if I was brave enough to walk downstream in the river without getting out.

That day the river was in mild flood, and Mum had told us kids a million times not to play in the river. But what kid listens to Mum when she is not in sight? So, here I am, up to my neck in water trying to hold onto branches of the overhanging trees so I would not get washed away. I guess I was about eight or nine at the time.

My brothers were walking on the bank of the river throwing fun at me and generally giving me a hard time. I do not recall them ever being in the river when it was in flood, but I had to so I could play with them.

Yes, I guess I learned to go past my fear and stuff my emotions very early in life. The only problem was that later in life I had to face the consequences and reverse the process.

Being very close to animals instilled a deep appreciation of nature in me, which I am only now beginning to understand. Being with animals also has its downside. I can remember when my little sister had a pet lamb that was being prepared for the local fair. She put in hours of work and had the lamb doing anything she asked of it.

The morning of the fair, Dad washed the lamb for her, and it looked so pure white and beautiful. He tied it up outside the milking shed while we all had breakfast. When we were ready to leave for the fair, the lamb was nowhere to be found.

Dad had unknowingly tied it to a longer rope than usual, allowing the lamb to reach an old well, which it had fallen into and strangled. I can still feel my sister's pain as she battled to deal with that death.

In those early years, I do not remember much disharmony between my parents, but I guess we block out a lot when we are young. Later, in my teens, the memory of their arguments became more vivid.

Our family was Roman Catholic and Sunday was church day. How Mum got seven kids clean, dressed and into the car for the forty-minute drive to the church for ten o'clock mass I will never know.

I can still see the pride on Mum's face as we seven little Hiestands all filed into a long pew, all done up spic and span with not a hair out of place.

After church, if an argument had not developed in the car and Dad was still in a good mood, we would stop and all get an ice cream before going home.

Sometimes in the summer, we would go down to Opunaki beach after church and have a picnic lunch. How I loved the beach! At last I could escape and be alone to climb the rocks and go right out to where the waves came crashing in.

I remember the thrill I had when I used to run as fast as I could, bouncing from one rock to another. Even then, I would push myself to the limit. How I never fell and broke my legs on those big rocks, I will never know. I guess my guardian angels had to work overtime even then.

Being on a farm, we all had our jobs to do, even on school days. Before school, we boys had to go to the milking shed to do our chores, and after school Dad always had jobs for us.

Of course, there were many fights among us kids, and at times Mum would get totally frustrated and angry with us. But when I was about nine or ten, I can remember Dad getting so angry that he became violent. Hitting us was his natural way of dealing with his anger - not just spanking us, but actually getting so violent that he was out of control.

Mum would try to intervene, and that would start an argument between them. As their arguing raged, we kids would scatter in all directions. Even so, when we returned we often felt we were responsible for the anger.

I can remember running away to my hut in a big hedge of trees and crying and asking God to kill me because I was so bad that I caused Mum and Dad to fight so much.

Those feelings of blame, of being bad, a naughty boy, of being responsible for Mum's unhappiness, really got to me at times. How could a nine-year-old deal with that?

The panic, the incredible fear I felt deep inside when I knew Dad was going to belt me or the other kids, is still vivid within me.

When working on the farm with Dad, we boys really had to work, which in itself was not bad, but Dad had only one standard - perfection. I always felt that what I did was not good enough, so striving for perfection at top speed became ingrained. Being the youngest boy, I always felt I was expected to keep up with the others, and I remember the incredibly deep hurt I felt when I was told to go home to Mum because I could not keep up with the workload.

One summer holiday we boys had the job of picking up rocks from a plowed field. Dad had promised us a very rare trip to the movies when we finished. The excitement, the keenness that we felt as we hooked the Farmall H up to the big wooden sledge and towed it out to the field soon left us as we started to load those rocks.

The day was hot and we four boys, three barely teenagers, soon got tired. Being the youngest, I wanted to drive the tractor, as the rocks were too heavy for me. So after a lot of moaning, my brothers finally let me. By this time the sledge must have had about two to three tons of rocks on it, and I kept stalling the tractor when the sledge started to move.

The sledge was connected to the tractor with a steel S hook, which slowly started to straighten under the load. My older brothers saw what was happening and told me I could not drive properly and to get off the tractor.

Maurice, the second oldest, then got on the tractor and as he started, the S hook bent out completely, and the tractor broke away from the sledge.

We all knew Dad would get angry at us for breaking the S hook and not finishing the job, so I got all the blame, even though we had simply loaded too many stones onto the sledge. To my brothers, it was my driving that did it.

Sure enough, as punishment we did not get to the movies - not just us boys, but the whole family. Needless to say, six other kids vented their emotions on me. It did not matter how many times I protested that my brothers had put too many rocks on that sledge; it was still all my fault. A pretty heavy burden for a nine-year-old.

There were also some marvellous, wonderful times when my younger sister Cathy and I used to walk out on the farm to the pine plantation. It was about six acres, but to us it was a vast forest. It was an adventure to experience the feel of those fresh, soft pine needles under our bare feet. The rich, soft, sweet and invigorating smell of the pines was heaven to our young hearts.

Many long summer days were spent exploring our forest, building huts with dead branches and pine needles, playing with imaginary fairies or being chased by imaginary monsters. Yes, the pine plantation was cool and private, a place to which I could escape. A love of pine forests is still with me today.

My father, who had emigrated from central Europe in his early twenties, had brought with him old-world, male dominant attitudes. I feel this was even more pronounced because he was Roman Catholic.

I remember in the Catholic convent school how the nuns and priests used to drum into us their perception of God. Their God was so judgmental; He had mostly don'ts, and there were so many wrongs. So much fear was instilled into us kids there that I can see why people like my Dad had such judgmental attitudes.

To me as an eleven-year-old, their God did not make much sense. The nuns taught us that God made us in His likeness and that He loved us all. In fact, we were told He made everything. But I could not understand why a loving God would also create hell, punish kids for using swear words, banish us from heaven if we kissed the girls or played with our own penis. Heavens above, Dad punished us enough for most of the things we did wrong - and for some things we never did - so why would God give us a double dose?

That seemed grossly unfair and unloving to this young kid. Even though getting angry was a sin, some of the nuns would go into a blind rage in the classroom at times. My father, who believed going to church every Sunday was crucial to being a "good" Catholic, was the quickest to anger of anyone I knew.

The convent school gave me other conflicting realities. There was one time when my class was being talked to by a visiting priest. Actually, he was more than just a priest: he was a Monsignor. He was trying to put the fear of God into us, and I asked him how God could be like he described and still love us. I can still see his reaction: He fumed and said, "how dare you question God," and sent me from the classroom.

It was at this point in my young life that I made a decision that this religion thing was all bullshit. For instance, the "thou shall not kill" thing was something I could not understand, as all the people I knew were either farmers or worked in slaughterhouses and were in the killing business either directly or indirectly. The nuns told us that was okay because we were allowed to kill the animals. But to me at that young age, the Ten Commandments did not make that distinction.

The more I thought about God and what I was being taught, the more confused I became. And of course, I soon learned not to ask the nuns or priests, because questions like that just showed I had no faith. That made more guilt to deal with on my part.

It amazes me that not every kid with a dogmatic Christian upbringing grows up to be a rebellious delinquent!

It was during these years that I spent a great deal of time alone. Sure, I played and interacted with the others in the family, but I was alone with my thoughts and feelings.

Withdrawing into myself was often perceived as moodiness by Mum and the other kids. I remember going down to the pine plantation and just walking or sitting for hours, letting my mind drift slowly through the cosmos. I often felt a oneness with God, but not the God the church taught.

When the little fantail birds would dart very close to me, catching the bugs that were disturbed in the trees, I would have an overwhelming feeling of closeness, of wonderment and pure joy and pride at being so close to those beautiful creatures. To me they represented God in more ways than I could express.

It seemed to me that the more I talked to them, the more they understood. In their joy they darted in and out of the trees and, oh, how close they would come to me! I am sure they could feel my hurt and were doing their best to cheer me up. And they did. Sometimes I would run as fast as I could to see if I could race them, but they would always be there first, showing off their superb aerial acrobatics.

It was hard for me to have many friends outside the family other than one or two other boys. To me, most of the other kids at school were childish and did not think the way I thought. I never liked group sports much because everybody kept telling me what to do and how to do it (God, I'd had enough of that at home). So even at school, I would often just go off on my own and be with my innermost thoughts.

Yes, eleven through fifteen were very lonely years for me. I guess I did a lot of emotional stuffing during this time as my weight went up and my brothers nicknamed me Fatso. God, how that hurt!

Around this age, my family moved to a new farm Dad had purchased with a large loan from one of Mum's brothers.

This began the most unhappy time of my childhood. I had two years left at primary (grade) school and moved into a new very small school environment as the only boy in my class.

The farming area we moved into was fairly well-established with financially well-off families. My family had the oldest car, and I remember my embarrassment when Mum drove it to school to pick us kids up. Luckily, it was not very often, as we usually rode our bikes to school.

I think my feelings of inferiority began because the girls in my class were all from those well-to-do families. They always wore the best clothes and talked la-di-da to each other. During those two years I never really got close to any other boy at school, so my younger sister Cathy and her friends became my friends.

Cathy was an outgoing, bubbly kid, but also had a quick temper, and at times was a right bitch. (I guess all sisters are at times from their brothers' points of view.) But she got on well with Heather, a girl who lived not far from our farm, so we spent a lot of time together.

Heather was one of those girls who had developed early, with extremely well-developed breasts and a naturally oozing sexuality for a twelve-year-old. It was with Heather that for the first time in years I felt accepted by another person. Kissing, holding hands, and "I'll show you mine if you'll show me yours" in the big fern bushes near her house on the way home from school and on weekends, allowed me to sort of feel good about myself.

God, it was so good to get away from the endless work and arguments at home! Home was developing into a war zone at this time. Dad, with his big mortgage and his drive to get things done, drove himself and us boys to the limit and beyond, emotionally and physically.

Mum, trying desperately to hold the family together, would intervene when Dad directed his cruel, emotional verbal abuse at us. She would try to stop him from beating us. God, the gut-wrenching fear and terror I felt when Dad turned his rage on Mum. Many times when Dad was belting me, I shut down my emotions so I would not cry no matter how much of a hiding I was getting. That was so Mum would not hear and come out of the house and try to stop him. I knew if she did, Dad would take his anger out on her. I would rather take all the pain silently than have Mum hurt anymore.

At times, Mum would cry for days on end and be unable to talk much, even to us kids. But the love and caring she gave us never diminished in any way. Her workload was colossal with seven kids, but we always had clean, pressed clothes to wear, lots of food on the table, and our home was spotless.

Mum always kept a large, beautiful flower garden that in later years became so well known that tour buses came by. She fed the whole family from her wonderful vegetable garden. A more incredible, loving and caring woman the world has never known.

Many years later, when I was dealing with my emotional hang-ups, I realized just how much those early emotional traumas had affected me. For years I had struggled to control my needing women as a way of dealing with whatever emotional pressures I had.

I was always attracted to women, and in fact have always found it hard to relate to men. Heather was the start of this pattern all those years ago. I felt safe with her so I developed a tendency to seek loving and caring women when I felt a need for emotional support. This in itself is not unhealthy, but it sure added to my emotional torment later during my marriage.

The programming most young males get is "men do not cry; do not show emotions; and are to be tough." As I think about it, when we grow up, a young boy's first feeling for another person outside his family often is his first girlfriend.

Up until then, most boys were allowed to feel anger, but never much love.

Girls have dolls and cuddly toys and plenty of cuddles from Mum and Dad, but boys are boys - fighting and in trouble, sparring with others to express their dominance. To be the toughest in your group was cool. You were a sissy if you cried or ran to Mum for comfort.

Yet when you got a girlfriend, a whole new range of feelings was allowed - tenderness, kindness, consideration, love, closeness and a lot more. And you know what? It felt really good. In fact, it bowled us off our feet. When we experienced our first crush, we were madly, obsessively in love.

All the shit in our lives would pale into the background when we were with "our" girl. And so the patterns were set. To be in love, to be loved, to have a new girl was the mechanism by which we subconsciously were able to handle, or override, all the shit in our conscious lives. Yep, to have a girl was the most powerful shit-suppressing drug a male could have. The world was, or could at last be, beautiful.

But of course that feeling, being only biological and a subconscious reaction to stimuli, soon passed, and it returned only when a new girl came on the scene. It is not hard then to understand that later in life when things get emotionally hard, a lot of men seek another woman. The pattern was set in our early teens.

If only young boys were encouraged, particularly by their fathers, to feel and express their emotions in a loving, caring and supporting environment and were able to feel good and safe in expressing those feelings in whatever way they needed around males, then the requirement to seek this comforting from women would not become so ingrained and obsessive.

Of course, when we got older, this urge translated into sex. I feel that if boys had different patterning when young, there would be fewer broken marriages and less promiscuity later in life.

There are a lot more people today bringing up their children who realize this to some extent, but in my day this certainly was not the case. When I think about it, I cannot once remember my Dad putting his arms around me and giving me a great big unconditional loving cuddle. Not once. I do not think he has ever looked me in the eye and told me he loved me.

I am not blaming him or judging him, but merely saying that this was how it was with him. He just could not express his emotions with us boys in that way, no doubt patterned after his own childhood. God knows how hard it would be to face that reality and then attempt to change it!

Many were the times when I have been in a group of men and the conversation (yes, men do gossip!) has been about somebody's buddy who was going through a hard time emotionally and was reacting with anger, and generally giving everybody around him a hard time.

Somebody in the group would say that he needed to go and get a good lay or he just needed a woman for the night and so on. Yes, I have been guilty of that myself. You see how ingrained this relationship between other women and men's emotional well-being is.

Some men use booze for the same reason, and as a result, get even more macho; some just get plain ornery with everyone around them. If they cannot express love, then the opposite must manifest.

I used women as well as anger to deal with my emotional hurt and loneliness. That is, until I was helped to take a good, hard look at myself. And that is when the real hard work started! But more about that later.

At thirteen, being called Fatso, alone and lonely inside, I started high school. Oldest brother Brian was working at home on the farm and the next oldest, Maurice, had started an apprenticeship in a nearby town. Maurice loved his work and was darn good at it. I can still remember how proud I was when he gained the highest marks in the country in his trade exams.

Maurice's success was Dad's pride. Not Maurice the person, but his worldly achievements. I say this because Maurice and Dad still had colossal arguments that became so bitter that Maurice came home to the farm less and less, until he eventually left for a working holiday overseas. I was devastated, my hero had deserted me.

High school for me was quite fun, on the outside anyhow, thanks in a large part to Cathy and all her friends.

Often at weekends she would bring home her girl friends; I was her big brother, so we all got along great.

Lots of holding hands and going for long walks on the farm allowed time for me to be with girls and have fun. I was never short of girl friends at school, but I recall many fights with other boys. It was quite a growing time for me, both physically and emotionally. I was at last starting to grow up instead of sideways and was thinning down as a result.

Being very strong and fit (lots of farm work saw to that), I did not shy away from the bullies and smart-asses, so more than one met his match, plus some. I was starting to come out of myself, even though I had only a few very close friends. Schoolwork was relatively easy, though I was lazy as all hell about it.

After years of struggling to be accepted by my older brothers and my Dad, I finally found myself in a situation that did not require that kind of struggle anymore. The girls accepted me just fine, and any bullies who did not, well, I just followed my Dad's example - got wild and belted them. I was starting to feel my power and I loved it. A lot of the fights I got into, or rather, ended, were a result of going to the aid of younger and smaller kids. Often Cathy or her friends would come to me and tell me that some poor kid or another was being picked on. I did not need to be told twice and I was into it.

I guess I must have been quick, because I cannot ever remember being hit back. Hell, my over-length arms and real farm-boy-sized hands packed one hell of a punch, so it was a brave kid who came back for seconds.

More and more kids came to me with their problems, even problems with teachers, when they felt they were being picked on. My arguing skills had been honed to a sharp point at home trying to compete with Dad and older brothers, so to take on some of the teachers was not daunting in the slightest.

School debates were great fun for me, and our team nearly always won. I even got into the finals of the public-speaking contest. Yep, I was starting to learn that you either got put down or you won. There was no in-between for me, and I realized darn fast just where I wanted to be.

I had spent most of my life feeling rejected, not good enough and put down, and now I had my chance to turn the tables. I was starting to feel alive and, hey! I could be in control. I did not have to be the underdog; all I had to do was to hit the hardest, run the fastest and argue with the most powerful emotions.

Anger in all of its manifestations was a winner. I had received expert training for fifteen years at home, so it was easy for me to excel and become top dog. It never occurred to me that I was becoming all the things that I did not like about my father. That took another twenty years.

Leaving high school after three years, my first job was in a bank. My Dad had encouraged me and had, in fact, made the initial approach to the bank manager. Fresh out of school and into the work force, I once again felt that I was the underdog. Well, not really the underdog, but when you go from being a senior in high school to the new kid at work, that macho role of being looked up to, of being important, goes out the door. Here you are, once more the new little boy still wet behind the ears.

Feelings of my childhood insecurities dominated my first few months of work, but I soon picked up what was required of me, and after six months I felt comfortable.

It was around six to eight months after starting work that I was able to purchase my first car, my pride and joy, a little English Morris Minor. Still living at home, the car gave me an unsurpassed feeling of freedom. At last I could get away from the farm on weekends and go to a local dance without having to beg my older brothers to take me.

Cathy started work in the same town not long after I did, and we started to spend most of our spare time together because we had mutual friends (in a town of only 500 people, it is pretty hard not to). We had dollars in our pockets, boyfriends, girlfriends, a car, booze and parties and no need to ask Mum and Dad if we wanted to go somewhere on the weekends. I mean to say, what else was heaven made of! And the best part was that there was always somewhere we just had to be on a Sunday morning, so we could not possibly get to church.

We still had a curfew at night. That was not so bad, as Dad never woke up. But Mum did; mothers have ears more effective than radar. Mum was a good sport and never told Dad when any of us got in late. I can remember many times coming home half drunk but on time, and Mum would never ask us what time we got in. But come in one minute late, even stone-cold sober, creeping in and not making a sound, you got it - Mum would know to the minute! Mothers!

These years from sixteen to twenty or so were great. I was able to let go of a lot of the anger, and I felt good about myself - well, most of the time anyhow. Home, more and more, became a place to stay away from.

After only a year and a half, I was totally bored with working at the bank. Needing desperately to get away from home, I handed in my notice and left. Dad hit the roof when he found out, and that was my cue. I packed my clothes into the old Morrie and hit the road, heading for the city sixty miles away.

I was going to start my life over, and this time I was going to do it my way. I was only seventeen going on eighteen.

CHAPTER 3
ANGELIC SEX AND
MY MACHO STRUGGLE

Getting a job, unskilled as I was, was still easy back then. My first job in the city was in an engineering foundry, breaking scrap iron. I found lodgings and made friends. Like many young males, I was car mad; I soon joined the newly formed Hot Rod Club. Having had the work ethic drummed into me by Dad, I always excelled at work. By this time my body was lean, mean and fit, and my work output was noted and rewarded.

Because I was now experiencing new friends and a change of work environment, I put everything into it. I was able to successfully file away in the too-hard-to-deal-with drawer all my previous childhood bitterness.

This working life was even better than high school. Fast cars and even faster women were like a narcotic to this young buck. Girlfriends came and went as did jobs, from working in sawmills and lumber yards to driving large bulldozers in tree logging, then going back to the iron foundry. It was during this time that I had my first sexual encounter.

It happened when I met an old girlfriend from high school at a party. Pauline was wonderful and we had a great time together for about six months. She had a terrific body and really knew how to use it. One of the most amazing memories of my early love life, and one that always helped me to hold women in the highest regard because of the beauty of what happened, was an experience that occurred one night around 1:00 am.

Pauline had left town to undertake nursing studies and we had not seen each other for about five weeks. It was a Wednesday night, and I had been asleep for about three hours when I was awakened by a feeling of awe about me.

Not a sound was made but I was wide awake, which was strange for me, as I am usually a slug when I first wake up, especially at that time in the morning.

I remember the room being pitch black as I turned over in bed to face the doorway. God, what a weird feeling I had! A real strong feeling of a presence, but of what, I did not understand and I started to get scared. My heart was really thumping, and just as I was about to leap out of bed and go for the light switch over by the door, I saw it.

I just froze, because about two yards from the bed was this slightly glowing and absolutely amazingly beautiful young woman. Remember, it was pitch dark, but I could see this thing, person, or angel very clearly and the body was clearly defined.

Recovering from my initial shock, I thought I recognized the person as Pauline. There she was, very slowly and deliberately taking off her clothes. Her movements were so flowing, delicate and angelic, it was as if her clothes were peeling off her rather than being taken off. When after what seemed like forever, she was completely naked, she smiled, and when she did, I felt this incredible wave of energy flood through my body.

It is hard to explain, but I had never felt anything like it. Not a word had been spoken by either of us and then, silently, she sort of glided towards the bed. I moved over and she slid in beside me. The incredible feel of her naked body against mine and the warmth that penetrated me, I will never forget.

Pauline and I had made love many times, but this was very different, way different. Yes, there beside me in the bed was, to all my awareness, a real live, human body, but somehow much more than that as well.

The loving, the pure mind-blowing sex I shared with that being that night was like nothing I had ever experienced before. Every movement, every touch, every action and reaction seemed to be in total harmony. This was much more than sex - this was loving.

Our bodies seemed to melt into a oneness where we were not two, but one, and the loving went on for hours. I can distinctly remember climaxing five times that night, a feat I have seldom equaled and never beaten to this day. (Must be getting old! Darn it.)

Finally, in the wee small hours, I fell asleep, totally exhausted. It was not until my boss, who used to pick me up at 7:30 for work, rapped on my bedroom window that I woke up.

I remember getting out of bed and almost collapsing on the floor in a sort of daze and bending down to kiss Pauline (or whoever, whatever this was) on the cheek and leaving, still without a word ever being spoken.

When I got home that night from work, my bed had been changed and made up perfectly. Pauline never made my bed. There was no note, or anything to show that I had ever had any company, except my very tired body. That was the last I ever saw or heard from her. To this day I still do not know if it was in fact Pauline, or even if it was from this earth. But it sure as hell was the best sex I ever had at that time, and it had a dramatic effect on my outlook.

My sister Cathy was aware of that inner shift and my struggle to reconcile my two selves. In fact, most women I met could see a deep, caring and gentle side of me, yet most men reacted only to my hard exterior. It was not until years later that I understood the struggle that was taking place within me.

The hard-driving, emotionally tough outer man was ego-driven. That was how I thought I had to be to make it in life, so I became darn good at it. The softer, gentler, feeling me was heart centered, and I was able to begin to express this part of myself more fully, as I began putting this book together.

This struggle between my two personalities and how I came to accept the other side of me is what this story is really about. That first heart feeling I experienced that night with

Pauline took a long time and a lot of emotional struggle for me to allow it to become a full part of my being. Whether it was Pauline or some angelic spirit is not the issue; the awakening that resulted from that experience helped me later to come to terms with myself.

Having operated an alternative health clinic for the past number of years, it is clear to me that a large number of men struggle with the same emotional torment: whether to be a "man" in this so-called real world with all its materialistic, success-driven goals and urges, or to be a human, who allows his deep inner feeling of spirituality and oneness with All That Is, to be the motivating factor in his life.

Material success never has been, and never can be, the source of inner peace and happiness. Yet, due to the society we live in, our whole life is geared to *this* "God." (Demon, or Mammon in the Bible.) It is only when we allow our hearts to open completely and receive our divine spirituality and oneness with All That Is that we can start to find that feeling of completeness.

Men have greater difficulty in accepting this, fearing the loss of their manhood and driven no doubt by their traditional perception as provider. If only they would realize that they would lose nothing in this change, but only add to their beingness, so much unnecessary mental and emotional anguish would be avoided.

Life is meant for living in the full consciousness of our whole selves, physical as well as spiritual. Feelings of incompleteness and aloneness are inevitable when any one of these is not part of our conscious awareness.

Acceptance of our spiritual nature does not mean going to church once a week, but completely accepting that we are spirit. I have counselled more people who go to church every week than any other group.

We are not humans having a spiritual experience but spirits having a human experience.

This simple fact has been stated in different ways by many great philosophers, including Jesus Christ. At last, I understand the fullness of that statement, and I hope each reader will also be helped to understand.

Approaching the age of nineteen, I found myself back working at the iron foundry in the city. I loved the work because I always got a tremendous feeling of creating something out of the earth itself. To take iron ore and sand and produce usable goods for mankind fulfilled something in me. I excelled at work, and the boss offered me an apprenticeship without loss of pay. As I was older than the usual apprentice, I had to apply to the local Apprenticeship Board for acceptance as an adult apprentice, which was granted.

This was a new experience, because now I was committed to working for five years at the same job. Realizing this, I decided to give it my best shot. If I had to be there for five years, I darn well was going to be the best.

As there were not enough foundries in my city to have an apprentice school, I had to do all the theoretical work by correspondence. I got one hell of a shock when I received the first assignment. It was three years since I had been in high school, so I had forgotten a lot of math. I had to go down to the bookstore and purchase all of the textbooks to relearn a lot of senior high math and physics.

As you can imagine, this was darn hard for me, as I was living in a flat in the city with a group of other guys, and when they were out partying I was at home studying. It was not long before I got sick of this and gave up this studying idea and joined the party set once again.

The assignments kept coming (20 per year) and the apprenticeship committee wrote to my boss because I was not completing them. They said that if I failed my national exams in November, I would be asked to leave the course. I got on very well with my boss and told him not to worry because, even though I was not doing the assignments, I was still going to pass the exams. How, I did not really know, I just felt inside that I would, and had no concern about it. He said he could not have me as an apprentice if I failed my exams, and it was my problem and left it at that.

The practical exams were in October. I had no trouble with them and was one of the top three in the nation. The theory exams were in November, with two three-hour exams on the same Saturday.

About one week before exam day, when I woke in the morning, I had this sudden idea about how to pass them. It was clear as a bell and I laughed at its simplicity, although I told no one. The day before exam day I asked my boss if I could have the afternoon off to study. He roared with laughter and told me it was a bit late to get concerned about my exams, but I could go ahead anyway. I was happy because I just knew my idea was going to work.

I went home to my apartment at lunch time, washed up and put up a big sign that told the others to party elsewhere that night because I wanted total quiet for ten hours. I got all twenty assignments and started with the first one, reading all that afternoon and all night until one hour before the exam the next morning.

As I read, I became aware of a feeling of being the words. A sort of transition took place and I could feel the *essence* of what was being said. It was as if I became one with the metal or was the furnace itself as I read. It was like going on an incredible trip into another dimension.

It was a bit like the night with Pauline. I sort of entered another world, but this time I stayed in this altered state the whole time and read the complete set of assignments. I remember going to the hall to sit the exam in a sort of daze.

Answering the questions was easy, for the state I was in allowed total recall of the assignments. I could still see the words in my mind, so I just wrote down the answers almost word perfect. As a result of this process, I got the highest marks in the country and was given the top award from the apprenticeship committee. I used this process for all six of my trade exams over the next three years and topped the country in all six.

At the time, I never gave much thought to this ability to concentrate at a level where I was in touch with my subconscious mind, as I thought it was perfectly natural. I also remember being able to use this process at work, to focus into the furnace and "see" the metal being melted and know its temperature before it was tapped out.

It was a time of great personal growth for me. I was made shop foreman with fifteen men under me at twenty-one years of age. A year later, I was manager of the foundry division with twenty-eight men reporting to me.

It was easy to focus my mind and know instinctively what decision to make, yet I always felt for the people in the shop as well. Of course, this ability and the power it gave me simply built up my ego at that age. I could do anything and achieve whatever I wanted, and I thought it was all my personal self.

The other, mellower, softer, caring me was still there, but it is amazing how material success overrides these deeper feelings. I continued on this big ego trip of me, me, me, and the more success, the greater my ego.

Of course, ego is not all bad, as it gives us the will to succeed in this material world. The problems start when we lose control of our ego, and as a result lose the ability to feel and to be in touch with a deeper part of ourselves.

Women, with their natural feeling ability (required for motherhood), have a great advantage; their ego functions non-aggressively. This is often seen by men to be a sign of weakness, whereas their own more upfront dominating and controlling ego is seen as strength.

Oh, how mistaken we men are, for in fact the opposite is the case! Luckily, a lot of women understand this and smile silently to themselves, letting the men play their silly games and not allowing themselves to be controlled and dominated.

But sadly, there are women who give in and become totally caught up in the material world and become dominated by men, usually their husbands. This often leads to feelings of worthlessness, emotional disharmony and torment as they go through life.

At this time in my life, I was heading down this usual male-dominating road, overriding all other parts of myself. Having just finished a stormy and intense relationship, I met my wife-to-be, Denise.

This incredible woman was to experience with me the most troubled stage of my life, to live through some of the most traumatic emotional experiences anybody could or should have to. She was to bear our three beautiful children and be an exceptional mother to them.

Here I was, about twenty-three years old, with a high-paying job, lots of friends and in control of my life, but increasingly I was feeling incomplete. Of course, I related this feeling to the material world and became increasingly dissatisfied with work.

For the first time since I started high school, feelings of incompleteness and aloneness were returning. Although I was rapturously in love with Denise and we were spending wonderful times together, there was real dissatisfaction and an urge to get out of the city. Denise, being born and bred on a farm, had an amazing and unique relationship with animals, so we decided to go farming when we got married.

Having made this decision, I left engineering and got a temporary job on a farm, so that when I applied for a good dairy-farm job, I could at least say I was working on a farm.

With our wedding coming up and a good job secured on a top farm, my emotions once again settled down. With this, the now-familiar, ego-driven, go-get-it self moved into top gear.

It was not until much later that I realized that these feelings of emptiness deep within me were emotional triggers that forced me to seek another direction in life, although the resistance I put up and the emotional imbalance that followed almost destroyed me in the meantime. However, I loved the new challenge on the farm and we gave it our best shot.

Within three years we were share-farming and milking three hundred cows. These were great times, even though very hard physically for Denise and me. But we were young and fit and nothing was impossible.

During this time, Denise gave birth to Mark, the first of two sons, and I slowly entered farm politics by way of the local farmers federation. My entry into farm politics was the start of a fifteen-year battle with a bureaucracy that did very little to support, let alone protect, its members.

On the personal front, Denise and I were getting on really well. Sure, we had some arguments, but as life was moving very fast for us, all our energies were spent working and being totally involved in the farm. Denise was a full financial, as well as working partner. In fact, she was a darn sight better with the cows than I was.

We were farming on some of the best dairy land in the Eastern Waikato of New Zealand's North Island and were stretched-out financially, as we had borrowed lots to purchase our cows. My first real big fight with the agricultural bureaucracy took place during the brucellosis eradication program.

It happened when the slaughterhouse workers went on strike and refused to slaughter the cows that reacted to the testing. As the program was nearing its end and a lot of farmers had lost many cows and lots of money, it was important for the testing of cows to continue so that farmers could identify the infected cows and keep them separated from the rest of the herd to stop cross-infection.

Since most of New Zealand's dairy farms are seasonal and the cows are not milked for two months in winter, it is this time when the share farmers move to new jobs or take delivery of more cows, so there are large movements of cows between farms.

All this movement adds up to hundreds of herds being split up and sold into many other herds. Many of the herds, as ours was, had been in the eradication program for a number of years, so it was important that any cows we purchased were tested by the government testers. That way, if they reacted we could at least keep them isolated until the slaughterhouse workers ended their strike. Otherwise, our disease-free cows could all get infected.

Of course, unions are not stupid; they always pitch their strike at the most difficult time for the employers. With this strike they had done their homework, so the workers were called out just at the time of this mass movement of cows between farms.

We had lost seven thousand dollars the previous year because of this disease, and there was no way we could stand the financial strain of a repetition. To replace the cows we had lost and to increase the number of our herd we had purchased fifty more cows for delivery on the first of June.

Written into the sale/purchase agreement was a clause that the cows were to be tested by the government testers. All was arranged, including the cattle trucks to bring the new cows to our farm on the due date, which was the day the union called out the slaughter workers.

The Director General of Agriculture, who has total control of agriculture for the country, issued an order as a result of the strike, that pulled all the government testers out of the field. All testing stopped.

I was in town on business that day, and Denise telephoned me at the accountant's office to tell me that the Agriculture Department had phoned and said that the testing of our newly purchased cows would not take place.

I immediately went to the office of the local Farmers' Federation to get them to phone the capitol and tell the Director General not to stop the testing of cows.

The Farmers Federation was already aware of the withdrawal of the testers, and the local chairman told me he was going to send a letter to the capital to inform them that this was not the best action.

I could not believe my ears!

"Write to them?" I bellowed,

"Why not just phone the idiots?" It did not matter what I said, I could not get through to them.

"One has to follow procedures," I was told, "and you do not just phone the Director General of Agriculture and tell him that he has made an incorrect decision."

Yes, the chairman agreed with me about the serious consequences of the testing being stopped, but you "had to follow procedures."

Well, I hit the roof! I mean to say, here was this person who was meant to fight for the farmers - that was what he was paid to do - and we had a situation not only of local, but potentially of national importance, that could cost the country tens of millions of dollars and this twit was following procedures!

God, I was angry. I left his office fuming and went to the office of the area headquarters of the Agriculture Department and demanded to see the area director.

I was shown into his office and, to my disbelief, I got the same argument. He admitted to me he was deeply concerned; many farmers were phoning in and trucking companies were pulling out their hair because no farmers wanted cattle moved without government testing clearance.

The one time of the year this mass movement of dairy cattle takes place and all hell had broken loose, yet all the so-called experts could say was, "Well, we have to follow procedures!"

Damn it, this directive had to be changed now - today, not tomorrow or next week. The infuriating thing was that everybody agreed with me but nobody in a position to do anything had the guts to do it. Who the hell was this Director General of Agriculture anyhow? Why was everybody afraid to just pick up the phone and talk to him?

I went back across town to the Federated Farmers' office and, yes, they were pulling out all the stops to resolve the problem.

The chairman had called a special meeting of the crisis committee for the next day. The next day? I exploded.
"What the hell is this country coming to?" I yelled.

"What if we had an outbreak of foot-and-mouth disease? Would you call a meeting for the next day, too?"

My exploding anger must have intimidated the chairman because he spluttered hesitatingly, "W..e..ll, the local Director of Agriculture has a special code to call the capitol in a case like that."

That was the breakthrough I needed. I just left the idiot standing there shaking in his shoes and bolted out of his office, down the stairs (too impatient to wait for the elevator) and ran to my car, a very fast Italian sports model.

As I hit the key and throttle simultaneously, the car leapt into life and, with tires screaming, rev counter going over the red line, and gear changes that would have made a Formula One driver proud, back across the city I went.

Arriving back at the Agricultural Department office, I ran straight into the Director's office without knocking. Lunging forward over his shiny mahogany desk, I grabbed him by his shirt and tie at the throat and pulled him forward over his desk. His chair shot backward as his legs flew out from under him, and with his head held down on the desktop with my enraged face about two inches from his, I gave him his options: he would either use his infectious-disease code to get through to the Director General in the capitol, or I would beat it out of him and do it myself.

With that, I gave him an almighty shove and he shot backwards and hit the wall before collapsing into a heap on the overturned chair. I grabbed the phone and slammed it down on the desk in front of him and said in the most bloodcurdling, power-charged voice, "Do it!" The poor guy was petrified, and with an instinctive reaction of pure self-preservation he reached for the phone and dialled.

Well, as they say in the movies "the rest is history." By 4 p.m. that day, full government testing of all cows was under way again and a crisis of national importance had been averted. (This is the power, and the lure, of ego-driven self. You can move mountains, but at the time are blind to the cost to your deeper self.)

Emotionally drained, I slowly drove back to the farm, reflecting on the day. I should have felt elated because single-handedly I had saved my country millions of dollars and hundreds of fellow farmers all sorts of emotional and financial stress. I had also done the impossible - turned a government ruling completely around in a few hours. But I did not feel happy with myself and I was not sure why.

Arriving back at the farm, Denise came out to greet me with a smile on her face.

"I hear you have had quite a day," she said. Apparently the Agriculture Department's local director had phoned her before I got home to let her know what had happened.

She was told to tell me that he held no grudge towards me for what I did and that if I had not put the pressure on him, he would not have got the testing started again as quickly. He also told Denise that after he had informed the Director General of the situation and it was changed, the Director General phoned him back and thanked him for going outside his normal authority and not allowing a crisis to develop in the dairy industry.

I just sat in the car and cried. The emotion and the power I had had to display was frightening. It came to me just how dangerous that sort of emotional power could be if it got out of control. I had achieved my objective, but there was no satisfaction with that success. I remember saying to Denise that I behaved just like Dad used to. Sure, I got the job done, but at what cost? I was emotionally shot to hell, and I knew it.

But you know, success is success, and after two or three days, the emotional hiding I had given myself was pushed to the back of my mind. I began to feel that I had done it all, and the whole incident became an ego trip. Once again, the two sides of my personality were evident, but the dominating, power side had had a big win, validating a pattern I had picked up from Dad when I was a kid. The gentle, loving side did not have a chance.

The terrible toll that this emotional power had on me did not become evident until about ten years later.

This pattern of behavior was so set that I used this ego power in all aspects of my life - with Denise, the kids, with anybody I had dealings with about the farm, and especially in farm politics.

Yes, sure, I was a nice guy most of the time and had lots of fun with our kids and all that, but look out if anybody did not perform to my very high expectations! My intolerance of slow, sloppy or ineffective work, or suppliers of goods or services to the farm triggered instant anger and a good tongue-lashing. God, I got results as people jumped when I said, "jump." I really thought this was the only way to get results.

More and more, I looked at other people's way of doing things or running their business as not good enough. Nobody was performing; nothing was done quickly enough.

I guess to all the people who knew me, I was becoming a right arrogant bastard, but I never thought I was. I just thought most people around me needed to wake up and get with it and start performing. The feeling side of me was still there, but its suppression was almost total.

More and more, feelings of frustration became the norm within my conscious reality. To counter the emotion and mood swings that were occurring as a result, I buried myself in even greater work efforts and commitment. By leasing more land and raising corn, combined with a silage contracting business, as well as the 300-cow dairy farm, I was able to fully utilize my drive for production and perfection.

Working fifteen to eighteen hours a day became the norm. I was in my ego element, spending long hours on tractors and other machinery.

It is strange really, but I always felt at home with machinery. I could communicate with it, feel it and always know if anything was going to go wrong before it happened. This shift in dimension to another reality was easy, and I became a part of the tractor.

I always used to modify the fuel settings and air intakes of the engines to give them their all. It was like they were able to talk to me and we were in complete harmony. There was no greater thrill than to work a tractor for fifteen or so hours at its absolute maximum and to know when to back off on the power and when to give it heaps; to take it right to the point of tipping on sides of hills, plus some, and talk it through the steepest part. Yeah, that was living; it was like a drug to me back then, and I was able to fully pour my emotional energy and ego power into sheer work.

During these years our second son, Craig, was born, and at least Denise got a break from my driving power, because during the small amount of time I actually spent at home I was quite easy to live with. I had no pent-up energy to express, so life settled into work and more work. At last I had found some fulfilment, some purpose in my life. At the time, I did not see the shallowness of this fulfilment. I was not yet to know the absolute despair I would feel when it all went wrong.

CHAPTER 4
ME AND MY EGO

After our third child, Karen, was born, Denise was kept very busy, as our oldest, Mark, was not yet four. Share farming was financially good, as product prices were moving up. Even though we had a very high debt, we were making good money. The contracting and corn growing, as well as milking 300 cows, engaged all my time and energy. Denise helped out on the farm whenever required, but as we employed full-time labor, she was able to spend most of her time being a mother to the kids.

Trips home to my parents became few and far between other than the mandatory Christmas visit, but visiting Denise's parents was always a trip worth taking. Her upbringing had been the opposite of mine, so visiting there was a welcome retreat for me into another world - a world where people came first, where nothing was expected of you, where you could just be yourself. I was always able to feel very centered there and very close to nature.

It was easy to see how Denise had developed her amazing ability to understand and interact with animals through her childhood environment. This would allow her to keep our farm running in the years to come when I would be emotionally unable to.

Even though I was very much into work and "making it," there were times when I felt an emptiness well up inside of me, an incompleteness, and that now-familiar aloneness. I took these feelings to be a sign that I was under-achieving. Or was that an excuse? I do not know. But to suppress these feelings, I pushed myself and everybody around me even harder.

Although we had many friends among the farming community we lived in, there were no really close ones that I could talk to about subjects other than farming. Thus, we were very lucky to make close friends with a couple who lived nearby and had kids of similar ages. At first, I thought the wife was a bit hoity-toity from the way she spoke, which was very correct and proper. But as usual, first impressions can change and we became very close. In fact, I turned to Jo when the emotional pressures built up.

At first, we used to meet and just talk. You know, having a special friend is very important. Most people need a friend they can always talk to from the heart about all their secrets - the things they would not dare tell anybody else, not even their spouses. It is sad that society practically prevents a man from having woman friends other than his wife. The same thing is true for a woman about having man friends, but it is usually the husband's jealousy that cannot deal with that.

I think it is part of our society's conditioning that puts men at a big disadvantage as far as being able to have women friends. We cannot talk to men friends like that because it is not manly or macho. Talking about emotions and things other than work or money makes most men very uncomfortable. Face it, most of us cannot talk to our wives about our inner feelings, can we? For goodness sake, that would be giving up our control, ownership and dominant position in the marriage, would it not? We could never allow that, now could we?

God help us stupid men because, heavens above, most of us cannot help ourselves. Well, I certainly could not at the time! So it was Jo who became my special friend.

The relationship was not about mad, passionate love; rather, she understood my need to have someone to talk to. Many times when we met, we did not actually talk much at all.

In fact, very little happened; we would just sit close to each other and the feeling of comfort and safety that would come over me allowed me to process or work through my feelings my way.

I guess a lot of people use church and other such groups for that safe, belonging feeling. I never had any guilt feelings as a result of our time together. Anyhow, I was able to hold myself together much more. That is probably an excuse, but nevertheless, it is true.

My swings of emotion were to become a major battle for me later. The more I pushed to achieve and, in fact, did achieve, the more empty and unfulfilled I felt and the more I needed my special friend. I was on this accelerating treadmill driven by success, pushing harder and faster.

I had no way of knowing at the time that these feelings of emptiness and unfulfilment were the triggers that would cause me to look beyond the physical and material world for the fulfilment I so desperately sought. How could I? I had rejected any spiritual ideas, even the idea of God to a large extent, as a result of my childhood experiences. My ego had taken over and I, me, was all there was to life.

However, deep down in my heart I knew that I would have to face some acceptance of my spirituality sometime. But at that time, I made sure that's where it darn well stayed, deep down.

In many ways I think I felt a fear that maybe I was wrong; that there was a God; that all my early Catholic teaching may have been correct. But I would be damned if I let that be true, so the alternative was rejection of all religious and spiritual thought. I had no other situation to base my beliefs on.

Face it, being brought up a Catholic meant being told that everyone else was wrong, that the Catholic view of God, and everything else, was right. That was all there was to it! The whole basis of Catholic teaching was judgment, blame, fear and shame, and you would be damned for all eternity if you even thought that some other teaching might have some truth.

I guess my reasoning was that if I rejected it all, at least I might escape the "be damned for all eternity" bit on the plea of ignorance: "I honestly did not know any better, your Honor,

Sir." So to allow even a few spiritual thoughts to come through would be asking the ego to release some control. And when the ego was as dominant as it was in me at that time, that was almost impossible.

So the battle lines were drawn, the ammunition inside me was primed, and the war that would rage in the future would all but destroy me. Yep, I was on a collision course with myself, but I had no way of knowing it.

It was years later, when I was professionally counselling people, that I realized just how many people, especially men, suffer this sort of battle between the ego's drive for success and a yearning for deeper meaning. Often it is the very successful businessman who has some of the hardest battles because, as in my experience, material success was not fulfilling at the deepest level. Realizing this is, indeed, a hard pill to swallow.

It was during these share-farming years that I was the furthest from really knowing myself. I was into agricultural politics; I felt the world needed to change and that only I had the sense to see what changes were needed and how to make them. I had a good friend nicknamed "Woodeneye." He got that name, not because he had a wooden eye, but because if anybody told him he could not do this or that, he would say, "Wouldn't I? just you watch me." He was game as all hell, a man of my own heart. So we all called him Woodeneye, and the name stuck.

He and I were one hell of a team in farm politics and were on the provincial (state) executive of the share farmers' association and had some right royal battles. I guess we thought we were always achieving something, but in fact we were probably alienating ourselves because of the way we expressed our points.

Angry young upstarts was how others probably perceived us. Looking back now, I realize just how poorly we were able to get our points across. But we had some good wins and a hell of a lot of fun in the process. I remember how I used to love to make fools out of the bureaucrats.

God, I was so judgmental. I guess I was also quite hard to live with, with all the work pressures and forever out to this meeting or that one, and always angry about something. It became a bit like at school; everybody came to me to take on their problems, which I did with great gusto. I remember once Woodeneye and I were in the capital for a meeting, and on returning home we got into a major political debate with a couple of airline pilots in the airport cafeteria. The debate got so intense we lost all track of time and ended up missing our flight home.

Here we were, two country boys playing big shots, and no way home. As there were only one or two flights which left for our destination, we were in rather deep shit. It was only a day trip to our meeting, so we had no money with us. We both had cows to milk the next morning, so getting home was a must. To convince the airline to allow us on the last flight, we had to use all our considerable persuasive skills.

We told the airline people that their speaker system informing the passengers of their flights was not good enough in the dining room and that was the reason we missed our flight. We turned the whole argument around so that the airline thought it was their fault, not ours. Needless to say, we were on the last flight and arrived home still cracking up with laughter. Yes, we were a damn good team and could bullshit our way out of most problems, and most probably into a darn sight more, but we did not see it that way then.

Looking back, I always had real deep feelings for the injustices that people had to put up with and the stupidity of many government decisions and programs. My driving urge was to correct all of these wrongs for the good of all. Even then, people were the most important reason to fight the system. The trouble was, I made the judgment that anybody who was not on our side was the enemy, and all was fair in love and war. But when the arguing was over, I was always able to be friends with the "enemy" because I was fighting the system, not the people. But to take on the system, I treated people as the enemy.

Many times I had to wrestle with my conscience over this. I would really feel guilty that I had to be so hard on people, and many times I would arrive home after a particularly hard fight feeling emotionally drained and not at all proud of myself because of the anger and power I had used against people. I spent hours trying to convince myself that there was no other way, none that I knew of. But it did no good, as something deep within me felt there had to be another way.

Often some of the biggest wins left me with a wrenching feeling of remorse. True, I was not using my fists like I had back in high school, but my ego-driven power with words was even more destructive and, damn it, I was starting to feel sorry for the individuals on the receiving end.

I was getting good at arguing and using a power I did not even understand. It became so easy to destroy people emotionally that winning an argument was never in question.

I remember Denise repeatedly telling me that I had only to look at somebody when I was angry to cut them down, and then, when I opened my mouth, they had no chance. Of course, there was no way I would admit to this, so I answered that they were just weak, and if they could not take a good argument they should not argue. But on the inside, I was really starting to hurt because of my ability to cause pain to others.

Often I would talk to Jo about these feelings, but Jo already knew that I was as soft inside as I was hard outside and that this inner struggle was starting to affect me. Of course, Denise knew also, but at the time I did not know how to let her help me. An outer wall of stone had been built up so well during the years since I had left home that no one close to me was going to see my real self, or so I thought. (The collision course with myself was starting to gain momentum. It would be a bloody rough ride before I finally ran smack into myself.)

At this stage we had been farming for six years. My need to move to even greater challenges to satisfy my obsession with success was becoming so strong that I looked around for a suitable farm to purchase.

Finding a farm that could be developed, I played all the financial power games I had learned and raised most of the loan money. We needed an extra $35,000 to finalize the deal, and since my oldest brother Brian had purchased the home farm from Dad, with Dad leaving most of the money in the property as a mortgage, I asked him to refinance some of Dad's money out so that Dad could then put it into my farm.

Brian was in full agreement with this, but as Mum and Dad were on vacation in Europe at the time, we had to set it all up with the lawyers to enable us to purchase the farm when Dad returned.

Upon Mum and Dads' return, Denise and I went to visit them to explain what we had set up. Brian and I could see that there were some real benefits for Dad, as his money would be secured by two farms instead of one and the income from nearly twice as many cows would offer him a greater guarantee for his interest.

I had agreed to reimburse Brian for the extra interest he would pay by having to get his mortgage money on the open market. We thought it was a real good move for all. However, Dad had different ideas. I could not believe it; he was angry about the idea and an explosive fight developed.

Dad argued that he wanted to keep his money in his farm. (It was not his anymore, as he had sold it to Brian about five years before.) Another point he tried to make was that we should continue share-farming until we could buy a farm outright with cash.

Damn it, I thought, what is this? He had given Brian a 100% loan to buy his cows when Brian share-farmed for him, and done the same thing when Brian bought the family farm! All of it, every damn cent! And now he was telling me I should save the entire purchase price to buy our farm.

How that could be done, even if I lived to be a hundred, I did not know. Besides, Dad had borrowed 90% of the money to buy the home farm from one of Mum's brothers. So to me, he had some contradictory double standards somewhere.

Anyway, the argument raged on for about three hours and Dad, as usual, vented all of his anger because we would not see his point. I was furious, as all the family could see the benefits, and my farm purchase would fall through if I could not get this mortgage transfer.

I was not asking him to write a check or give me and Denise cash. The money was already tied up in land; the only difference was that less than fifteen percent of it would be transferred to another piece of good farming land.

When everybody had finally become emotionally worn out and things cooled down, Dad agreed to come and look over the farm we wanted.

Needless to say, he really liked the place. He agreed to make the transfer, and that started a whole new chapter of giving control of my life back to my father. I should have realized at the time that once he had money in the farm, I was under his control, as far as he was concerned.

This ensured that the old pattern of domination and his differing perceptions and attitudes would lead to many arguments and build up much emotional stress later, especially when farming went through its biggest financial depression since the thirties. As extra security, over and above the registered mortgage, I signed over to him an $8,000 insurance policy.

I am not relating this part of my life to be hurtful or judgmental, but to express that even though our family had many emotional upheavals, I still felt a strong connection and a deep sense of belonging. After all, we kids had worked our butts off on the farm; without that work and those improvements, it would not have possessed its present value.

We never received wages or pocket money as school kids, and to my knowledge none of us ever asked for cash, just mortgage assistance from the family assets, which was to be paid back in full. Hardly a parental handout. More like a normal business agreement, using the assets we all helped to create to help us get started. Well, that is how I looked at it, anyhow. I also reasoned that I was a damned good risk due to my track record.

When we share-farmed, we secured from the Rural Bank the biggest single loan they had ever given a share farmer. At the time their limit was $11,000, but our loan was approved at $16,000 due to the production we had achieved. I put up quite a fight to get the bank to go beyond the $11,000 limit due to the fact that many share farmers were starting to milk two to three hundred cows and more. Eleven thousand dollars was like petty cash to an operation that size.

Denise and I were also the first people in the country to get a bank loan on cows with a budgeted production level of 500 kg of milk fat per hectare.

This was regarded as the four-minute mile of pastoral (grass) farming and, at that time, very few farmers had achieved it. We were very fortunate that prior to going share farming we had worked on a farm owned by Bernie Davis, who was right at the leading edge of pastoral farming production. In fact, the year Denise and I milked and ran the farm with Bernie as 29% share farmers, the farm achieved a national first by becoming the first commercial, privately owned farm to achieve the 500-kilo level. So we were right up there with the top guns of pastoral farming in a country that was and still is regarded as the leader in pastoral farming in the world.

By being well-known in farming politics and at the top 5% in production output, we were able to break all the bank's borrowing rules, and in so doing, we had a large part in changing the rules for hundreds of share farmers in the future.

I recall that on completion of our first year of 50% share-farming, when we had achieved 495 kg/ha from a target of 500, the Rural Bank brought all the area appraisers out to our farm for a day to show them how we had done it and to give them a greater understanding so they would believe other young upstart farmers when they put in loan applications that might seem outrageous.

It was from this background that we approached Dad on his return from Europe to ask if he would make the transfer from Brian's farm to ours of a small parcel of mortgage moneys. The incredibly deep hurt and feeling of rejection I felt when he resisted so much stayed with me for years. For God's sake, I would think, the biggest rural lending bank in the country is backing me way over their limit, the dairy company is backing me, my track record is well and truly proven, and here is my own father giving me a hard time!

Is there anything I have achieved that is good enough for this man? What in God's name does he expect of me? What do

I have to do to get his approval? I guess I felt the same deep hurt as I had when years before my brother Maurice got the highest marks in the country for five out of his six trade exams and was taken out to dinner and praised at family gatherings, etc., but when I achieved six top marks out of six in my engineering exams, I never got as much as a postcard from Dad saying, "Well done son." To this day I have never heard those words from my father.

You know, it is amazing how this lack of acceptance by parents, especially father to son, affects us. At the time I took this to mean that I was not good enough, so to be good enough I had to achieve more and more. As Dad was a material world achiever, I needed to be this too. This incredible urge, this drive deep within me, overshadowed all other parts of my being. And of course, when we suppress parts of ourselves we start to get screwed up emotionally.

It was years later that I realized that by trying to be accepted, I had become very much like my father, even beginning to treat my kids the same way. It was only when I came to the conclusion, that I did not need my father's approval; that I had a right to be me for my own sake and to feel good about myself; that I did not have to be the best or to achieve the most in the shortest time, that I then started to treat my own kids differently and to love them for themselves, not for what I thought they should achieve.

They have this God-given right to be themselves and to be accepted, loved and cherished just for being, just as I had the right to be. It was at this point that I really started to grow and change the me in myself.

It was not an easy process, and in some ways I am still going through it. The biggest single outward change occurring is that slowly I am losing the anger that was in me. I am feeling more and more love, and as I change I become "more" (fulfilled), and I express what I now am.

Sure, I still get angry and frustrated with people, but it is a damn sight less severe and it soon passes. I seek serene, gentle places to be and try not to attack people emotionally anymore. Yes, I think I am changing - well, at least I like myself a whole lot more. So I hope that rubs off and maybe other people like me a lot more.

You see, when we like and approve of ourselves, we do not need approval from others. Then, and only then, can we be ourselves. We cannot really love others until we love and accept ourselves. It is simple really. We cannot share something we do not have.

It took me a long time to dissolve my anger with the world - well, most of it - to stop blaming my father; to stop blaming the financial system; and to realize that the person who looks back at me in the mirror holds all the responsibility.

Yes, we certainly can be programmed by our parents and society, but it is up to us to take responsibility and stop hurting others. To do this, we must first stop hurting ourselves. This requires complete self-acceptance and self-love, and only we can achieve this for ourselves. Nobody can do it for us. Sure, we can be helped, but in the end it is only ourselves who have the power to change who we are. Yep, it is that face in the mirror that we have to talk to. The world may well be an asshole, but maybe it is allowed to be that way so we can recognize it and then make sure we are not.

The farm we purchased was much smaller than the one we had share-farmed, milking 130 cows instead of 300, but there was a lot of work to do that kept me busy.

Within three months of moving onto the farm, the bank approved a development loan which allowed us to re-fence it, put in lanes and upgrade the water supply.

The best production that had been achieved on this farm was about 330 kg/ha, but we were going for 500 once again. As the farm's land surface had rolling hills and a bit drier soil, this goal would be very hard to realize.

Being the young upstart that I was, we financially stretched ourselves like a guitar string, purchasing more cows and starting the season with 185. The locals thought I was stark, raving mad, as the farm was only 128 acres and nobody in the area was milking more than a cow per acre.

I had total confidence that, with the development I had in mind, we could milk that many cows. Anyhow, the more people said we could not do it, the more certain I became that we could. I remember that my emotions were fairly even during this stage. I still visited Jo on occasion; we often talked about spiritual things and generally enjoyed each other's company.

With the farm ticking over just fine and Denise able to handle the cows on her own with ease, I developed the contracting business even more. In the first year, we reached our production targets and immediately I started to get bored. Hell, running the little farm was just too easy for us, so I began spending more and more time on the tractor contracting.

The second year was very dry and we did not reach our production targets, but cow and land prices were moving up, so our financial position looked pretty good.

More and more, I started to feel that I wanted something more, a greater challenge. That old inner drive was really coming to the fore, so I began to look for bigger farms. Denise was really happy with the present farm, but she understood my need to be pushed to the limit.

As land prices had moved up, there was no way we could afford a 300-cow farm in our area, so I started to look farther afield. Weekend after weekend, I would drive for five or six hours to other areas to look at farms, and it was during those drives that I could always move to that other part of myself.

I would drive very fast, and it was like I was not driving at all; I had very little conscious perception of the actual driving. My whole being was sort of moved to a different dimension. I loved the feeling, and I remember the time after arriving at my brother Eddie's farm about five hours' drive north, having to sit in the car for five minutes or so to bring myself back to everyday reality.

It was like I had been flying through another plane of existence; the five-hour trip felt like it had taken only a half hour or so. My whole body would be vibrating with energy. It was a really neat feeling, but I never really gave it much thought, as I had come to expect it when I was able to drive alone for long distances.

At that time, I had not made the connection between this experience and my ability to focus into and become part of the metal in the furnace back in my engineering days, or the experience with Pauline as a teenager, or my ability to focus on a problem and feel the thing I was concentrating on and see the answer.

The same thing used to happen on the tractor when I could feel it starting to slide or tip on very steep hills; I would just talk to it and immediately it would feel safe. Many times I would look back at where I had driven and wonder how on earth I did it without tipping over.

The farmers I used to contract for would just shake their heads at the places I drove tractors. I remember one farmer for whom I was harvesting a particularly steep and hilly field sitting in his pickup all night watching me.

At about three in the morning during a break for coffee and something to eat, I told him he did not have to stay up all night watching us work. He said there was no way he was going to bed, as he just had to watch. Never before had that part of the field been harvested, and to see me drive my tractor and harvester around the sides of those hills without even slowing down was utterly amazing. Why the whole thing did not just tip over, he did not know.

I only laughed and said, "it would not dare tip over with me driving it, as tomorrow there are other farmers expecting me."

Hell, I did not realize then that my intense concentration was a form of mind power that had the ability to slightly change normal reality. I certainly had no idea that I was getting lots of help from forces that were not traditionally associated with so-called "normal" reality. I always could feel that my body was very different after these times. It would be buzzing and had a sort of inner heat for up to a half hour after I stopped, and my mind would be a little hazy, making it hard to think normally. Often I would have to splash water over my face to clear my mind.

At the time, I had no idea I was using an energy or power that ancient gurus and teachers had spoken about. In fact, the ancient Egyptians and other races knew how to use this ability, but I just thought it was all me, never giving it another thought. It was just my normal self, and I used this ability in arguments to make things happen, to destroy people emotionally and to allow me to know, really know, what and how to do things.

Face it, my ego-driven self was having a field day with me. I did not know it, but somebody (guess who) was setting me and my ego up for a big fall, which by now was not too far away.

I was reasonably happy with my home life. Well, Denise and I usually got on pretty good. Denise was the type of person who could get on with most people. She was always so beautifully centered, but I was really pushing myself. I did not like normality very much, as I got bored very quickly.

By pushing myself toward success and achievement, I was able to put myself into this other dimension. The buzz I got was becoming like a drug. To the people around me, I must have acted like an egotistical bear with a sore head. A right pain-in-the-ass was what some people probably thought, and I guess they were not too far off.

By the third year on our own farm, land prices had nearly doubled, so we put our farm on the market. After a couple of false starts, we got it signed up at nearly twice what we had paid. Then, I had to find another farm before the next milking season; as the third season had also been rather dry, the irrigated Canterbury plains of the South Island became worth looking at.

A friend and I decided to travel south to have a look around, and while there I found a suitable farm. It did not have the most desirable soil type for milking cows, and at the time it was running sheep. But it was in my price range and it sure would be a challenge to convert it to a dairy farm.

It needed a lot of work and development, but that was what I was looking for. As land prices were still moving up with no end in sight, I figured that the sooner I purchased, the better. Getting all the paperwork together did not take me long and soon we were the owners of 336 acres of flat, irrigated, second-class sheep land.

If people thought I was mad trying to milk as many cows as we did on our North Island farm, then they were sure I had lost all my marbles intending to milk any cows at all on our new farm.

Most people organize their money before they sign up for a farm purchase, but that was too easy for me. I signed up for a $386,000 farm and then went out to find the money to pay for it.

For the first time in years, I really had to push to find the cash. Nobody would believe me when I said that the farm could carry milking cows. I was dealing with the same bank but in a totally different part of the country, and the appraisers were so damn conservative it was appalling. I had one hell of a fight to raise the cash, and it was only our past history and the personal intervention of the bank's national manager that made it possible for us to get the purchase money.

We also needed a large development loan, and that proved even harder to get. Being me, I just went ahead with the conversion anyhow. We had the new milking plant built and ready for milking, the water supply to all the paddocks installed, the whole farm re-fenced - before we even had a dime to pay for it!

It was three months after we took over before the development loan was finally approved. But the bank had attached some strings. For the first time in its history, it had granted a development loan for a one-year term on the condition that if I did not reach my production target at the end of the first year, they would pull the skids from under me. But if we reached the production target, the loan would be granted a normal table mortgage.

Boy, it was shapeup or ship-out time in a big way! Every cent we had ever earned was now at risk. I loved it! I was in my element. If I had wanted a challenge, I really had it now. My ego and I would really have to dance for our supper this time.

CHAPTER 5
MY EGO AND I TAKE A TUMBLE

Before we even moved onto our new farm, we had all sorts of financial problems. Like when Dad wanted $12,000 paid back to him, even though he knew we were going to be stretched out financially with all that had to be done on our new farm. And then the old farm property appraisal was reduced by $50,000. The farm had been a leasehold property, and when we prepared to sell it as a freehold, we had to apply for the freehold price from the government so that we could determine the selling price.

The first purchaser did not complete the deal, so we had to put the farm up for sale again. The resulting delay was longer than the three months the government had given us for converting it to a freehold.

This is not normally a problem, as that price is usually stable. But in our case, an employee at the Valuation Department was interested in purchasing the farm, but did not have the necessary cash deposit, so he told us the farm was too expensive.

When we signed up the final buyer and informed the Valuation Department that we were ready to pay them the cost of freehold, they informed us that because more than three months had elapsed, they would have to re-evaluate the farm.

Many lawyers' letters went back and forth; I even went to see the area head of the department. The farm's purchase price was not a penny more than the first time, so their argument that land prices had gone up just did not hold water. But no amount of talking and argument would change their minds. It was going to cost us an extra $50,000 to freehold the place. God, I was mad! We had no way out but to pay the extra money.

Only later we found out from the real estate agent that the employee of the Valuation Department who handled our file was the same person who wanted to buy our farm. Because we would not lower our price for him, he made damn sure it cost us the fifty thousand he had wanted us to reduce our farm by. He used the expired three-month time clause to re-evaluate our farm and increase the price.

It was an easy thing for him to do, as he was a senior appraiser. Our lawyer told me later that the department had never done that to any case he have handled before.

I was in favor of taking the Valuation Department to the high court, but our lawyer said, as it was a civil case, it could take two to five years, and in the meantime we would not be able to sell the farm to anybody, and as the new purchaser wanted the land now and as freehold, we could not do a damn thing.

The most infuriating point to me was that between the time the purchaser saw the farm and actually signed the papers, a different purchaser appeared who was prepared to pay cash above the leasehold price and then freehold the farm himself later.

I declined, as I had agreed to sell to the other party. I chose to stay true to my word, even though at that time I was under no legal obligation to do so. That little bit of integrity cost me a cool fifty grand.

I can laugh about this now, but at the time I could quite easily have cut the balls off that bastard in the Valuation Department for that dirty trick. He did not get our farm, but he made sure it cost us the fifty thousand.

The next kick in the guts we got was when the Rural Bank would not accept the cost of trucking all the cows down to the new farm as part of the development costs. They would not accept that cost in the development loan.

I had earlier looked into this when I was doing the preliminary costing before I purchased the farm and had been informed by the bank that the transportation cost would be part of development.

Since there were not enough cows available for purchase in the sheep-farming part of the country, we were naturally going to truck our cows to the new place. But the bank in our new area saw it differently, probably because they thought we would not be able to milk cows there, anyway.

Or maybe I was pushing the bank manager's comfort buttons due to the way I operated. Anyhow, here we were on the new farm with $112,000 less cash than I had budgeted for. Fifty grand less for the old farm than we had thought, fifty grand for trucking and twelve grand we paid back to Dad. All cash that I thought I had available to me when I signed up for the new farm. Talk about pushing shit uphill with a garden rake!

The challenge I had wanted was turning into a monumental impossibility. At the time I never even thought of bailing out, even though that probably would have been the wise thing to do.

The next few months were hectic, what with getting the farm ready to milk cows and fighting with the bank to get the development loan approved. Long days and even longer nights were spent building the milking shed to handle the three hundred cows.

I was totally absorbed in work and, as was usual for me at that time, everything had to be done yesterday. Thus, my suppliers of building materials, etc. were on the receiving end of my impatience. But when there were many cows due to calve in a matter of weeks, we just had to have everything ready.

I had hired a friend and his helper to assist in the concrete work on the new milking shed while I did the engineering. We started with a bare field on May 5 and had the milking shed finished on June 10, ready to milk cows. I was in my element!

Things were happening and it was like a phoenix rising from the ground as the whole farm was transformed. I never even doubted that I would not get the development loan; I just would not take no for an answer. Finally it was approved - with strings.

That first year on the new farm was the hardest I had faced up to that time. We were always short of money, due to the shortfall of cash. Having to get money on the short-term money market to pay the trucking firm, we were always late in paying our bills. To purchase the supplies and materials that we needed, I just kept talking with total confidence. But inside, I was starting to feel the pressure, and even though I would not admit it to myself, I was getting hard to live with.

The continual borrowing from Peter to pay Paul, the never-ending work and battling cold winter weather, all took their toll on me. But I was in too deep now. Although I had dug a bloody great financial hole, there was no way I was going to give up.

Unknown to me then, our move south had started a whole train of events that would push my emotional health beyond the breaking point. The incredible pain would finally force me to look at myself and start the changes I have since gone through.

It is hard to pinpoint the one thing that starts us on another path, because our entire life experience bring us slowly to that point. But moving to that new farm certainly put things on fast forward.

When I think about buying a $380,000 farm and spending another hundred thousand on it in the first six months, then having to borrow the $112,000 we were short on the short-term money market, unsecured and at an average of 22% interest, I realize it was worse than a living hell.

We could not get this money on a normal mortgage because the Rural Bank and Dad had first and second mortgages for their small amounts of money. This led to another big battle when the bank finally approved the development loan.

They wanted a second mortgage, so I asked Dad to move his remaining loan back to third. "No way" was his answer, but the bank insisted they wanted second and it was a bank policy not to allow family money to have prior mortgage.

There I was, desperately needing this money to pay for the cow shed and other bills, and we could not get the money that was approved because Dad would not move his mortgage back. I was at my wits' end, with creditors pressing me from all sides, and I just could not get Dad to move.

In desperation, I asked my brother Brian to talk to Dad and even he had a hard time (I found out later that they had a massive argument). Finally, Dad gave in and signed the papers.

Meanwhile, we were still needing more money to survive and I was negotiating with the trading bank for a small $10,000 overdraft. The trading bank, unbeknown to me, registered this loan, and as a result, a million-to-one problem occurred.

With thousands of mortgages being processed through the registration office at any one time, it was unbelievable that Dad's mortgage transfer to third and the trading bank's small overdraft mortgage documents ended up right next to each other and were stamped with the same day and time seal.

This was technically not possible, but it happened! When we found out later, we realized it was the start of my most bitter battle to date. You cannot have two mortgages with the same ranking. One must rank ahead of another, and because these two mortgages were stamped one after the other in some great pile of documents, they were both equal, which was not legally possible. This, in effect, made both mortgages invalid.

The shit really hit the fan this time. The day the bank manager phoned and asked me to come in and see him was the first I knew about the problem, and at first I laughed at the amazing coincidence. The funny side of it soon left me when the bank manager told me he was withdrawing the overdraft because he had no security.

Hell, I could not believe my ears. It was not my fault, and surely he could sort it out. Why the hell did he want the overdraft secured by the land anyhow, when he had second charge over all the livestock, which gave the bank plenty of security? Then he said, "the bank should also be in front of Dad!" That would put Dad back into fourth mortgage.

I knew that would be like expecting hell to freeze over in summer. I can still feel that sick, gut-wrenching fear that came over me that day in the bank manager's office when I realized just how much of a slime bag the manager was and how much trouble I was in.

Here was a power play, and I was in the middle. What frustration, anger and absolute rage I felt! I argued with the pious idiot for hours! I was emotionally sick, my stomach in knots, and he just sat there saying he could not do anything about it. Bullshit! I had an overdraft of up to thirty thousand, unsecured, in the North Island with our small farm and now we had an operation with twice the cash flow, so what was his problem?

You see, the thing that was getting to me was that part of the short-term money I had borrowed was from the same bank. To get that loan, I had had to sign over to the bank all the income from the dairy company, so the dairy company, instead of paying us every month, paid all the money to the bank.

Because I really had to fight to get this short-term money, the bank manager was taking this opportunity of using this "no legal mortgage" situation to legally take all the proceeds from the dairy company and pay off both accounts. That would take every damn cent the farm would earn for the next three months, due to the fact we were not into the highest production months.

We also drew our living expenses from the farm account that had the overdraft and that was now being closed down by the bank. As the short-term money account had priority over the farm account for the dairy company proceeds, it would be at least three months before Denise would get any money transferred to the household account. How the hell could we feed three kids, ourselves and pay power, phone, etc., if we had no cash for three months?

I was livid. I all but thumped the bastard. He was arrogant as all hell and told me that all I had to do was phone my Dad and get him to agree to go back to fourth mortgage and he would file the papers with the legal people that day and we could then use the account.

It did not matter that I told him a million times that you just could not do that with Dad. Dad was a very hard person to deal with over money and we had previously had such a problem in getting him to accept a third mortgage that we knew that he would never agree to move to fourth.

Anyhow, Dad had a right to be third, as that was the agreement between the Rural Bank, Dad and us. The trading bank had known this and had tried to pull a fast one by registering the overdraft in the hope they would get in front of Dad's mortgage, but got caught in the unbelievable coincidence of both mortgage documents ending up next to each other in the land-transfer mortgage office.

It was hard to believe that with thousands of documents coming in from all over the country, my two ended up next to each other! If Dad's lawyer had filed just one hour earlier, the problem would not have existed! I was beside myself. One minute I was yelling with total rage at the manager and the next I was pleading with him with tears in my eyes.

I knew that with no money from income to pay the bills that were already late and no food for the kids, the emotional torment for Denise would be too much to ask of anyone. Somebody would surely file in court for payment of an overdue bill, which could be enough to push our very dangerous financial position over the edge into bankruptcy.

In New Zealand there is no Chapter 11 protection. You fall over like a great big Humpty Dumpty and all the king's horses and all the king's men just come and walk all over you.

Everything was going wrong! How could we run the farm with no money? The bloody bank approved the loans less than a few months earlier and now, just as the income was starting to come in, they were making it impossible to survive. What the hell was their game?

We argued for hours, and in the end I was emotionally and physically depleted and felt totally destroyed. I had lost and the bank had won. The bastard had me. I walked out of the bank not knowing whether to cry or go home and get the .22 and shoot him. Hell, I was almost ready to shoot myself! My ego had taken one hell of a licking, and for the first time in my life I really did not know what to do. I felt totally devastated. How could I go home and tell Denise she could not pay for food for our family? Could not get shoes for the kids?

Leaving the managers office, I slammed my fist into the concrete wall on the outside of the bank. What had I done wrong? Everything had been coming together. The farm was milking cows, the revenue was about to come in, all the hassles of getting the money together were behind us - and now this! I just could not understand it!

Looking down at my now very painful hand, I saw I had skinned my knuckles and blood was oozing out of my wounds. I had really hit that wall hard.

Seeing my hand so beat up unleashed determination not to let some bank branch manager destroy my life. I thought, this idiot must have an area manager in the city.

As I just had time to drive there, I should be able to catch him before he finished work for the day. Without another thought, I went straight to my car and broke every speed limit in the fifty-mile drive, arriving about ten minutes before bank closing.

The wait at the reception desk felt like eternity while the area manager was located. I must have looked like I meant business because the receptionist told whoever she was talking to on the phone, that this man looks like he will not take no for an answer.

No doubt my anger was showing all over my face in a way that would have backed off a raging bull. Later, I felt quite sorry for that poor girl, as I probably gave her a real fright. I was still dressed in my farm working clothes, and with the anger I was feeling, I must have been really intimidating.

However, it worked, and I was ushered into the area manager's office without delay. The drive to the city had given me time to go over in my mind just what I was going to say to this man.

Just as I was going to let him have it with no holds barred, he, nice as you please, asked me if I would like a drink and gestured for me to take a seat, not at his desk but on the lounge settee. He then walked over to the wall cabinet and brought back two glasses and a bottle of whiskey, commenting that I looked like a man who took his whiskey straight.

This turkey was good. He really knew how to defuse an angry young farmer with murderous intentions. (It is a bit hard to bore into somebody when he brings out the whiskey, especially Johnny Walker Black Label!)

A great feeling of relief came over me as he handed me a large, freshly poured whiskey and, with a big smile, said, "You look like you have a problem or two." That did it! I just rolled my head back and laughed out loud.

That was the understatement of the year. Yeah, I could get along with this guy. So I told him the whole story. Yes, he was familiar with my account and accepted that things would be tough for a year or two, but I had nothing to fear from the bank, as they were in with me for the long haul.

There was a problem with the legal situation regarding the mortgages, but in the meantime, until it was sorted out, he would authorize the transfer of funds into the household account from the farm account to pay power, phone and other day-to-day farm expenses. He would talk to the branch manager the next day.

You could have knocked me over with a feather! Good God, I had spent most of the day beating myself to death trying to get the branch manager to see reason, and here we were with the same set of facts and this guy had no problem with it at all! I was dumbfounded. It was just too easy. The change in attitude from one man to the next was beyond understanding, but I guess that was why this guy was area manager and not still some branch manager in a small rural town.

Driving slowly back to the farm, I had time to reflect on the day's events. Physically and emotionally, I felt that I had been in the ring with Mohammed Ali for a few rounds. I could hardly keep my hands on the steering wheel, but I began to think about the difference between the two bankers.

I had often heard from other farmers that a bank manager could make or break a business, but I had always thought they were just moaning. Now I was starting to understand. What had happened to me that day showed me that if one individual could have that much control over somebody else's life, maybe the whole financial system could also be under the same sort of control! Maybe farmers were not in control of their farms at all. That was a frightening thought, and it was there and then that I stopped trusting the banking system. I made a decision to find out more about the financial system and who really pulls the strings.

The more I thought about the day's events, the more uneasy I felt. I could not really understand the feeling, but it was like I had a really deep need to look at the banking system, to understand just who made what decisions and to what end. I knew right then that the whole financial system was corrupt. If I had known then what I was going to find out over the next seven years, I think I would have gone home, sold the cows and gotten out, then and there.

I would find out, that I knew. I had been knocked around that day and by God, the feeling I had in my heart, in my gut, was so strong that I vowed somehow I would expose the banks.

It is funny, but if the branch manager had not been so arrogant that day, I would never have had the urge to find out how the system worked. I think the thing that really got me going was the amazing difference between the two managers - same facts, same farm, same farmer, but totally different answers. Face it, two and two makes four in all schools - and if they do not, as in this case, there is obviously a rat somewhere.

Arriving home that evening, I phoned my good friend Eddie Glass. Eddie was a member of the area's Farmers Federation (union) and was without a doubt the most honest man I knew. He always stood up for the man on the land. I told him the day's fun and games, and Eddie said he would phone the area manager the next day on my behalf as an extra push.

I left the house very early the next morning to catch up with the work, so it was Denise who took the phone call from the branch manager. Well, the bastard started to get into Denise about my going over his head by going to the city to see the area manager. He tried to tell Denise that we could have sorted it all out in his office with a little bit of understanding.

Because I had told Denise the whole story, she knew that he was reacting to the call he had undoubtedly gotten from the area manager, who no doubt ordered him to transfer the money to the house account, etc. Denise is usually a very quiet lady, but this time she, too, had had enough bullshit and let him have it. I was so proud of her over that!

Eddie had a good long talk with the area manager and told us to deal directly with the city office. But this still left us with the problem of registering the mortgages, so I told the bank that if they wanted theirs in front of Dad's, they could write to him, as it had nothing to do with me.

It was four months before it was sorted out. The bank took all of the farm's income other than day-to-day living, and in the end, they still had to agree to fourth mortgage because Dad had written the bank a nasty letter that left them in no doubt where he stood.

By the time all this was sorted out, we no longer had an overdraft or short-term debt, but as we had paid no farm bills during that time, the city manager authorized a small overdraft to pay some of these.

That was the thrilling start on our new farm. God help us if this was the way things were going to go. If we had only known what lay ahead...

My ego was bruised and I felt bitter, but we had survived. Much now depended on the weather. A dry year would make it really hard for the farm to perform. In the first six months there were problems with the health of the cows due to a lack of minerals in the soil. In fact, the cows stopped having their menstrual cycles, which was very serious. With an emergency treatment of a specially formulated mineral salt lick, we soon fixed that problem.

The area had a reputation for cows failing to get in calf and we were on some of the poorest soil, but after the mineral treatment we had no further problems. I had sold all the contract harvesting equipment when we left the North Island, but as the local contractors were not up to my standard, I purchased a small harvester for our own use. As soon as I did, I was asked if I would harvest silage for a friend, and so the contracting started once again.

Once other farmers saw us operating, they wanted us to do their harvesting too. Very soon I could see that there would be a good business for a switched-on operator. In the meantime, with my small gear, I did enough to help the cash flow and pay some bills. The grass harvesting season did not last long that first year, as the weather turned really hot and dry. Damn it, it just could not be a dry year - the area had had one of its driest years the year before, and droughts do not usually come two years in a row.

The rain came just in time that summer. Sure, it was dry, but not a drought. The locals told us that if we could keep the cows milking through that year we would be okay, because it was about as dry as it would get. This gave me great hope for the future, and as we were getting very close to our target production, I informed the Rural Bank.

They wrote me that their area manager would be out to the farm in three weeks for an inspection. The report he would send to the head office would determine whether we got the development loan rolled over onto a permanent basis or not.

I had three weeks to make the farm look great. The production target would be passed by then, so that was not a problem, but this manager had to be really impressed. I had been farming long enough to have picked up some tricks.

I ordered some nitrogen fertilizer and got it spread over all the grass paddocks and negotiated with my neighbors to swap their irrigation roster days so that I got their water as well as mine. In that way I irrigated the whole farm. I would give them my water the next month.

Three weeks later the city boys came out to see it. It looked like an oasis, with green grass growing everywhere. They were impressed - amazed would be a better word. All smiles. Yes, I would get my loan extended, no problem.

The nitrogen and extra water had really done the trick, but a month later when I gave my water allocation back to my neighbors, the farm did not look so good. I often wonder why the bank gave me a three-week notice for that visit. I guess I had a guardian angel after all, but at the time I took the opportunity to score lots of points.

I often look back at that incident and chuckle to myself. It was a real neat trick; the farm looked great (nitrogen and water sure makes grass green).

It was now into autumn and our-next door neighbor offered us some of his land to rent. This would allow us to milk 400 cows, which would make a real dairy farm. To do this, I would need to get more money from the banks for the extra cows, so I applied to the Rural Bank because they were so impressed with what we had achieved.

The loan was approved without any hassle. The nitrogen trick had really paid dividends, and the second winter was spent changing fences to accommodate the extra cows. Product prices were up for the next year and we had survived the first year, so things looked good.

It is amazing what effect the prospect of a good year has on farming folk. Everybody is happy and keen to get on with it. Money is spent on things put off in the past; the wife does not get bitched at when she wants to go into town to get something for herself, clothes and even new shoes for the kids.

Even though I had taken some knocks, my emotions were fairly stable and I had the ultimate farm - yes, 400 cows - so we were big time. Hell, I was big time! Here we were milking 400 cows on 300 acres of irrigated land that only a year earlier the experts were saying could not carry cows. Not only that, but I was aiming for that 500 kg per hectare production figure. I intended to blow the experts away so completely that they would have to rewrite the textbooks. For if we achieved 500 kg per hectare from that farm, the textbooks really would have to be revised.

Starting the milking season that second year, we had great hopes. Denise and myself, with the help of our very young kids, handled the farm and cows without extra labor. God, we worked! There was never any letup; as soon as the spring rush was over, I was away on the tractor contracting.

We would milk the cows in the morning and do what was urgent on the farm, and usually I would be away by 11 a.m. Denise would milk all the cows in the afternoon by herself. We had a really good milking shed, so she would take only about half an hour longer on her own than with the two of us, and on weekends the kids would help.

That second year the rain just kept coming. Everybody wanted me to harvest the surplus grass, so the contracting business was really busy. The rain made it real easy to manage the farm. Lots of bills were paid that year and we really made some headway. Production prices came up to expectations, so I figured that we would be able to afford to employ labor. But the farm needed a second house for that, which would require more money from the banks.

What the hell, I thought, there was no way we could keep up with the workload by ourselves year after year, so I applied for a house loan. The Rural Bank was really good, saying that if I reached our production expectations, the loan would be approved. That was okay by me, and we passed that figure with two months of milking still left.

I expected to receive in the mail a loan application to sign, but instead I received a loan authorization. To this day it is the only loan I have never signed for. The Rural Bank was true to its word; we did the production and they supplied the funds for a second house on the farm.

Dad and Mum paid a surprise visit to us and Dad was quite impressed. In fact, he came back to help with the finishing touches on the new house. The two weeks he stayed with us were great, and I thought he could see the reasons that we went big and how product prices could be critical to our success. It was one of the few times in my life that I remember getting on with my father. Well, I just left him to do his thing on the house and I went about the farm work. I felt good about him helping, even though I had to pay his air fare both ways. He never did anything for nothing, but still, I was pleased to get all the finishing touches done properly, as Dad was super fussy.

So that was the first few years on our new farm. I had gotten over the initial hassles of getting money together. We had had a darn good second year, and the bills were being paid. I had met my own very high production targets, reaching 516 kg per hectare in the second year, an all-time high for that part of the country. I had justified all the pushing and proved the experts wrong. I had done it.

We were on a high and looked forward to reducing our workload a bit, as we interviewed people to take up the position on the farm and occupy the new house we had built. Sure, we had been through some tough times with the banks at the start, but I had put that behind me and my ego had recovered somewhat and was expanding to be the old powerhouse. This would be a rather short-lived recovery.

We started our third year with great hopes, but very soon they were dashed, largely as a result of a government change that allowed the international banks to have a free reign in trading New Zealand dollars on the international market.

As a result, the exchange rate of our currency went up. This had the effect of collapsing the milkfat price, so the dairy companies had to lower their payment to us farmers. The biggest financial crisis in the country's history had begun.

Living in a country that earns its living by agricultural exports has its problems. Only about 20% of the work force produces the farm exports that earn the country's income, while the other 80% spends that income on imported goods.

With one person having one vote, it is very hard to get the right people elected - those who have the strength and guts to run the country with a bias toward the producers.

Very few people in the cities understand where the money comes from that allows the French perfumes, new cars and fancy shoes to fill the shops. If New Zealand farmers stopped producing and exporting, 60% of all consumer goods, fuel and other materials would disappear from the shops and markets.

It is sad but very true, that politicians play their own power games and do not look out for the good of the country. As a result, one of the biggest political upheavals in years took place, ending with a political party in power who had little desire to understand New Zealand's rural-based income and even less guts to be honest with the people. They pandered to the masses in the cities and did it well - the money shufflers got their way.

There was a time after the elections that 90% of the money coming into and going but of the country was simply yuppies buying and selling dollars and shares on the world markets. Only 10% was from trade in real goods.

Because we had one of the highest interest rates in the Western world, money flooded in to take advantage of this, and our dollar went sky high due to this buying pressure. This rise in dollar value against our trading partners' currency had the effect of dramatically lowering the price that farmers were paid for their exported produce.

As New Zealand farmers exported over 90% of their production, this fall in income had the effect of sending the whole country into a severe depression that put more people out of work than the global depression of the thirties. Of course, the farm lobby voiced its warnings loud and clear.

We organized a big public march in the capitol, but to no avail. The government, who by now was under the control of the money traders, took no notice and kept telling the people that the money traders could earn the country more income than the farmers anyhow.

Of course, anybody with any sense could see that this was a load of bullshit. Any kid could tell you that when you try to build a house with a pack of cards, it will sooner or later fall over. The share market crash of the late eighties proved that point, but by then the damage had been done.

The change that occurred in the financial market had a devastating effect that almost destroyed my family financially, as well as emotionally. In fact, it did just that to many other farmers.

Going into our fourth year, our high hopes were very short-lived. No sooner had the season started than the dairy company announced greatly reduced product prices. That was all we needed, with our extremely high debt load.

I felt devastated, shocked, and angry; a heavy cloud of doom seemed to descend around me. I spent hours and days going over and redoing the farm budget, but try as I might to raise the production figures and lower the costs, I still could not make it work. Our interest bill had shot up to over $100,000, because our base rate had gone from 7.5% to 21 %. For the first time in my life I was having trouble sleeping.

What could I do? It seemed like every week the bank would send us a letter informing us that the interest rate had gone up. I spent days with my accountant going over the figures. I hired a management consultant to go over our operation with a fine-tooth comb to see if he could pinpoint any room for improvement.

The bank manager just kept saying he could not do anything and that it was our problem. Our problem, hell! What could we do? What could anybody do when their costs tripled and their income was cut in half? I felt like a trapped animal and I was getting about as dangerous as one. I was fighting like hell with the farm leaders to do more in the capitol to give the politicians a hard time. I joined newly-formed pressure groups and became actively engaged in all protest movements against the government and the banks.

On the farming front, we decided to increase revenue by raising 400 beef calves and pushing the contracting as much as we could. Of course, this had the effect of doubling our workload, as if 400 cows were not enough on their own, but what else could we do?

Out most nights to one meeting or another and working hard all day brought already fragile emotions to the boiling point very quickly. As a result, Denise and the kids took much more than their share of my anger. They were going through the same pain as I was and did not need me giving them more, but that is what happens when emotions get stretched to the breaking point.

A glimmer of hope shone through when a neighbor who was close to retirement asked me if I would like to lease his farm. This got me thinking, as it was one thousand acres of sheep land. I knew there was no money in sheep, so we looked at beef. All the experts said this was the most stable product, price-wise.

Since we already had the harvesting equipment, I decided to set up an open feedlot to raise the bulls to two-years-old. When we did this, the price for beef was $2.80 per pound and we had done all our figures using only $2.00 per pound. When I researched the project, I found that only once had the price ever dropped below $2.00, so it looked quite stable. We kept all the sheep that were on the farm, but took out 400 acres to grow silage crops to feed the bulls.

Everything was holding up really well until six months into the season, when the world market for beef had the biggest single drop ever recorded. It was slightly larger than the late sixties drop that put many farmers out of business.

It is hard to believe, but over a four-month period, the price dropped to $1.50 per pound! Everything I touched was falling apart! I took the only way out I could, and that was quick. Selling the half-grown bulls on the local market was quite easy, because they were really good; the price we got enabled us to just cover costs. My big, dangerous but calculated jump into big-time feedlot farming nearly cost me my shirt.

At the time no money could be made out of any kind of livestock farming. Everything was down and the people were full of doom and gloom. It really got bad, especially at meetings, because all the farmers were so depressed. The whole countryside was in a state of shock, and some pretty gruesome protests took place.

One of the most dramatic was when the sheep farmers organized a mass slaughter of old sheep to protest payments so low that they were all going broke. Nobody blamed the sheep men, because the slaughterhouses were offering only one dollar a sheep.

This mass slaughter is now part of the area's history and it took place not far from our farm. A great big pit was dug about 20 feet wide, 30 feet deep and 200 feet long. On the agreed day, the farmers came with all their old sheep.

The site was all set out like a selling yard with pens, yards and lane ways, all made from netting and pipe gates. There were unloading bays where the farmers could back their trucks and pickups for unloading and on the other side were the small pens the sheep were herded into, ready for the farmers to grab.

There were about ten cutting pens right next to the pit, and as the sheep came into the last pen, they would be caught, hauled out onto the boards and their throats cut and then tipped over into the pit.

Throughout the day hundreds of farmers came in all manner of vehicles, some bringing one or two sheep in the trunk of their cars and others bringing truckloads. By evening there were over 3000 sheep with cut throats lying dead in that pit.

What a bloody hell that was! There was blood all over the cutting boards, and people were making small trenches with shovels so it would flow over the side and into the pit. The whole side of the pit was a sea of slowly oozing blood, glistening in the late afternoon sun. I can still picture in my mind the great mounds of dead sheep lying along the length of that pit; the sight of 3000 carcasses stacked up is one I will never forget.

To get as much impact as possible from this protest, the local farm leaders had let the news media know it was going to take place, so the event (if you could call it that) was covered by local and national papers as well as national television.

That night every city person who was watching the six o'clock news on their television had this mass slaughter brought into their living rooms in full color. God, what a public outrage! The papers were full of letters to the editors. The TV stations were inundated with complaints. In general, the city people just did not like to have to deal with the stark reality of the farmers' plight.

I was one of those farmers and I fully supported and took part in that protest. Face it, what else could we do? Here we were in late summer, having come through the area's biggest droughts with no feed on the farms.

The shortage of feed had pushed up the price of any available hay or straw, so that it was costing us farmers fifty cents a day to feed one sheep - if they had any money or credit left with the banks. The slaughterhouses were paying only one dollar per sheep when a year earlier the price was eight dollars.

The protest action came from the farmers' reasoning that it was better to kill the old sheep quickly than let them starve slowly on the dry, grassless farms. That way the slaughterhouses would not get the sheep, which would force the companies to increase their prices. I am not sure who won the sympathy prize, because a lot of people were against the action taken by the farmers. I think the slaughterhouses got the message, as it was not long before the price for this class of sheep was up to five dollars a head.

The argument about the action taken by the farmers will go on for years, but it sure as hell had a big impact on the nation. The impact on the farmers was even more pronounced.

Farmers are a hardy lot; they learn to take in their stride droughts, floods, disease and good or bad years. Still they keep on producing food for a hungry world. But that day I saw grown men - and I was one myself - hardened from years of battling the elements reduced to tears at the sight of all those slaughtered sheep. One moment we were full of gaiety, feeling we were going to show the companies and banks a thing or two, and the next moment we felt gut-wrenching sick and fearful of what we were doing.

We saw white wool slowly turn red with blood as the heaps in the pit slowly got bigger and bigger while the afternoon wore on. We had dedicated our lives to tending and caring for our animals, and here we were, cutting the throat of perhaps the very sheep that, as a motherless lamb, we had warmed and fed in our living room by the fire.

Many wives came along, but some could not get out of their cars. I certainly had conflicting emotions, and felt deep down there must be another way. But what, none of us knew.

It did not escape the notice of local farmers that the heads of the national Farmers Federation did not endorse the action. That attitude, as far as I was concerned, typified the gutlessness of most politicians to get off the fence and stand up for the people they represent. Even though the Maryfield sheep slaughter (as it became known) was a gruesome sight, the logic of it was valid. But it certainly added to my emotional turmoil, as it no doubt did to many other farmers.

It was some time after this that the drought really started to bite, and before the end of the season I had to beg an extra $90,000 credit from the local stock and station company to feed the cows. I arranged this credit on the surety of raising another 400 beef calves the next spring to be sold through the company.

They would then collect the proceeds and the loan would be repaid.

Of course, this type of finance was at the top end of the interest-rate scale, but we had no other choice. The emotional strain I was under, with all our debts, the drought, low product prices and by now failing land prices, was really starting to take toll. As the land values came down, the banks started to get jumpy, as any equity we had was dissipating fast. Very soon we became technically insolvent.

If the interest rates had not been so high, the demand for land would have remained and land values would not have fallen. Because costs exceeded income, too many farmers wanted out, some were being forced out and nobody wanted to buy. Farmers expect to handle droughts, low product prices and high interest in the course of a lifetime, but when all three happen in the same year, the only word to use is disaster. Everything went wrong; it did not matter how much we produced, how hard we worked, how efficient we were, the bloody sums still did not add up.

Every Tom, Dick and Harry was pushing to get his bill paid. Every month I had to figure out who to pay and how much; if this company would sue or would wait a bit longer; whether to get more hay to feed the cows better or use that money to pay off some bill. It was a never-ending battle that went on and on. Sometimes I would scream with rage.

The fear that I could lose everything brought feelings of failure, of not being good enough, of being judged a poor farmer. I felt totally inadequate and in a constant mood of despair. And every day the sun just kept shining, with no rain in sight. Another hundred dollars of grain and hay had to be fed to the cows! When would it end? If only it would rain, if the banks would only back off the interest ... if only, if only. I was going mad with the pressure.

The power, the drive and the will to succeed had been replaced with the daily grind of forcing myself to function physically. Even thinking and working out the next move became a nightmare. Arguments with Denise started to become more and more frequent and any noise at home, especially from exuberant young children, was met with overbearing, reactive anger.

I started to put more and more pressure on our young boys to help with the work, expecting them to perform like men. When they made mistakes, I responded with mad-man-like rage.

I was aware I had become reactive and always angry, giving the kids a hard time. I hated myself for it, but it is strange that although I could see these behavior patterns, I still could not change myself. It became a vicious, self-destructive spiral. The more angry and reactive people become, the more they hate themselves, which creates even more anger. Highly charged anger can become extremely dangerous. What an asshole I had become!

With this sort of emotional torment, it was no wonder I started to suffer the first signs of depression. Not just feeling down, but real, clinical depression. Just getting up in the morning became a battle. Instead of facing up to all the bills, I would just stuff all the mail, unopened, into a drawer. Why look at the bills when there was no bloody money to pay them? Life was becoming a nightmare... no, life was a nightmare.

My world was about to come crashing down. I was a failure - I was useless, no bloody good. What was there to live for? Life was a bitch, a bloody nightmare where some god somewhere had pushed a button so it would go on forever. What warped humor did he have to watch us self-destruct like this? But wait, there is not a god, anyhow.

To let people suffer like this, there cannot be, can there? No, all that stuff is just bullshit. Tonight I might as well shoot myself. Why not? If I stay alive, this bloody drought or the banks will do me in anyhow. I would go to sleep hoping I would never wake up.

It was during this time that I hit rock bottom emotionally. Unable to function, I laid on the living room couch all day unable to get up, my mind a fog of unconnected whirling thoughts.

The few times I moved I would wander aimlessly around the farm for hours on end. Sometimes I would carry the rifle with me, telling the kids that I was going to shoot some rabbits. But my thoughts were about killing myself.

On one such evening I took the rifle and went walking, I cannot recall how long I was out, but I remember knowing that this was going to be my last day of pain. Through my fogged mind I had worked out that at one minute before midnight I would pull the trigger and that would be the end, no more pain, no more hurt. My last day had come.

Denise must have felt that something was wrong when I was late coming in and called the neighbors who started to search for me. I was found at about 11:30 p.m. at the back of the farm, sitting staring into the night with the loaded and cocked .22 up under my chin. Helped home and into bed, my emotional recovery would be slow and long.

CHAPTER 6
DIVINE INTERVENTION

Autumn started to make its presence felt with cooler days and longer nights. Surely the autumn rains must come soon. We had kept the cows milking with an extra $100,000 that would have to be paid back the next year. What an emotional strain to carry over the winter - what if the next year was a dry one? That was too painful to think about.

Unable to face the problems, I stuffed my reality by simply not thinking about anything. My days were almost a haze of blurred thought; I just refused to accept the problems around me as real, like putting all the unopened bills in a drawer - if I refuse to look at them, then they do not exist. That was the only way I kept my sanity, or what was left of it.

I could not do any work on the farm because every time I started the tractor, it cost money we did not have, and any other jobs always took materials that had to be bought. So we just milked the cows and did the essentials. It was like being in jail - total economical strangulation. My emotions were unable to handle the strain, so I shut myself down and became a zombie, going through the motions of living but not really being alive.

I would spend hours reading the daily paper over and over, every word. What for, I do not really know. I guess it allowed me to keep my mind off the farm and our situation. I had to pass the time between milks somehow.

One Saturday morning while going over the classifieds once again, my eyes were drawn to an ad to drive a camper van to the North Island. I had no reason to go there, but this ad kept drawing my attention. I felt an urge inside me that I had not felt for months. I could not understand; what was I feeling? It kept nagging at my mind like a tune that haunts you all day, only from much deeper within.

By Sunday morning the urge to phone the company that had placed the ad was totally overpowering. Although my conscious self had no say in it, I found myself phoning. I was on automatic.

The company was based in a northern city, and as the tourist traffic was mainly south, they had too many camper vans located in the South Island and were offering a free week to anybody if they would drive the seven hundred miles north. I have no idea why, but I said I would go the next day.

Afterwards, I thought I must be crazy. How could I go, with the farm to look after? What would Denise say? I delayed telling her until that evening, and to my surprise, she thought it was a good idea. Knowing the emotional state I was in, I certainly needed a break, but she told me later that she also knew in her heart it was for much deeper reasons. I left Monday morning on what was to be an amazing saga.

Driving up the east coast of the South Island always brings joy to my heart. Its steep mountains on the left at times extend their towering ruggedness to the ocean, leaving barely enough room for the road, which in places clings to the edge of thousand-foot cliffs and at other times tunnels right through the very heart of rock millions of years old.

On the right is the crystal-clear Pacific Ocean, its waves endlessly crashing against the cliffs. Out behind the breakers you can see dolphins and whales leaping from the sea in their ecstasy of being. As the road dips down from the cliff face to wind its way along the rocky shore, it is unlucky not to catch a glimpse of sea lions basking in the autumn sun on their favorite rocks.

The little dots bobbing up and down about a mile and a half off the shore are the cray (lobster) fishermen checking their pots in their ridiculously small boats. There are quaint fishing villages where a pause in the journey demands a feast of freshly cooked cray.

Following the gorges made by fast-flowing alpine rivers, you come back out onto the flat planes at Marlborough, where you can almost taste the hundreds of acres of grapes ripening in the sun, ready for the harvest that turns them into world-class wine.

The drive north along the coast is beauty personified. All too quickly I arrived at Picton, at the foot of Queen Charlotte Sound, but that brought its own magic. Then onto the ferry for three-and-a-half hours of awe-inspiring sights, first up through the sounds that at times are so narrow I felt like reaching out from the ship to pluck the wildflowers from the cliffs. Then out into Cook Strait where, seventeen miles away in the clear air of this part of the world, the North Island emerges from the Pacific.

Entering the narrow neck of Wellington Harbor, I imagined all the early sailing ships and the bravery of the sailors who had negotiated that passageway between the reefs and cliffs that seem ready to pound their ships from under them for a single mistake. Moving on into the harbor, the ferry swung slowly left and headed for the capitol, nestled below high hills and spread around the harbor in all directions. Finally, the ferry gently backed into its dock to an accompaniment of soaring, acrobatic, noisy sea gulls.

Leaving the ferry and travelling out of the city, I was soon driving through the world of lush green pasture that New Zealand is noted for. Yes, the North Island is as famous for its green as the South Island is for its scenic grandeur.

It felt like I was going home. The road was familiar and I was happy. I had no idea what I was doing other than heading north, but it did not matter. It was like I had left the farm behind, with its financial hassles and drought. More than that, they ceased to be part of my present world. I felt as if I were being taken on a mystery tour. I was the driver of the van, but not the driver of me. The happiness I felt was incredible. I was actually enjoying the scenery. I was enjoying everything, even myself - and that had not happened in a long time.

Nightfall was gently settling in when I arrived at my good friend Jo's place in the familiar territory of our share-farming days. Explaining to Jo and her family the reason for my unexpected arrival was a bit difficult, as it is hard to tell somebody why you are six hundred miles away from home when even you do not know why.

Jo, being the friend she was, did not ask questions or push the point. She and her husband made me feel at home in their usual wonderful way. We did not talk much after their kids had gone to bed, because after about twelve hours on the road, I was ready for a good sleep.

If I had hopes of awaking feeling normal, I would have been disappointed. I awoke feeling even more out of myself and even less in control of my mind. I could not concentrate on anything. Everything seemed hazy; the thought process just was not there. I could hardly think what I had to do next. Jo could see I was not myself and gave me my space.

About midmorning I was feeling more in control and decided to go and visit a good friend who lived nearby. While I was visiting there, I decided to go see some people who lived about an hour away.

Bidding farewell to my friends, I drove down their drive in full realization that I was going to turn left at the road - but the next second my hands were moving the steering wheel the other way. The van swung back to the right, using all the road.

What the hell was going on? I was shaking, sweat was dripping down my face. I had no idea why I was heading north. I did not even want to go this way, but I had no option. I was in the van driving it, or so I thought, but I sure as hell had no control over my actions, either physical or mental.

The van was accelerating up through the gears; I still wanted to stop and turn around, but I could not. I was really scared; it was like something had taken total control of my physical actions. I remember having strange thoughts of God and other spiritual feelings, but did my best to dismiss them.

Finally, I give in to this unseen control. I decided to keep going north for a few miles and call in and visit a friend who used to work for us when we were share-farming in the area.

Arriving at Peter's farm, still very shaken, his young worker informed me that Peter was at the milking shed. As it was only a hundred meters across the paddock, I walked over to see him, but he was nowhere to be found. That was strange, because his worker told me he had just left the house to go to the shed a minute before I arrived.

I went over to the other sheds around the farmyard and even yelled out his name. No answer. It was only a small farm, and I could see over most of it from where I was standing. It was like he had just disappeared from the face of the earth. I must have called out to him a dozen times, to no avail. Thinking how strange it all was, I went back to his house. His worker was as baffled by my not finding him as I was. Oh well, I thought, I will now drive south and call on the people I had first intended to. So into the van and down the road I went.

When I came to the road to take me south - which I had a full conscious intent to do - the bloody van turned north again! I remember looking down at my hands in amazement. What a strange sensation it is when your mind knows where you want to go, but your hands are turning the steering wheel the other way.

I broke out in a sweat of fear. I yelled out loud at myself, desperately trying to get control of my actions, but to no avail. The bloody van was going north and that was that. Somebody or something was making me drive it that way. I thought I was going mad; that this must be a dream. Terrified, I can remember yelling out for somebody to help me. I was on a trip; to where, I had no idea.

I was not in another dimension like when I drove fast. This was very different. This was really scary stuff; it was like nothing I had experienced before. Imagine that you are you, but not you; sort of, a bit like you are a robot but with a human head that can experience and feel your actions, but cannot control them. A bit like your own movie of yourself, except that it is taking place while you are watching. It is hard to explain. If I could have stopped that van, I would have run like hell.

As I turned into a side road, I realized I was heading back to the area where we had once share-farmed. That was okay, I thought, I will be able to look at the old farm again as I drive past.

Approaching the old farm, I wanted to slow down, but I could not. I remember trying to look back to get more of a view as I went on by. Damn it, I could not even slow the van down when I wanted to. It got worse by the minute.

About three miles down the road was the farm of my good friend Stu. I had known Stu since we had first started farming in the area. He and I had similar views on most things - like we were the reason things happened, and that God or spiritual things were for the churchgoers and not us. We were real men and did not need anybody else.

I had heard that Stu had got all religious since I had left the area, and I had laughed it off as just a tall story. I could not believe the Stu I had known would change like that. Nearing his farm, I started to feel all sweaty again and as the van got almost to his gate, an overpowering urge swept through my body.

My foot left the throttle and hit the brakes. The van just stopped dead as if it had hit a brick wall, and the next thing I recall, I had driven into his drive and had stopped right outside the front door of his house.

I was a mess. Sweat was dripping off my body, saturating my clothes, and my entire body was shaking uncontrollable. I felt weak all over. I just sat in the van for a few minutes because my body would not move, let alone walk. What was I doing at Stu's place? I did not want him to see me like this, but after a few minutes, I was suddenly given the strength and the urge to get out of the van.

I almost ran to the house. Neither Stu nor his wife Chris had come to the door, but I went straight in. There were Stu and Chris and another person, standing in the living room with arms outstretched welcoming me. Stu came straight up to me and put his arms around me.

Stu and I were not into cuddling each other, so this was a surprise, but what he said next just floored me. "I'm glad you made it; we have been expecting you." I burst into tears.

Chris came up to us and put her arms around us as well, and the three of us all cried together. Here we were, three grown people crying our eyes out in each other's arms. For God's sake, what the hell was going on?

Finally my legs just collapsed from under me and I fell to the ground. Chris pulled up a lounge chair and helped me into it. Then she went out and got me a drink of water.

I did not know what to say, so I just looked at Chris, tears pouring down my face, and asked, "Why?"

Chris came over to me and knelt down in front of me, took hold of my hands, looked me in the eyes and said in the most gentle but knowing voice, "You have been called. You have been asked to do God's work. You have been brought to us so that we could make you aware of it."

God Almighty! I thought as she said this. I felt a prickly feeling come all over me and goose-bumps broke out over my entire body. This was too much. I could not take any more and ran from the house out the back door. I did not get very far and collapsed onto an old tree stump in their back yard. There I completely broke down and the tears came by the bucketsful. My sobbing was uncontrollable and unstoppable. I was terrified and felt totally destroyed and broken. I felt that I had been kicked until life itself was flowing out of me.

I guess I was there for about an hour before I went back inside, where I was introduced to the man who had been waiting all this time. He was a minister from the church that Stu and Chris attended. They had all planned to visit the city that day, but when it came time to leave they had all felt a need to stay at the house and pray instead. It was during their prayers that Stu got the feeling an old friend was going to arrive unexpectedly and they were to wait for this friend, as it would be important to be there to receive him.

This friend would be guided to the house by Spirit for his learning and understanding and to help him change his life. Then he could undertake his own spiritual growth, which would lead him to his life's work. Stu was also told by Spirit that this old friend would be very troubled on arrival and would need lots of help.

When I heard all of this, I could not believe it. No wonder Stu had said they were expecting me when I arrived. I was just floored. I sat down and told them everything that had happened to me during the past three days. It seemed unbelievable.

I was shaking once again. The coincidence was just too much. How could all this be true? How could it happen? I was trying to think of ways to convince myself that it was all bullshit, but there was no way. There were too many things pointing in the same direction. All of my shutting out thoughts of God and all that stuff was being turned on its ear. I was being forced to really think about all this now. If all this was real, then I was being given one hell of a kick to wake up and face things I had not allowed to be part of my life.

Maybe God, or my guardian angel, had organized all this for my benefit. Bloody hell, my mind was starting to spin. Hey folks, hold off; slow down; I need some time to think about this. I had enough problems back at the farm without all this. Why now? Why me? What had I done to get all the religious stuff thrown at me? There was a world full of people out there to pick on, damn it. I had not seen God help out with the problems at the farm and the drought, so why ask me to believe in all this?

I was trying to argue my way through my own thoughts. I was desperate, really looking for a way to rationalize the events of the last three days and especially that day. But it did not matter how hard I tried, I just could not. Something was going on here, something was really happening to me. I was forced to think about God and all that stuff.

I went outside again to try to think it all through, but that did not work, so I went back in. The four of us talked for the rest of the day and at times the other three prayed over me. The minister told me that I had been called for a very special reason and that I would be made aware of it as I accepted my spirituality.

The power I had in my physical life was to be used in service to others. This power and the ability to become part of other dimensions was a gift that I had not been using the right way, so now I was being shown that there was something more to life. He also told me that my life would change if and when I accepted the calling, but it was my choice.

This was all too much, but so many things, really weird things, had happened that day that I just did not know what to think. There was no doubt about it, I was certainly guided. Guided, hell! I was driven to Stu's place, and I had absolutely no control over or say in it. In fact, during the last three days I had been influenced by another power.

Was this God at work? Had I made this promise before I was born and was now being kept to it? I did not know. I needed time out, time to think, to cry, to run away. Run away to where? If some power could make me drive a van to where it wanted me to go, it was surely no good trying to run away, as it (or whoever) could control my body. Damn, damn, damn! This cannot be real. It is okay, I will wake up any minute now and it will be over. But no, damn it, it was for real and I was experiencing it, all right.

Somewhere deep inside me, I had sort of known this day would come, but I had never allowed myself to think about it. Now, I had no choice. The more I allowed myself to think about my life, the way I was taught religion at convent school and my questioning of the priests and nuns and some of the things I had felt over the years, the more things started to make sense.

I started to calm down and went for a long walk around Stu's farm, trying desperately to put it all together. This was very different from normal Christian teaching, but it sort of felt right. That was the frightening thing about the last three days. No matter how hard I tried to dismiss what had happened, I could not, and deep within me I felt almost relieved. That was weird, but it was as if at last, I would not have to struggle to keep my thoughts suppressed. That was okay for me, but how the hell could I tell Denise about it? What would my friends think of me? I did not really know if I was going mad, so how in hell were my friends going to think otherwise?

It was really strange how I felt. I seemed to be much lighter: my head had become clearer than it had been in weeks, and I did not have the heaviness pressing in all around me. I did not want to feel happy. I wanted to be angry, but the more the day wore on, the happier I became. I had so many conflicting thoughts and emotions that when I got back to the house, I had another big talk with Chris.

She talked about how she had changed, about the emotions she experienced and about her understanding of spiritual things. Then she told me about a trip she and Stu and others from the church took to the Fiji Islands and the amazing healing and other things that took place with those very spiritual islanders. She again said, "Maybe you should think about all that has happened to you over the last three days, as just maybe you are being given a chance to respond to a spiritual calling."

By this time, evening was drawing in and I was feeling quite good and in control of my emotions, so I bid Stu and Chris farewell.

As it was too late to travel to my other friend, the one I had intended to visit at the start of that crazy day, I drove back to Jo's place. This time the van went where I wanted it to go.

Arriving at Jo's, I told her and her husband about the day's events and how I had felt. They did not rubbish me, but seemed to understand and gave me lots of support.

Later that evening I felt I should go and visit my old boss, as his wife was a very spiritual lady and might be able to help me understand things a bit more. Relating my story to her, she was not surprised and also said she thought I had been given a powerful message.

Later that night as I lay in bed, tired as I was, I spent hours thinking about everything that had happened. It was hard to really understand, as none of it fitted normal Christian teachings. I had never read about anything like this, and some stories I had heard I had always dismissed as imagination working overtime. Maybe all this had been my imagination - but no, it was real. Well, hell, it *felt* real. I finally fell asleep, hoping the morning would reveal that it had just been a dream.

Jo woke me by bringing in a cup of coffee at about 9 a.m. the next morning, as she had to leave for town soon after. Any hopes I had that it had all been a dream were dashed, as I could remember everything. I was feeling very different inside. I still had a sort of light feeling, and the farm and its problems strangely seemed to be a million miles away, almost like I had left them years ago.

I seemed to be in another world, a world that totally revolved around thoughts of God. What was happening to me? I just could not get my mind off these thoughts. I was going over and over all sorts of questions: Who could I go to and talk to that would understand? How could I ever get back to normal? But what if this was normal and my other life was all wrong? That was a hard one to debate. Then I remembered that my old boss' wife had told me that I should talk to the priest that had married Denise and me, since I had gotten along well with him.

We had spent hours talking about religion, but that was about eleven years before and I had not seen him since. She thought that he was now in Wellington and that I should call in and see him on my way home.

Yes, many things were going through my mind, but because I had to get the van back to the city depot, I said my farewells to my good friends, hoping that they did not think I was going loopy. Face it, I did not know what was going on, but I surely felt more loopy than sane.

Being more than a bit frightened about driving the van and not sure if I would be able to make it go where I wanted it to, I delayed leaving as long as I could. Finally, I found the courage and the fifty-mile drive to the city was uneventful.

Upon arriving, I spent the remainder of the day with an old skiing friend I had met down south. We had a very beautiful afternoon at Auckland's beaches. Nicky was really good therapy for me, and that night I stayed with her at her parent's house, where I was made to feel at home.

Nicky's father and I got on well, and I was able to have a really restful sleep that night, no doubt assisted by the fact that we sampled most of his very comprehensive liquor cabinet. I was not in any state for thinking that night, thank God. My emotions certainly needed a rest, and I went out like a light.

Nicky and I spent the next day looking at the city and talking a lot about my experiences, which by this time seemed like a fairy tale to me, as I was starting to feel almost normal.

The thing that surprised me was that my constant worry about the farm was no longer with me. Of course, I would think about it at times and wonder how Denise was coping, but the deep worrying fear was not there.

It was really strange, as if that part of my consciousness had been dulled. Sometimes I would even try to reason with myself about why I did not have the worries on my mind. But even that thought was lost very quickly. It was as if I was not allowed to think about it. I remember wondering why I felt this incredible happiness deep inside, something I had not felt in a long while. We had a nice easy day and spent the late afternoon swimming. I returned the van last thing and stayed at Nicky's home again that night.

I had planned to fly back to the South Island from Auckland the next day, but once again my decisions were not exactly mine, and I had an overpowering urge to rent a car and drive down to Wellington, and from there catch a plane to the South Island.

I booked my flight for late that night and headed south in the car. Now, this drive takes about eight hours. I knew what time I had to be at the airport, so I gave myself about an hour extra. For the first part of the drive, I was on time and the miles seemed to just fly by. But about halfway, I stopped to give a hitchhiker a ride, and from that point on things started to go haywire.

Jim, the hitchhiker, lived in a town about two hours out of Wellington, so, as it was not far from the highway, I said I would run him right home. We were getting on really great, talking nonstop, and my driving speed must have dropped a bit, but I never realized that time was starting to be important.

Arriving at his home, his mother invited me in for coffee. As is usual with rural people, this ended up with a full meal, and what was meant to be a fifteen-minute stop stretched out for about two hours. I had lost all perception of time. I was in a daze again and nothing seemed to be important. I remember feeling incredibly happy, really enjoying Jim's and his mother's company.

I finally pulled myself out of the fairyland and forced myself to bid my farewells and leave. Here I was again, my body overheating and allowing me little control over my actions, but it did not scare me as much this time. It was almost normal by this time to be "taken over," and I was starting to allow things to unfold without the resistance and panic I had felt before.

The final two-hour drive into Wellington was rather strange. The time seemed to compress; I can remember driving really fast, zooming in and out of traffic and feeling high and excited. I cannot remember much else about that strange drive, but I remember arriving at the airport too late for my flight home. In amazement, I tried to work out where all the time had gone. It was probably due to the stop at Jim's home, but even with that stop I could not really account for all the time.

Realizing that I had no way home that night and no money for a hotel room in a big, strange city, I came down to earth really quickly. Just as my concern about my predicament started to become anxiety, I remember being told that the priest who had married Denise and me all those years ago was now living in Wellington. Great, I thought, that was one human being I knew, and this allowed me to feel much better.

Slowly getting my brain under control, I called the residence of the priests and asked for my friend. He was not there, but I was given two other numbers. I had no luck with the first, but with the second, the voice that answered the phone said, "Brian Sherry here."

My heart missed a beat, as I had not heard his voice for eleven years or so. Not really knowing what to say, I hesitated, and I could hear Brian say, "Who's there? Do you need help?" I finally found my voice and said, "You probably don't remember me..." and with that, he butted right in and said, "Oh, yes I do. How the hell are you, Denie?"

I nearly fell over. How could he possibly know my voice after all these years? When I said that to him, he just laughed and said he was thinking of me that day and had a feeling I might be contacting him soon. So when I phoned, he immediately recognized my voice. Shit, I thought, this priest is psychic.

Father Brian insisted I stay the night with him and gave me directions. Leaving the airport and motoring down the freeway, I suddenly realized I had no idea where to go. The directions I had been given had vanished from my mind. Damn. It was dark and it had started to rain, and I did not have a clue where I was going. I took the next off-ramp, ending up downtown, and tried to find a street name I could recognize. I could remember Brian saying he lived on Hill Street, but after about a half-hour of driving around in the rain, I was more lost than ever.

I was frustrated and pulled over into a side street and stopped. I slumped forward onto the steering wheel. With my anger building up, I thumped the wheel with my hands, lifted my head up and with my eyes looking at the roof of the car, yelled out loud, "Damn it, God, you win! You got me in this mess and if you are real, prove it. Get me to Father Sherry's place. I'll drive, but you turn the steering wheel."

With that demand, I slammed the car into gear, let out the clutch and we were off. Down the side street the car went! I had my hands on the steering wheel but I was not making any conscious decisions about where and when to turn. I was just allowing that to happen. The car and I turned into another street and immediately entered what I thought was a maze of warehouses.

There were small, narrow alleys and tight curves everywhere. The car never went down a blind alley and I never turned around and went back the way I had come. Finally, I came out onto a proper road and stopped.

What was that? There in the headlights, across the street, were big stone pillars on each side of a driveway going up a hill, and on the right-hand pillar was a brass sign. Peering through the rain, I could just make out the words; "Catholic Presbytery Residence, Diocese of Wellington."

I froze. I felt an instant fear, and the hair on the back of my neck stood out. A cold shudder rumbled through my body. I could hardly believe my eyes, and as the realization of what had happened sunk in, I started to cry.

Fifteen minutes earlier I had been hopelessly lost on a dark, wet night in a strange city. Now here I was, after asking a God I was having trouble accepting, looking up the driveway of the place I was meant to be.

After all that had happened during the last week, this one took the prize. I had asked and God had delivered. There was no way I could talk my way out of this one. I was shaking so much that I just sat there trying to allow my mind to come to terms with the situation. Was it a fluke? Was it chance? No way. Finding my way through about three city blocks of warehouses with dozens of entrances and exits and coming out at this particular one was not chance.

Looking back now, I feel it was at that point that deep inside me I knew there was more to life than just us people. This was the most powerful example of help and guidance from the spiritual realms I had ever experienced, and I was blown out of my tree.

Finally, I regained my composure enough to drive the car across the street and up the drive to the front door of the large building. There, with a big smile and outstretched arms, was Father Brian Sherry.

I could barely climb out of the car. My knees were like jelly, my coordination was all to hell as I staggered up the steps like a drunk, into the welcome support of Brian's arms. I promptly broke down into deep, uncontrollable sobbing. I guess we stood on the porch on that wet, rain-drenched autumn night for at least several minutes until my sobbing subsided, and it was only then that Father Sherry gently guided me into the house. Once inside, Brian helped me calm down with a good, stiff whiskey, and with that, this farm boy let out like a flood, all that had happened over the past few days.

I did not try to understand it at all, I just told it as I perceived it. Brian, being the incredible man he was, allowed me to tell it my own way. God, it was good to talk to somebody who made no judgments, who just allowed me to talk. I felt he actually understood me. During the course of the night, we left the residence and went into the city for a meal.

On the way back, Brian showed me the large area of government department offices and warehouses covering at least three blocks that I had been guided through to find him. We sat in the car and looked at each other, and I think Father Brian was as overwhelmed as I was that I had actually got out of that maze of alleyways at all, let alone right across the road from the priests' residence. Brian commented that he had seen some prayers answered, but this was amazing.

We talked well into the early hours of the morning, and Brian really helped me understand the significance of what had happened and why. He also made it quite clear to me that as far as he was concerned, there was a major interest in me from the spirit world and the time had come for me to take notice of what they were trying to tell me. He also told me that if I took no notice, I would probably be kicked harder in the future. His inference was that I was being called to change my life and start my work for God, and not to be so preoccupied with myself and my earthly success and perceptions.

Hell, that was a biggie, as I was being asked to serve a God whose existence I was having trouble even accepting. But then, how could I explain the past week and the happenings earlier that night? It was just too much.

The more I thought about the last few hours, the more I could not get away from the fact that somebody had guided me through the warehouse complex, and that guidance sure as all hell was not human. I just had to accept that maybe a God did exist and we were able to communicate with it, him or whatever. My perceptions were really getting stretched. As sleep finally overtook my tired body and very confused mind, I was glad to sink into oblivion.

Father Sherry woke me at 6 a.m. and asked if I would like to accompany him to early morning mass. I remember thinking to myself, as I struggled to gain consciousness, that I had not been to mass for at least twelve years, and that I must be weak in the head to get up to go now. But somehow I felt I must. I also felt that it was okay to have doubts and that I could really trust Brian not to attempt to convert or pressure me.

Mass was at the nearby convent, and other than a dozen nuns, I was the only other person there. Brian took the mass, and many times during the service our eyes met and produced in me an immediate emotional outpouring of tears. My body got very hot and I could feel a surge - a shaft like wave of energy coming into me. I had never before felt anything like it. It was different from all my other energy experiences. It felt as if the energy was coming straight into my heart and filling my body with love from the centre out. As the energy flowed in, my emotional energy poured out. It felt like Father Sherry was connecting me straight to God. It was like the mass was just for me and that all the power of the prayers and the sanctity of the mass were being directed through me.

Toward the end of the mass, the intensity of energy in my body had become tremendous. I felt much lighter, so light I could almost float. My skin felt like it was expanding under the pressure from inside. I felt a fullness and a completeness that I had never experienced before. At the end of the mass, I just sat in that little chapel, feeling total wonderment. I was wet through with sweat, my whole body was vibrating. I was in total awe of the experience I had felt and was still feeling.

When Brian had finished his priestly duties, he came out and we just sat together in silence for about thirty minutes. Finally, as if we both knew, we got up and walked outside. "Wow," I said, "what the hell happened to me?"

Brian just laughed and said, "you have experienced a little bit of the power of God, and you allowed the Holy Spirit to enter you."

The walk back to the house from the chapel was made in silence, as I was trying to accept what Brian had just said to me. Good God, what was happening to me? Was I going off my head; had I finally fallen out of my tree, or what? But my body was not lying. The feeling I had experienced was real. My body was still feeling as if it would float away at any moment. I felt as if I wanted to be alive - here on earth... and that was a very different feeling for me at that time.

Having breakfast with about six other priests, and all their small talk, came as a welcome release, as I was able to stop thinking about what was happening. After breakfast, Father Sherry and I excused ourselves and moved into the study, where we had a nice long talk, trying to help me put everything into perspective. It was still hard to accept that the past week had been real and that all the events had actually happened.

Brian was wonderful; he made no judgments, but just tried to help me come to the understanding that God really did exist and that at times some of us really do experience some amazing spiritual events that can change our lives. He also explained to me that there was a great hierarchy in the spiritual world (which I realized later was an amazing understanding for a Catholic priest) and that there were many levels on which we could be helped.

He said that not everybody had these experiences, and to those that have them, it is a true calling to become aware of their spirituality and to serve God by helping people on this earth. Of course, I argued the "why me?" bit and all that, but Brian just said that this was not the point. I had been called, and it was up to me to accept or not. He advised me to go back to the farm and try to get on with life, letting the events of the past week have time to settle into my consciousness. When I was ready to talk some more, I could contact him. I said I would do this, as at the time he was the only person I felt comfortable talking to. Blimey, I did not even know how I would be able to tell Denise about what had happened, let alone anybody else.

The time had come to leave Wellington and, dropping the rental car at the depot, Brian drove me out to the airport. Neither of us said very much, and when we arrived at the terminal, I felt rather afraid. It was not a fear of going back to the farm, but of having to face a new reality. A reality that, even to me, was so far-fetched that I was having trouble accepting it. A realization that from now on I would have to include thinking of God, angels, spirits and all that stuff. I was going to have to turn about-face, and I did not know if I could handle that.

What would my family say? What would my friends think of me? Hell, they would laugh and say the twit Hiestand had gone all religious on us. How could I face them? The only way was to tell Denise, and nobody else, about it for the moment. God, I hoped she would understand. Those and many other confused thoughts occupied my mind as the plane winged its way south and all too soon arrived at Christchurch. Even one of the world's most spectacular views, the snowcapped

Southern Alps, was not able to bring its usual joy into my heart due to my confused mind.

Leaving the airport and busing into the city to pick up my car, I finally started to get control of my emotions. After that, I was able to still my mind somewhat. I needed to start thinking about the farm again, because no doubt there would be things that would need my input and decisions.

I had rung Denise from Wellington, so she was expecting me home that day. She had said everything was okay on the farm, but I knew she would say that anyhow so I would not worry. Damn, that girl was great. She somehow knew that I was going through all sorts of shit. She was a strength to the family, as well as being able to keep 400 cows milked and the farm running.

I felt really strange heading back to the farm. I was having to bring myself back into another world - a world of no money, no grass, no rain and lots of problems. Yet I did not have the worry or the pain I'd had before. It was almost like, although the farm was there, it had less effect on me. Of course, that feeling of detachment was not to last for long.

CHAPTER 7
TURNING POINT

The reality of a hard, long winter soon brought me down to earth, and I pushed my experiences of that week to the back of my mind. I had found it quite hard to tell Denise all that had happened, because it was hard to believe it all myself. But over the next few weeks most of it came out, and she never expressed any doubts, or judgments, nothing but support. I was the one with the problem of acceptance.

Within three months, I had totally suppressed all that had happened and was back to my old ways, although with less depression and anger. More and more work for less and less was the order of the day; the treadmill was still going strong. I sort of put myself on hold emotionally and just went about life with no real meaning, doing the day-to-day things.

At times I enjoyed being with the kids on skiing trips or such, but most of the time I just stuffed all emotions and kept my mind dead. The newspapers finally told us that we had been through the worst drought in over one hundred years, as if we did not already know. But somehow it made me feel a bit better, as we had survived and you do not get two like that in a row.

Spring was just around the corner, and as usual all of us farmers got keen again. The hard work from the year before is always forgotten when we look forward to the cows calving and the milk flowing, the grass growing and the bloody bank manager rubbing his hands together as the money starts flowing.

We must be fools, I thought. The whole country gets its living from our exports, and we do all the work, take all the risks, pay all the interest and still pay the mortgage. And we keep doing it year after bloody year.

But it is amazing what happens to farmers when spring arrives. Well, to this farmer anyhow. My whole emotional state seemed to come out of the winter blues and, like the unfolding of the first spring flowers, I felt the joy of being alive. On the farm everything bursts into life, new and renewed life; but this year that good feeling did not last long as we got into the tremendous workload. I was purchasing up to 100 week-old calves every week for four weeks, as well as helping our own 400 cows calve in a seven-week period, so we hardly had time to stop and pick our noses, let alone take time off.

It is incredible what our bodies went through those days. Both Denise and myself would lose twenty to thirty pounds of body weight over the spring; we just could not eat enough to replace the energy we burned up. Our days started at about five in the morning and we usually did a final check on the calving cows between eleven p.m. and midnight. If there was any calving trouble, we got to bed still later.

No sooner was the calving rush over and the milking and calf-feeding routine established than it was grass harvesting time, and I was away from the farm with contracting equipment making silage. This usually lasted about three months - three months of pressure, and go, go, go as everybody wanted their harvesting done yesterday.

We had a good crew of men and by this time some good gear, but we still would work fifteen to eighteen hours a day to get the work done. Denise would be left running the farm with the staff, usually only one, and the kids helping a lot. With all this work going on, I did not have time to think about anything else, especially things like what had happened back a few months in the autumn. In fact, the only time I was brought back to that reality was when I learned that Father

Sherry had died suddenly. He was a young man and a darn good one at that, so why, if there was a God, did he allow that to happen?

At the time I simply thought, there goes the one person I could talk to about spiritual things, so now I have nobody. So I just filed my experiences away in the too-hard-to-deal-with part of my mind and threw away the key. That would be the end of that, or so I thought.

As the season moved into summer, the weather started to play tricks on us again by being unusually hot and dry. Bloody hell, two dry seasons in a row would be too much for anybody to take. My emotions were holding up reasonably well due to the amount of work that had to be done, but of course I was only delaying the inevitable smash against my brick wall.

It was in late summer that I met the woman who was to have a major influence in my life and, in fact, who probably saved me from totally self-destructing. It is strange how things happen that lead us unexpectedly into different paths and understandings. This was one of those strange events.

This woman, who was from Australia and travelled around teaching some natural health things, suggested we try to solve some of the soil pesticide problems we had, problems accentuated by the dry weather, by using some experimental homeopathic treatments. Of course, I jumped to accept this help. What did we have to lose? Anyhow, who knows, it might even help. God knows we needed all the help we could get.

Meeting this woman for the first time was quite an experience. Sue was about fifteen years older than me, rich (and looked it), world-wise (and knew it), sophisticated, wore only the best clothes, and obviously only the best was good enough. Even though she was over 50, I could tell by the clothes she was wearing that she had a body that would put most twenty-five year olds to shame.

She oozed self-confidence and would have easily made most people feel inferior. Of course, to me she was a real challenge, and we spent most of the night in a mental sparring match.

This lady was good; her mind was like liquid lightning, and it was sometime in the wee small hours she really started to get to me. Damn, this lady was starting to get in my head. That was enough for me, so I excused myself and went home.

We had arranged for me to pick her up the next morning to travel to the mountains to get pure water for the homeopathic treatment. As it turned out, that next morning was to be the start of a changed me.

Arriving to collect Sue about midmorning, with clear blue skies and the sun once again drying out the last bit of moisture from the grass, I felt despondent as the drought was getting as bad as last year's.

Sue came to meet me with an overly cheery smile and a "good morning, good morning, isn't it a lovely day," all dressed up and carrying a picnic basket and thinking the world was wonderful just because she was out in the country.

Miss bloody rich city bitch, I thought as she climbed into the pickup, trying not to get her neat city dress soiled by the farmyard dirt that all but covered the Toyota.

Heading out the gate, I turned toward the mountains for the three-hour drive that would take us into the Mt. Cook region, where there is some of the world's purest water. Sue tried to wipe the dust off the seat of the pickup and arrange everything nicely and neatly (a hell of a job in my farm truck).

At last, she sat back all satisfied and looked across at me with a big smile and said, "Oh what a **lovely,** lovely day this is, the sun is so bright and shining. It's just such a lovely day!" Well that did it. I could not hold my emotions together any longer and I let her have it.

My anger just flowed out my mouth and I yelled at her, what the hell was the matter with her? It's a nice day? It was a bloody lousy day - the sun was shining and the animals were starving as the drought took hold. Could she not see how dry all the farms looked. How were the farmers able to survive without rain? "Look at what you are wearing," I said to her. Everything she had on either came from farmers or was imported with money that was earned by farm export. How the hell did she and her city friends think that the shops were able to get all the nice things to sell? If it did not rain soon, there would not be many farmers left in this area to earn the country's income. So what was so bloody good about a sunny day, when all we all needed was a good week of rain?

I went on and on. It was as if a floodgate had been opened in me. I poured out all my pent-up emotions and frustrations. The poor lady took the lot. The more emotional I became, the faster I drove and Sue did not have time to get a word in edgewise.

Two hours passed before I stopped. I was wet with sweat and felt completely drained. I could barely hold on to the steering wheel. I had let out all my anger about the droughts, farming, politics, the inequities in life, the struggle we were all having with the banks and so on.

I looked over at Sue half expecting her to respond with anger. Because I felt like a beaten, hollow man I just did not care anymore. But Sue did not react as expected. She began to say something, paused, then bent over toward me and ever so gently touched my arm. In the softest voice she said, "It's okay, I understand. I can help you if you will let me." Her voice had an angel-like quality and, combined with her touching my arm, had the effect of melting me.

I just let go of my control and started to cry. The crying came in ever greater waves until I could not even drive anymore. I pulled over to the side of the road and just sobbed and sobbed, as wave after wave of emotion welled up in me and rolled out through my tears.

My head rocked back and forth, one minute resting on the steering wheel and the next on the head rest. My shoulders heaved up and down and my breath came in great gulps between sobs that seemed to originate in the depths of my being. I was racked with emotion, and every cell in my body seemed to be letting go. There was no way I could stop the sobbing.

Sue did not say a word, but just sat there being with me, allowing, understanding, letting me experience my hurt. I guess we sat there for about thirty minutes. When my sobbing subsided, I realized the engine was still running. Still without any speech, I put the pickup in gear and continued our journey.

Although the beauty of the Southern Alps was before me, I was unable to take it in. My mind was in a haze, not really focusing on anything. I guess I was just allowing things and thoughts to happen. I seemed to have no fight left; my body was like jelly. As we drove deeper into the mountains, I became aware of a quiet peace slowly coming over me.

Nearing the water collection place, Sue asked me if I would like to take a detour, as there was a place she would like to take me, about an hour and a half's walk into the mountains. The day was still young and I really needed a good tramp in my favorite mountains, so I readily agreed.

We packed the picnic lunch into a backpack and headed off on foot. I was feeling quite good at this stage and Sue and I were talking quite freely, in fact joking and generally giving each other a hard time. At no time did she even mention my two-hour outrage.

At one point along the trail I stopped and chipped a small rock out from the side of a bank formed by earth movement. A sense of wonder came over me as I realized that I was the first human being who had ever held that rock, and it was also the first time in tens of thousands of years, maybe billions of years, that the sun had shone on it.

I remember looking up at Sue with wonder in my eyes as I was squatting on the ground looking like I was talking to the rocks, realizing just how insignificant our human problems really are. I realized how our focus on our problems keeps us from taking joy in just being alive. This rock I held in my hand had waited all this time to feel the sun, so why were we humans in such a hell-fired hurry?

Moving deeper and deeper into the mountains, we were soon climbing quite steeply, until at last Sue said the place was just around the next bluff. Rounding the bluff, we came onto a small plateau, and there before us was the Caroline face of Mt. Cook towering straight up into the heavens, so close it made you feel like you were under it.

It was awesome, the pure power of the place. Every five minutes thousands of tons of snow and ice would break off and fall thousands of feet with a deafening roar that reverberated around the mountains.

There are not many places in the world where within an easy two-hour walk you can be in the midst of some of the biggest mountains in the world, where in every direction the earth towers up to over 14,000 feet, seemingly an arm's-length away, where you can feel the power, the strength, the pulse of the planet. It is no wonder people from all over the world are drawn to New Zealand's Southern Alps, and in particular the Mt. Cook area.

Finding a nice spot in the mountain tussock, we set out the picnic food. Sue then sat me down in front of her and put a set of earphones on me, saying she wanted me to hear a special piece of music.

As the tune started to play, she gently drew me back into her lap and slowly stroked my head. Lying there in her lap, taking in the grandeur of the mountains, allowing the gentle music to penetrate my body, was heaven.

Slowly my mind became still and I could feel the tightness in my body relax. As the tune finished, Sue started to talk very softly and slowly to me, first about my reactions in the pickup. She explained the reasons for my anger. She went on to tell me that I was or had been in denial of my spiritual self most of my life, yet I had power within me that was very great, and if I chose to, I could use this power to be of great help to others.

She went on to say it would be a hard road for me to completely accept this and to change, but she would help me if I wished. She said that she knew what the drought and the fall in product prices were doing to us and how emotionally destroying it was for us to see our life's work going down the drain, but maybe now was the time to really take a look at my life.

She was so gentle that I just lay there; I never reacted. I was so calm it was amazing. The whole time, she never stopped slowly stroking my forehead. Many of the things she was saying were similar to what Father Sherry had said, but Sue had met me only the day before, and there was no way she could have known anything about me. The things she was talking to me about were right on target, especially the things about my anger and frustration.

She talked about forms of healing and health care I had never heard about. How these methods used no drugs, about the amazing amount of knowledge that was out there to learn, and she said, "life is much more than work, work, work."

Probably for the first time in my life I did not argue back, even though some of the things Sue was saying had no reality for me at the time. It was strange, but deep inside I felt most of the things she was saying were true. Even though it was largely new to me, it felt right - almost as if I knew it all on another level and now it was being brought to my awareness. At no time did her voice sound demanding or strong, but was soft or even angelic in tone. We must have been communicating like this for about two hours before we realized how hungry we were, as by now it was the middle of the afternoon.

Finishing the remainder of the picnic lunch, we again started talking, but this time I was questioning Sue as much as she was giving information. This gentle opening of my perceptions was so consuming that the sun had dipped behind the peaks and the chill of early evening arrived before we realized we had better get off the mountain before dark.

Heading down the mountain as darkness closed in was one of the most wonderful experiences I had ever had. I felt so light. Sue had helped me put so many things in place, almost as if my life had at last found a direction. The way Sue had explained everything allowed me to see all the things I had been struggling with, logically and simply. Yes, she had brought in the spiritual aspect, but not in a church type of way. She made sense by the way she explained it all; life could be simple and happy. She explained that shit happens, but life did not have to be a bitch. It was largely up to us how we reacted to life's tests. We could react with anger or other emotions, or accept the shit, stay happy within and carry on - the choice was always ours. It was not the things that happened to us that was the problem, but our reactions to them.

Sue went on to explain that I had always reacted to things around me because that was the pattern I learned as a child. It probably had served me well when young, allowing me to survive, but now I was taking in far too much energy from all the problems and reacting only negatively.

I realized I was like a great big sponge, soaking up all the negativity I came into contact with, trying to solve all problems with the same energy. My feeling for other people and all the injustices in the world drove me to try to help and to change everything, but I was using the same negative energy, and I was getting nowhere. In the process, I was pulling in more and more negativity, which manifested as anger, frustration and feelings of self-worthlessness. I was, as Sue told me, so full of this negativity that I was on a path toward total self-destruction. I had better wake up or there was a very real possibility that I might completely fly apart.

She also told me that to change, to open my awareness, to become the real me that was suppressed, would be the hardest thing I would ever experience. She added that very few people get to where they actually want to change, and even fewer succeed. She also told me that I could make that breakthrough because of the help I would get from my spiritual connections, even if I did not believe that at this stage (which I did not). Sue went on to say that she would help me and stay with me for as long as it took. She would ask nothing in return because to see me become who I truly was would be payment so great that no other was necessary.

Yeah, that walk down the mountain was quite a learning time for me. For years after, I would remember that walk and think about my feelings and what she said, and every time a new understanding and a greater realization would come to me.

Arriving back at the pickup, we drove on and finished our journey to the high alpine stream to collect the water. I had enough containers to collect about 150 gallons, which when full would weigh about three-quarters of a ton.

As it was a climb of about 30 feet down to the pool in the stream and a difficult climb back up over boulders with two full five gallon buckets in the dark, I had my work cut out.

Luckily, it was a moonlit night and I could see just enough to find the foot holes in the rocks as I balanced the buckets against my weight and momentum.

It was not long before I stripped down to my shorts, with sweat glistening on my body in the moonlight as I stepped from rock to rock carrying an extra hundred pounds. One wrong step, and it was a broken ankle or split skull, yet I bounded over the rocks as if defying gravity.

As I was well-tanned, lean and fit, every muscle could be seen as it contracted and expanded to move my body. Sue, sitting on top of the bank watched this poetry of motion and strength in the moonlight.

Swinging the last of the full buckets onto the pickup, I stepped back, satisfied with a job well done. Sue gently slid her hands over my glistening body, commenting on the amazing way my body worked. The power, grace and ease with which the job had been done amazed her.

I commented with a laugh that I was surprised as well, and that maybe I had had some help. I had meant it as a joke, but looking back later I realize there was no way I could have moved that water up the bank in the dark in that short time without feeling totally stuffed, so maybe my half-hearted joke had more truth than either of us realized at the time.

With the water all secured and the buckets tied down, we headed back through the mountains toward the eastern plains and the farm. We did not talk much, and I allowed my mind to drift over the day's events to let everything sink in. I was not trying to put everything into place yet, just experiencing my thoughts and feelings within. So many things had happened, and I was starting to understand, though not yet accept. At least I was allowing myself to look at the overall picture of events.

The pickup was almost out of petrol when we pulled into the last village before the final pass out onto the plains. Finding everything closed because it was 11 p.m., and not being the tourist season, there was no all-night service station.

Well, that was that, I thought. There was no way we were going to get out of the mountains that night, so Sue went across to the tourist lodge to organize rooms for us as I parked the pickup away from the road. Catching up with Sue as she came out of the office, she cheerfully said we had rooms overlooking the lake, and led the way to the other side of the lodge.

As I opened the door to her room I asked her where my room was. Looking at me with a big grin, she said, "Right here. You are going to be treated with a little piece of heaven tonight." With that, she gently took my hand and led me into the best suite in the place. As I was going to come to know in the months to come, this lady only had one standard, and that was the best.

"Right," Sue said. "Go take a shower, and then you're going to get a full-body massage for all the work you did getting the water." Wow, I thought, this could be good. Never had a massage before.

Finishing my shower and not having a change of clothes with me, I wrapped myself up in the big bath towel and walked back into a transformed hotel room. Sue had turned the heaters up high and the room was warm as toast. She had towel-wrapped the table lamps to subdue the lights. The same music was playing on her Walkman that she had played on the mountain, but this time the Walkman was connected to small auxiliary speakers. A stick of incense burned slowly on the bedside table and she had used her silk scarf to create a beautiful flowing sarong (the things this lady carried in her picnic basket!). She looked absolutely stunning. If this lady was a grandmother, she must have some secrets for staying young, I thought to myself.

I must have stood there for quite a while in amazement before Sue came up to me, gently and slowly slid her arms around me, letting her body melt against mine.

She kissed me tenderly and then, drawing back, pointed to the king sized bed and said, "On your stomach, young man." As I moved toward the bed she reached out and took hold of the towel that was around my waist so that it came away from my body. My heart missed a beat. Shit, here I was in a hotel room with this stunning lady I had met only two days ago, with not a stitch on. Perhaps there was a God after all. It was almost a relief to lie there on my stomach. At least it was easier for me to keep my mind under control. As for my body, well, that is another story.

I can still feel those hands, moistened with oil as they slowly coaxed my tight muscles into letting go. Sue's hands moved expertly and intuitively, seeking, searching and with loving tenderness seducing my body into relaxing, one muscle after another. If there was a heaven, then this had to be pretty close to it. Sue was rapidly becoming a goddess as far as I was concerned. She worked on my legs, up over my buttocks and finally to my shoulders, my body felt more relaxed than I could ever remember.

Lying there, I could allow myself to sink slowly into a state of total bliss as Sue's warm, gentle, soft hands poured pure love into every fiber of my being.

Folding one side of the covers back, Sue then rolled me over onto the open sheets and started to work on my chest and stomach. I was so relaxed that I started to sink into a semi-sleep as her hands softly moved over my upper body.

Sue gently hummed to the tune from the Walkman as I drifted away with the fairies in pure and total ecstasy. I remember thinking how wrong the churches were when Sue slipped off her gown and eased her warm, naked body beside mine. Cradling me in her arms she drew my head into her bosom. You do not have to die to go to heaven, I thought as I drifted into a blissful sleep.

Not wanting to open my eyes for fear that my feeling of total peace would melt, I lay still in Sue's arms listening to the birds in the trees outside the hotel room. I struggled with my thoughts, yet not wanting to, thinking of last night - was it a dream, was I really alive? My hand gently squeezed Sue's leg and as she rolled over, her warm, yielding body melted onto mine.

I realized that no dream could be *this* good. Gently caressing my face, she slowly turned my head, and as our lips met our bodies became one in total harmony. The movement of our bodies, the incredible peaks of feeling, the flow, passion and beauty of our loving went on and on as if time ceased to exist. I felt totally at peace, complete within myself, yet fully sharing my essence and innermost emotions and receiving another's, something I had not experienced to this depth since that night with Pauline all those years ago.

The pure power of those feelings were fuelling my sense of awareness, so that every movement, every touch, was like an explosion of sensation, new and wondrous. I could feel myself expanding, expanding into a reality I knew was attainable but seldom achieved.

My conscious reality moved into another dimension, difficult to explain, but I knew the feeling. It was as if my whole being was energized to a different frequency. I could feel every cell in my body; I was alive, more alive than words can describe. As we loved, I opened up to even more energy, more feeling, until I broke through a barrier that exploded like a million galaxies throughout my body.

This was not just a sexual climax, as physically I was long since spent. This was opening to a completely new level of feeling, almost like going through a doorway of dimensional reality, expanding feelings and awareness to a level never imagined.

My body felt as if I were plugged into a high-voltage socket. I was tingling - no, almost sparking - from every pore in my skin, yet within in my heart I had this incredible peace, a feeling of total acceptance, of total harmony.

Our bodies at last parted, dripping wet with sweat, the sweet aroma of complete loving permeating the room. Sue propped herself on one arm, looked at me and said, "Wow! What happened? Are you human? That was goooood."

Lying there, chest heaving up and down, I could not say a word, not because of the physical effort but because of what I was experiencing. The expansion of feeling, the wondrousness of it - I cannot explain it, I just was! I was buzzing all over.

At last I recovered a bit and looked over at Sue. We both collapsed into each other's arms and held each other, not wanting to lose any part of the experience, the feeling. We both knew we had experienced something different, but incredibly real. Hours later we finally forced ourselves to face the real world, got ourselves together, filled the pickup with petrol and headed back to the farm.

It would be years before I would find out what was happening to my body during these times of strange energy charges. I have now experienced this expansion of myself many times, and each time I have experienced increasing energy as it pulsed through my body and felt, really felt, like I was about to become conscious of a very different reality.

Many things, I realized, could trigger this change in me. Making love was one of the more enjoyable ways, but with it I had a certain amount of anxiety, because not every time I made love would my body move into the other plane. And once my partner had experienced this other me, there was no way that anything less was acceptable. As one of my partners said, "To have experienced loving on that energy level made all other experiences pale into such insignificance that one might as well have been a virgin!"

Do not get me wrong, I was probably even more amazed than my partners at the incredible power, feeling and pure mind-blowing experience of having my body energized like that. Obviously, my body would transfer a lot of this energy to my partner, and we would both experience an incredible energy connection, which had an amazing effect on both our bodies.

Sometimes for hours after, my partner's body would be tingling with energy, feeling like it was floating because the feeling of lightness and well-being was so strong. I remember one incident years later in the U.S. when after an "energy experience," my partner was able to discharge a spark on the bed's brass work by holding her fingers an inch away from it. This was an hour after we had stopped making love, and she still felt so energized that she could not sleep. She said she was feeling too alive, too wired, to even think of sleep.

Another instance, again in the States, happened when I was working with horses. In this case, the man shoeing my friend's horse got one hell of a shock as a charge of energy shot through him from the horse's rear foot when I placed my hand on the horse's head. He reeled backward from the horse and told me to keep away from the animal until he had finished shoeing it. It was really quite funny, but the farrier did not think so at the time.

There were lots of unusual energy anomalies over the years, but at the time I had no idea how to control it, where it came from or what caused it. But I knew all my experiences were connected, starting with learning to focus into things back in my engineering days, to the feeling I could get driving fast or operating the tractor on hills, to the altered states I was in when the energy came into my body. At least it did not scare me anymore; but I never allowed myself to think it had anything to do with anything spiritual.

Another strange thing was my incredible body heat, which I was coming to realize was also connected. Nearly every one of the people I have been close to have remarked about how hot my body gets. My wife Denise always complained about it, and in fact we always had to have a king-sized bed so she could get far enough away to be able to steep. I thought she simply had a low tolerance to a differing body heat, because I never felt that hot.

As was usually the case, Denise was right once again, because after our marriage ended every single one of my partners have all said the same thing. In fact, I have been kicked out of bed on more than one occasion to cool down my body when my partner was unable to handle the radiated heat I generated. As my awareness and sensitivity increased, I, too, became aware of how different my body temperature can be.

Later, after I left farming, and for the first time in years I was getting enough sleep, I began to understand what was happening and how to control my body. I would wake up at night realizing how hot I was and would be absolutely wet with sweat and just lie there in wonder as energy pulsed through my body, producing more and more heat until every cell would tingle and pop like it was ready to explode - an incredible sensation, I can assure you. It was usually about this stage that my partner would wake and literally order me out, because sometimes the whole room was so full of energy that it felt like an oven.

Strangely, as soon as I left the room, it would immediately feel normal again. I came to refer to these times as being "plugged in." In due course, I was able to plug in on demand, and some amazing things in healing sessions and seminars would take place, but more about that later.

As we headed home, Sue, taking the lead, started to talk about all the things I had told her about myself on the mountain. She suggested that each time she was in the country we spend time together so she could start to teach me some basic natural health techniques and share the knowledge she had about the body's electrical system, its meridians and so forth.

Half of the words she used I had never heard before, but I had an incredible urge to learn all she could teach me. It was as if finally, after all the years of searching and struggling, here at last, was the road I was meant to follow.

The clarity, the knowingness that this was my direction, was amazing. I had never been so sure, so keen and so overjoyed, as I felt during that drive home with Sue.

It was as if I had at last turned a corner and could see an opening through the misery and despair I had increasingly been feeling. God, I was happy. When I think about it now, it was one of the most important crossroads in my life.

The trust I had in Sue was total. Never before had I let anybody get inside me as she had done. I took in her every word. For the first time in my life I was open, and when all my shit began pouring out, Sue helped me replace it with goodness and love. The process was to be long, hard and painful, with some incredible ups and downs.

Had I not totally accepted Sue after our incredible connection that night, the work she was able to do with me in the months to come could never have taken place. We were to experience a wonderful physical relationship (after that first night, how could we keep our bodies apart when the opportunity arose?), but I can see clearly that our physical relationship was first the catalyst, and later the anchor that kept us together.

This became increasingly important as I began to penetrate the core of my emotions, which resulted in my becoming extremely reactive. Without this strong physical tie, Sue would never have been able to reach me like she did. And I would never have been able to deal with my incredibly deep and painful issues.

She was able to bring up most of my difficult behavior patterns so I could face them and then deal with them. Without a means of keeping us together for that purpose, I would have run a million miles to keep them buried. I give thanks to God every day and ask blessings for Sue for the time we spent together. Without her, I surely would not be alive today, and certainly not doing the work I am now doing.

For two years, I experienced profound changes that equipped me for the next step and moved me progressively towards the knowledge I now have. More than that, I was able to gain my self-respect, and with that, my respect and love for all humanity.

CHAPTER 8
HEALING POWER

Denise and I had gotten through the farming season in reasonable fashion, and we were all glad to have a break from the twice-daily routine of milking the cows when winter brought shorter days and cold nights to our southern isles.

With more time on my hands, I was able to spend many days with Sue because she worked in our area on her travels through the country. I was present when she worked on friends and others using kinesiology and other muscle-testing techniques to balance their meridians. Because Sue had given me a full muscle balance, I knew how much better my body felt after this simple procedure. The technique was similar to the "Touch for Health" program taught throughout the world, but enlarged and incorporating much more than just Touch for Health techniques. It was a method taught by the International School of Cell-Electrology in New Zealand, Australia and England.

I watched peoples' reactions and noted their happiness and satisfaction because they felt so much better as a result of this simple technique. It was the catalyst that cemented my desire to understand what was actually happening within the body to bring about this change. I remember how I would feel after Sue "balanced" me and how much easier it was for me to handle my problems and the stress of everyday living.

You know, I used to think people who were involved in all these sorts of strange alternative-health things were all a bit weird. But here I was, working, learning and listening to this weird woman I had a connection with. I was rather embarrassed to tell my friends what I was learning.

Often after spending time with Sue, I would even tell myself that it was all bullshit, that it was our imagination that we could feel better after using these techniques. I guess that was my ego struggling to hold on to its power and control.

One of the things that really got to me during this early time with Sue was when we were together in the mountains. We used to go there together as often as we could, and she would put me through a pressured learning and emotional detox. One time Sue gave me a small gold pendulum as a gift and said I should learn how to use it.

With it came a little book explaining pendulum use and some exercises. Amazingly, when I tried the first exercise, the pendulum moved along the different lines in perfect order. Blimey, I could not believe it! I sure as hell did not deliberately make the thing move, but every time I focused my mind on a different group of exercises in the book, the pendulum would instantly change the direction of its swing and conform to what I was focusing on. I was totally intrigued and must have spent most of the afternoon playing and experimenting with my new toy.

I had known about divining because in a rural community many farmers get a diviner (dowser) to find where to drill a well by using divining techniques. I had seen some diviners use pendulums, but I had never thought I had any abilities like that. But here I was, dangling this thing that looked like a short fat bullet on a bit of cotton, and it almost seemed to have a mind of its own.

It seemed as if it could read my thoughts because by the end of the day I could ask questions and it would circle clockwise for yes and counterclockwise for no. I was like a little kid at a Christmas party; I just could not stop playing with my new toy. But this toy could communicate with me in strange ways. I remember thinking, I can divine, I am a diviner. I was happy as could be, really tickled pink about it.

Sue had an extensive library, and she would lend me all sorts of books as well as urge me to purchase those I needed to study. Also, my local town had a good library, and I think I read every book it had on different health and healing work. I was excited because I was learning something new, as well as things about myself I had never suspected.

With the farm finances slowly worsening, the occasional weekend with Sue was a welcome break, a break into another reality. Sure, I thought some of the things Sue would say and some of the books she would ask me to read were a bit weird. Some I disregarded as bullshit, but generally everything was settling into place in my mind. Well, so I thought, anyhow.

Often, when Sue would be balancing someone she would feel that person's pain or seem to know where the problem was in their body. The first time she asked me to put my hand about three to four inches away from someone, slowly moving it over them as they were lying on the massage table, I could detect different feelings on my hand over the area of an injury or problem. It was strange, but I could really feel a difference. As my hand reached that point, my body immediately got hot, and a surge of energy would pulse through me. I could feel what I can only describe as a very slight breeze coming out of and surrounding my hand.

Later, as I became more aware of myself and what was happening, the feeling became so strong that I could swear there was gasoline evaporating from my hand - that is how real it was. There was some energy transfer going on somehow, and my engineer-trained mind was determined to find out all about it, and understand it, by hook or by crook.

We were working on a small child one night, and while Sue was balancing his meridians (circuits), I was casually scanning his body with my hand when I got this knowingness, a sort of strong thought in my mind, a bit like something had hit me and there was this thought. At the same time my body became really hot with an energy charge so great that I had to leave the boy and sit down.

I tried to tell Sue to stop working on the child because I had picked up something really important, but she told me not to be silly, since she was feeling okay and she wanted to finish the balancing. Being new at this wacky stuff, I got upset, not because I was angry at Sue, but because my urge was so strong to do something about what I felt.

I could not tell Sue what that was, as the kid's mother was right there and what I had picked up was that the kid had a faulty heart valve. I did not want to mention that in front of the child's mother. Also, an urge built up in me more and more strongly to go back to the child and place my hands over his chest. I thought, I cannot do that, what would everybody think? But by this time my body had a full energy charge and was completely "fully plugged in," as I had come to call it. Sweat was running down my back, in fact I felt like I was going mad because my body was about ready to melt. I felt faint, and I had an overpowering urge to "heal" the kid.

I had never felt anything like it. "I cannot heal anything," I tried to tell myself, "let alone somebody's heart." My mind was in total denial as the logical me was fighting with a me that I did not know existed and that was coming through strong.

I started to panic, as the urge to go to the child and place my hands over him was so strong, but I resisted. Blimey, I had come to terms with being driven all over the country by some spook or force or whatever and I knew a bit about energy by now, but this was ridiculous, it was just so bloody powerful.

Once again I tried to get Sue's attention, but again I was told to wait and not be so emotional. "Bloody hell," I said, "do you think I like feeling like this?" With that, I lost control of myself and ran out of the house crying my eyes out. I remember hardly being able to breathe because my body was so hot, so charged with energy that my chest muscles would not work. It was horrible. I was experiencing a power like I had never felt before.

Sitting outside with tears pouring down my face, I could still focus into the kid's heart and almost see and touch it with my mind. I felt that if I put my hand out, it would reach into his body and touch his heart - that is, if I went back to him his heart would be healed.

My mind turned over at a million miles an hour. My body felt as if it would never be the same again. My emotions were shot to hell and, most of all, I was scared out of my wits. I thought, I really am going mad. What am I trying to do, thinking I can see the kid's heart, thinking I can fix it. Sure, I used to focus in on the furnaces and see the molten metal years ago, but that was metal and I was in control and using my power of concentration (or so I thought) and all that stuff. This time I simply passed my hand over a body and blam! - this vision hit me like a ton of bricks, my body went haywire and I got this urge to heal. No, this was all too much, I was falling out of my tree. Time to get out of this voodoo stuff. I was becoming terrified of the whole thing and I wanted out.

Sue and I argued that night over what happened. She did not think the child had anything wrong with him and that I had not handled myself at all well. Hell, I did not need her telling me that. I knew I was out of control and was blown away. When she said I was wrong about what I had picked up, I made my decision there and then: no more. No more weird stuff or natural health shit for me; it was just too way out for this farm boy. I was scared shitless that night and I needed time out.

For the next eight or so months, I concentrated on being a farmer, not allowing myself to think much about my last weird experience. I told Denise about it and said, "as far as I was concerned, I reckoned that that young boy had a fault in his heart." Even though I had no way of understanding how I knew it and in spite of the fact that I had stopped working with all this stuff, I never changed my mind about the child's heart.

It was early afternoon and I was out on the tractor when Denise called me up on the radio and asked me if I remembered the boy with the heart problem. I said I did, and she went on to tell me that when I came home she would tell me the full story but in the meantime I could feel good, because I was right.

I could not wait to get home to find out how she knew all this. Finally the job was done, and I headed the tractor for home. Over a coffee Denise told me about it.

Apparently the boy was not at all well, and even after Sue had worked on him he was still tired all the time and was not growing as he should. His mother, becoming concerned, took him to a doctor who sent the child for tests at the city hospital. These tests showed up the boy's bad heart, just as I had explained to Sue. The mother called Sue, and Sue called Denise to tell me I had been right all along, and that I had better start to work on people again. She said I had better realize that I have the wonderful gift of healing.

Well, that put the acid on me, not that I was right about the kid's heart problem, but now I had to contend with my emotions and attitudes about this healing thing. It is all very well learning about the body's energy circuits and this and that technique and all that, but this healing thing was another story altogether.

Face it, the Bible says that Jesus did things like that and that Jesus was related to God. As I was having trouble accepting God at the time and Jesus and I were not exactly the best of mates either, I did not think this healing thing was for me. Yes, I had picked up on one person's problem - how, I had no idea.

I do not think I really wanted to know, because that would force me back into that wacky world again. I think I was just too darn frightened to learn any more at the time, but looking back, I really was not given much choice.

Patrick, Sue's friend from Australia, came into my life when Sue brought him down to our farm to assist with the homeopathic treatments for the pesticide problem in the soil. This problem had the potential to totally ruin us financially, as the dairy company had picked it up in our milk.

Patrick was an older man, but his mind was as sharp as hell. Sue asked me if I would look after Patrick for a few days. That is how I came to spend time with this crazy old man. Crazy, not because he was a bit mental, but because the things he could do would seem weird to most people. Patrick was a highly skilled diviner and could feel with his body the earth energies and divine the exact spots to drill wells, build houses and plant trees, etc.

Having Patrick on the farm, I asked him to treat a sick cow. Patrick's treatment was to go up to the sick animal, hold out his hands and point his fingers at it, remaining like that for about five to ten minutes. Then he would say, "That's done," and be on his way. He was so matter-of-fact about it, as if it were an everyday thing that he did. I soon realized that it was what he did nearly every day, and to him it was the most natural thing in the world.

No big hullabaloo, no big emotional display, no hallelujahs, chanting or crystals or anything like that. This guy just stood there and fixed sick cows. I had been a farmer long enough to know a sick cow when I saw one, and I also knew when a treatment helps a sick animal. With Patrick, I have seen with my own eyes sick cows and other animals improve and even get up and start eating within minutes. I have seen young calves given up by farmers as hopeless get up and start sucking my hand after Patrick did his thing for a few minutes.

After seeing Patrick work for a few days I got interested in all this energy stuff again. As a result, I spent as much time with him as I could. We used to talk for hours, but he never got tired of my probing questions. As he was an electronics expert, he had an excellent understanding of energy and was only too happy to give me as much of that understanding as I could take.

At the time, he was the first person I had met who could take things that most people thought were weird and a bit occult and explain them in a scientific way using his knowledge of energy and things electronic. A lot of the things that I did not understand and most people dismissed, Patrick could explain and make it seem quite simple. He was and still is a truly amazing man, and it was no accident that Sue "happened" to bring him down to our farm.

Patrick was just like everybody else. He did not worry too much about what he ate and he was not opposed to a drop or two of the hard stuff. In fact, it was over a whiskey about midnight one night that I told him I wished I could do the things with my hands like he could. The old guy gave me a funny look and said, "Can't you see anything?" When I asked what he meant, he told me to put my hands on my knees, which I did. Then he told me to turn them over, palms up. He then came over and placed his hands over mine. He appeared to be taking a reading of my energy, because I felt no energy input. As I had seen him work many times, I knew he was not working on me, and after about one and a half minutes he withdrew and sat back down.

Looking directly at me he said, "There is nothing that you have seen me do that you cannot do better. In fact, your ability, if developed and used correctly, will be truly amazing. Young man, you should learn as much as you can about all different understandings, but always remember, everything is only energy, energy in many different frequencies. Then when you get your emotions sorted out and let go of the anger you have got locked up, you might then be allowed to use the awesome power that is waiting for you."

I was stunned. Patrick did not say much, and this was a major speech for him. But what he had said to me made me quiver. I think I asked, "Why me?" He answered, "Do you think everything that has happened to you was a fluke? No, my friend, you are being asked to do this work, and it is about time you realized that."

I sat there in the living room for a long time without talking. I think Patrick got up quietly and went to bed, leaving me to my thoughts. Wow - do not ask the question if you cannot handle the answer, eh? I had an answer that was going to take some getting used to.

Here I was, just a country boy struggling to accept all these strange things that had happened. I had taken one step forward by stretching my mind to give them credence, then pulling myself back abruptly, somehow sensing that this path would destroy the view of reality I had held all my life and leave me without solid footing. I lived one life struggling with the farm and another where all this energy stuff was coming up. (The Gemini in me?)

When I was with Sue or Patrick it was easy to be positive and believe this was what I was meant to be doing, thinking of spiritual things and the like. But when I was back on the farm (which was most of the time) with its never-ending problems, it was hard to believe any other world was real.

Often I was stretched so tight between the two that I felt like a guitar string. And, like a guitar string, there were times that I broke, literally flying apart emotionally. It was amazing to me that Sue would either phone or show up every time I hit one of those brick walls. She always seemed to know how I was feeling. Dealing with one life is hard enough, but I was trying to come to terms with two, totally different, realities.

It is hard now to recall details of the emotional roller coaster I was on. Part of the time I was in a daze or emotional never-never land, a sort of void, giving my subconscious mind a chance to sort out my beliefs. On one hand, my ego was saying, go for it, you must be somebody special, because everybody is saying that you have this unique energy, that you can be a great healer, do God's work and become famous. But the other side of ego, doubting that I could even survive on the farm, scathingly dismissed such thoughts as idiotic delusions.

I knew for years I had tried to deny any recognition of God. Only a week after an experience I was telling myself how crazy I was for even thinking that half of the things had actually happened. The cynical, disbelieving voice in my head might well have been trying to anticipate, and thereby protect me from, similarly cynical judgments that might come from others.

In good old Kiwi language my emotional state could best be described as really fucked up, and if Sue had not been available to keep me together during this period, I would not have made it.

I was into denial so completely that there was no way I could talk to Denise. I would have had to admit my doubts and failures, real or perceived. I felt forced to put on a front, but inside I was tearing myself apart. I remember the excruciating, emotional pain and torment I felt at times; often, without any real reason, I would go into violent rage then immediately sink into a deep despair. I became so reactive that Denise and the kids had to tiptoe around me for fear of upsetting me and setting off another rage and/or depression. I think Denise sighed with relief each time Sue came and took me away for a few days.

Looking back I am amazed at how self-absorbed I had become in my emotional hell. It never even occurred to me at the time to wonder how my behaviour was affecting those closest to me, especially Denise. I give thanks every day for having Denise with me during that time, as she was the rock of stability, holding everything together when I was flying apart. Thank you special lady, thank you.

That is not to say my behavior was any better when Sue and I were together. In fact, by now I was dealing with so many internal issues that I became unbearably defensive, and argued, questioned and challenged Sue in every possible way. One minute we would be sharing a gentle moment and the next we would be in a violent argument.

Sue was strong, and she used to bait me to draw me out. It did not matter how angry I got, she would keep on pushing me to face myself. Many times we got so engrossed in this power play that Sue would get as emotional as I was, and we would yell at each other for hours. She would never let me get away with denial and codependency.

Because I was around anger most of my life, I used the same energy to detox myself. Of course, at the time I had no idea what I was doing. I was like an onion, with layer after layer of stuffed emotion wrapped ever tighter inside each other; as I peeled off one layer, the next would be exposed. Then as I dealt with that layer, the rest would have to be dealt with in turn. As I got deeper and deeper into very old emotional problems, the newly exposed layers that were bound so tightly would explode with a force that erupted like a series of bomb blasts.

The weather was up to its usual tricks, and another drought set in. During this time, Patrick had divined water near the surface of our farm, so I irrigated ninety more acres and grew enough extra feed to counter the dry year.

With some development going on and progress being made, my emotional state improved somewhat. But when I went to dig the well, I found out that the stones Patrick had placed on the ground to mark the spot had been moved by our daughter Karen to make way for her horse jumps. I hit the roof. How the hell was I to know where to dig the well. I was really angry about this, and poor Karen got an earful of abuse, but of course, it was not her fault. She had no idea that the stones marked a well site.

Days later I was still stewing over this; I could not get Patrick back as he was in Australia. Then Denise asked me why I did not just go out and divine for the water myself with my pendulum. I had not thought of that; I was too busy being angry. After thinking about all this for a while, I went out into the field to see if I could do it. Sure enough, as I walked up and down the field the pendulum would spin only in certain places and by crossing at different angles over the field, I was able to find the center of the strongest swing.

Feeling that was the spot to dig I organized for the well to be dug, and sure enough we found water. Now, this is in an area of the country that was not recognized as having water anywhere near the surface. We enlarged the well to form a pond; this became quite a talking point among the community. People used to climb the fence and cross the field to look down in amazement at water only 20 feet below. Most wells were well over 300 feet or more and cost tens of thousands of dollars. Well, as for miracles, most people, myself included, thought our surface water came pretty close.

I wrangled enough money out of the system to put in pipes and pumps to irrigate fifty acres. By this time it was late spring, so I planted it all in corn. As our farm was not on good soil (or so the experts said), crops like corn had never been grown in our area. Here I was, once again making history, but by now the locals had come to expect strange things on our side of the fence.

I had grown corn years before in the North Island, so I knew what I was doing as far as growing corn was concerned, but even to me the crop exceeded all expectations, with the plants ready to harvest by autumn. Yes, the cows were well fed that winter and on into spring. At last we could see some light, because now the farm was drought-proof. The money side of things looked much more stable - that is, if the prices for milk held up.

With production back on target and cash flow increasing, we developed the remaining forty acres for irrigation that winter. Now the farm development was complete. Come hell or high water (or no rain), we would not have to worry so much about the weather.

Now, you would think a man should be happy - a wonderful wife, three healthy kids, a 400-cow dairy farm, a contracting business, and a new water source that drought-proofed the farm. But I still did not feel good inside. In fact, the torment I was struggling with was greater than ever.

Sure, I had my moments of feeling good, but often that was only because I refused to allow that deep anxiety to get to me. Many times, I would walk around the farm in the evening trying to understand why I did not, or could not, feel happy. I had achieved everything I had set out to do, yet somehow it was not enough. Or maybe I was just sick and tired of farming. Milking cows, yes; but farming, no.

I had pushed myself hard for years to achieve, achieve more and more, but I was not able to feel happy. Maybe achieving was not the answer, but what the bloody hell was all this holistic health and new-age spiritual stuff? Sure, that was interesting (what isn't when it is all new and you are learning?), but there were so many things that did not add up and were not logical in that direction, I would not let myself get carried away with it.

Then I thought about all the things that Patrick had said to me, all the strange things that had happened and all this energy I felt. So what, I thought, maybe everybody had things happen to them like that, or maybe I was going insane. I often thought about that last possibility, but I always argued myself out of it. No, I just could not be mad. I had a brain, I could work things out, I could see things. I was too quick with my head to be mad. Well, that was my reasoning anyhow. My arguments with myself would go on for hours. I could never come to any conclusions, and I would usually end up just going to bed to let sleep take over, so I would not have to listen to myself or face the unanswered questions.

Ah, sleep! It was always my escape from this crazy world. Even as a kid, when I was in deep shit with Dad, I remember going to bed and sleeping. Things never seemed so bad when I woke up, mostly because Dad had time to calm down. I had carried this escape technique into adulthood. I remember Denise getting quite peeved because when she got overly stressed, there was no way she could sleep, but the more stressed and depressed I got, the more I would sleep.

Sue and I were still spending a little time together, although I was not learning all that much, because I was so reactive that we spent most of our time together arguing. I was still reading all the books she would get for me, but not really putting it all together. I was so greedy for knowledge that I was studying too many different facets at the same time. This created more questions than it answered, but in my emotional state then, I could not see that.

Thinking that the worst in farming was behind us with the drought of the century and all that, our confidence was soon shot to hell. The product prices for the next year fell again, and the dairy industry went into another slump.

Farmers were stunned; young men who a few weeks earlier were full of hope now looked like old men. We thought we had been to hell and back financially. What else could go wrong? To steady my emotional equilibrium, I immersed myself even more in farm politics.

For the next few months I became a right activist, organizing protests and generally venting my frustration and anger. I was invited to the U.S., expenses paid, to study the protest movement that was set up during their farm crisis a few years earlier.

During that five-week trip I spoke to about 3000 people in 13 states; the biggest meeting I addressed numbered 1200. During that time, I found out how the banking system really worked, and that farm product prices in the US, New Zealand and Australia were being totally controlled and manipulated by, and for the benefit of, the international business and banking cartel. This may seem unbelievable, but it is true (but that is another book).

Back home, our fight for survival revolved around restructuring our debt and expanding our contracting business to the limit. God, I was working. The tractor was going day and night and we had even purchased a new grass harvester so we could do the really big jobs. A good silage harvest was our only hope to balance the books. We had the gear, we had the know-how, good staff and reputation.

The harvesting started out with good weather in the late spring, but then the unbelievable happened. Hot dry winds came and within one month there was no bloody grass left. Yes, we were into the second major drought in three years. There was nowhere to move; I had all this expensive harvesting gear but not one leaf of grass to harvest.

The dairy farm was going broke, and now the contracting company was heading for a fall. It did not matter which way I turned; I was trapped. The bloody banks did not care, they had the attitude that the share market and the yuppies could make the country's money, so why help the farmers?

This time I was running out of fight; emotionally I did not have the strength to keep going. I was a beaten man, physically as well as emotionally, so I let the contracting company go into liquidation, my first financial failure.

In twenty years of farming, this was the first spring drought I had encountered, and it went on to become even more serious than the drought two years before. We had had it all, two droughts, record low product prices, record high interest rates and a government that did not have the intelligence to see how much damage it would do to the nation.

With all this pressure the farming community went into severe recession and farms and rural support businesses went broke everywhere. I was so dead emotionally that when the men from the company's office came and took away all the records and furniture from my contracting company I just stood numbly by. For months after that, life had no meaning; I kept suppressing and stuffing all feelings. I was a failure.

Days went by and I never even looked in a mirror; I did not want to see my face. I thought, I do not even want to be here, I might as well use the .22 on myself again. Oh hell, that is no good - I cancelled my life insurance to save money during the last drought.

We had taken some hard knocks over the years, but it was getting harder and harder to recover. This one was the real biggie. I think it was at that point I gave up wanting to be a farmer. It was just too hard; we worked ourselves to a frazzle and got destroyed emotionally. Our dreams were shattered, and I was a shell of my former self.

I remember some days when I could hardly recall things I had done one hour earlier, and there was no way my mind could plan the day's work. I became a zombie. Denise seemed to be stronger emotionally, so she carried on and ran the farm. I would think, "Why can't I just die? Please, please God, let me die." But damn it, every morning I would wake up again, there was no end to this torment. By now I had no belief in anything remotely spiritual about myself. I even stopped reading Sue's books. Nothing interested me anymore. I was in a bottomless pit of self-pity, and it was getting deeper and deeper every day.

Going over and over the farm budget to find ways to keep expenses down without limiting production was becoming a way of life. I would spend hours in the farm office continually redoing the cash flow, to no avail. I had eliminated fertilizer and cut all spending to the bone, but product prices were just too low. There was just too much money going out on interest payments. The bank, after a lot of pressure, froze the interest payments on one loan, but that was still not enough. How we were going to get through the year I did not know.

The farm was becoming a jail; we were totally tied to it. We could not sell because land prices had plummeted so far we would not even have covered our debts. The only option was to sell some of the cows to pay bills. But how could we keep production up with fewer cows? We were on a treadmill going backwards. After nearly twenty years of farming, we were facing the very real possibility of losing everything. Farmers all around the district were going broke. The only thing that kept me going was that I was using my last bit of will and drive to protest the government policy that brought about a lot of this living hell.

It is hard to remember the exact sequence of events. My emotions had strung me out so far that my memory of that time is hazy, but around this time Sue got me to travel to Auckland to attend a course about energy in and around the body. Because she volunteered to pay my fee, I decided to go. I sure needed the break.

The ten days I spent with enthusiastic and supportive people did wonders for me. It also got me thinking about this energy thing again. The course included all the things that Sue had taught me, so I found it very easy and graduated with flying colors. The vacation from thinking about my insolvable problems really helped, and I started to feel alive again.

About a month after I returned from the course, some friends told me there was a clairvoyant visiting from England who had an excellent reputation; she was quite famous and had been on the radio and all. They convinced me that I should see her. I had never been to anybody like that, so I went along, more out of curiosity than anything else.

After being shown into the room, I was asked to sit on a chair across the room from her. The room was fairly dark, as all the drapes were pulled, so my eyes had to adjust before I could see her clearly. She was sitting there, not saying a word but looking very intently at me. I did not know what to do or if I was meant to speak to her, so I just sat there looking back at her for what seemed like ages. I became a bit nervous under her fixed gaze, and I was almost startled when she finally spoke.

"May I ask you something I have never asked anyone before?" she said.

"Sure," I answered, wondering what was coming next.

"May I come to you and hold your hands?"

"Fine, that is okay by me." She got up out of her chair and moved across the room. As she came close I held up my hands for her, but before she took them she asked me to turn them over so the palms were facing up.

As she placed her hands on my upturned palms she knelt down in front of me with her face down and I had the feeling she was becoming emotional. Lifting her head to look me straight in the eye, I saw a tear trickling down each cheek. In a very soft, almost hushed voice she told me that I was the most spiritually connected person she had ever met. She went on to say that this connection would allow me to use my hands as a healer, a healer the likes of which this earth had not seen for a very long time.

"Amazing, amazing, unbelievable, you are so blessed, you have so much." She went on and on, not really talking to me, but more like she was just talking to herself.

I did not know what to say, so I just sat there. I remember that I was hot and sweat was running down the inside of my shirt. But that was not unusual for me. It was just one of my energy surges, certainly nothing connected with spiritual things or healing - or so I tried to convince myself.

She again began to speak, but stopped herself. Then with an intense, almost angry look she asked me how much I knew about myself. I did not want to say much, as I thought clairvoyants were meant to tell you things, not the other way around, but I did say that I had been told that I was a healer and that I was having trouble accepting it.

At that point she got up, let go of my hands and went back to her chair across the room. She almost seemed to be angry. She just sat, silent for a moment, then asked me if I had had any spiritual training or teaching. I told her I had rejected most of that, but because some really weird things had happened to me, sometimes I would think there was something to it, but most of the time I was having too much trouble dealing with earthly things to think of anything else. Then not really talking directly to me, almost as if I was not there, she said, "Why, why wasn't he born into a spiritual environment? Why didn't he learn as a young boy. Why the hard life, why the struggle, why in New Zealand? He doesn't even know...."

I looked around the room to see who she was talking to, because it sure was not me. She was quite agitated and flustered. Then looking toward me again, she seemed to collect herself and I could see a calmness sort of ripple down her body. For a moment she let her head sink down into her hands, then lifted it, her face now soft and gentle.

She came to me again and knelt in front of me. Then speaking in a whisper, she said it was more important than I could realize then, that I stop being afraid of my spirituality.

She said, "Go to a Spiritualist Church to contact people who can understand and help you. Use your healing powers. Know that you are blessed…" She paused and then added, "No, you are the one who blesses others." She stopped again and dropped her head. Then she did something really strange. She grasped both of my feet, looking straight into my eyes, and said, "It has been my greatest privilege to meet you. You are to go out into the world and do your work. You will always be protected and looked after. You are not a farmer anymore, but some call you the shepherd. Do not be afraid, just do it. You will be shown, you will always be shown. I am blessed by your presence."

Returning to her chair, she told me she could not say any more to me other than she hoped I would someday understand all that she had said. That was it, the end of my session.

I got up and left the room not knowing whether to laugh or cry. I was so shaken I was hardly able to walk, my mind in a daze. What was the lady on about? Yet it was not too far from what Patrick and others had said, only this time there was much more. And what did she mean, "I was the one who blessed others?" Did she think I was a priest or something, or did she mean more than that? I did not know what to think, but I was sure glad for the cup of tea given to me by the folks in whose house the sessions where held. My hands must have been shaking, because I spilt the tea over my jeans and a sweet old lady had to get another cup for me.

I could not stop thinking about the session. I had never met the lady before, deciding to see her only that morning, so there was no way she could have known anything about me. Yet there were things that she was right about. How did she know that I was a farmer or that I was ready to give up? What about my life and all the struggles?

Life had been a struggle, all right, but how did she know? And she said the same thing as Patrick and Sue about the healing thing. There was no way she could have known about that. Blimey, only about five people in the world knew about it at the time. And who was she talking to if it was not me? There were times she seemed to be discussing me with somebody else, yet I could not see anybody else in the room.

It was all a bit too weird for me, yet somewhere deep inside I felt a truth in what she said. It made no sense at all, but I was drawn by her words and knew that I would be trying to understand my spirituality and would find peace when I did. Try as I might, I could not get that day out of my mind.

Of course, Denise wanted to know all about it when I got home, as she also had an appointment. I told her only about the healing bit, that the clairvoyant said I was very spiritually connected, that she had got a bit agitated and had talked to some spook I could not see, and left it at that.

How could I tell her about the other things that were said? I needed time to think about them first; most people would get locked up for saying things like that. It probably took me about a month to finally tell it all to Denise.

As usual, she responded with the understanding and support I needed. I do not know how Denise handled all my crazy emotions and weird experiences and still kept the house and farm running. She had an amazing ability to be accepting, as if she knew I had to go through all this for my own good. A person with less staying power would have walked out on me, but not this lady. She was always there for me, even taking over for me when I was not functioning. If there is such a being as a human angel, Denise must surely qualify.

Settling back into normality, I was soon given another push in the direction of healing. A farming friend had a bad accident with his motorbike, sustaining severe bruising to his thigh which left him unable to move his leg.

When Mike called I said I did not know what I could do, but I would travel to his place that night and try to help him.

Arriving at his farmhouse, I was shown into the living room. Mike was lying on the floor with his left leg propped up with cushions and pillows. I was shocked by the severity of bruising on the upper outside of his leg. It was the size of a football, pitch black with ugly dark red blotches around the outside.

"Bloody hell," I said, "is your leg broken?"

"No, just incredibly painful," Mike replied.

"When did you crash the bike?"

"Four days ago."

"Can you move the leg?"

"No way, when I try the pain is unbearable."

"I can understand that," I said. "I've never seen a bruise like that. That's a real humdinger, mate. It's a pity you didn't call me straight away after the crash, because now you have all this blood trapped around the muscle tissue that is going to take some time to go."

"Yea," he said, "and I can't lie here for three weeks. There's cows to milk."

"Well, I don't know if this energy healing stuff can help a leg like that, but I'll try and we will see what happens."

Kneeling down beside the injured leg, I slowly passed my right hand over his leg about six inches above it, in the auric field. As my hand came closer to the bruise, I could feel a definite change in the energy of the aura, and as my hand moved over the bruise, the energy felt heavy and cold.

This was the first time I had felt a change in the energy with my hand. I could really feel the difference, it was a real, physical feeling on my hand. The temperature and the density of the energy field over and around the injury was very different from the rest of the leg. What surprised me was how easy it was to feel the difference. Even when I closed my eyes, I could easily locate the center of the bruise just by the feeling I sensed with my hand.

I was like a kid with a new toy, moving my hand up and down over Mike's leg at different speeds and at different heights. If I went too fast, it became very difficult to pick up the change in energy. Moving too slowly made the change in feeling hard to perceive; but with a steady movement up or down the leg I could easily feel the difference. Height did not seem to make much difference. I could still feel the changes when my hand was about two feet away, but it was easiest to perceive at about four to six inches. It was really strange. The further away my hand was, the wider the area I could feel, and as I moved my hands closer the area became smaller.

It was as if I could hone in on the problem purely by feel. It felt like the energy field had been disturbed by the injury, and the further my hand was away from the body, the greater the radius of disturbance would become. I could feel a big cone of energy with the narrow end over the injury and the wide end about two feet or more from the body.

Because this was my first attempt at healing, it was all new and rather exciting. Not that I understood all that I was feeling, but the fact that I could feel the disturbance in the auric field caused by the injury to Mike's leg was enough to really excite me.

I was brought back to the job at hand when Mike moaned in agony as he tried to move his leg in an attempt to make himself a bit more comfortable. Okay, I thought, let's see if all this wacky stuff works. Rubbing my hands together (I do not know why I do that even now, but it sort of puts me in gear), I moved my hands in circles about a foot apart until I could feel a good strong energy movement between them. Then I placed my hands each side of Mike's leg.

Almost instantly a surge of energy flowed through my body, my body temperature shot up and an amazing flow of energy started to move from my right hand through Mike's leg to my left hand. It was strong, I could really feel it. It was sort of pulsing, and my hands felt like they were on fire. It was so powerful that I looked at my hands expecting to see some sort of breeze or light wind around them. Mike sort of moaned in agony and tried to move his leg. Looking up at his face, I was shocked to see him with his mouth wide open, head strained back and very obviously in real pain.

"What's the matter?" I asked, not thinking that I had anything to do with his discomfort.

"My, my leg," he said. "What are you doing? It feels like you're tearing it apart."

"Nothing. Hell, I am not even touching your leg." I said, and I was not. My hands were a good six inches from each side. Mike looked down in amazement.

"Blimey, I can really feel that. All hell is breaking loose in there." He paused and again he wriggled in pain, clutching his leg above the bruise. "Christ, that hurts!" he said. The poor guy was in agony, but there was no way I could stop my hands. Once again my body was not being controlled by me.

"Hang in there, buddy," I told him, "I don't know what is happening, but sure as God made little apples, something is."

My hands were about to explode and sweat was oozing from every pore on my upper body. My hands were held in place as if some great magnet had locked them there, and still the energy was flowing. At times it came in with great waves pulsing out from my hands, and at other times it came in a steady outpouring. On and on it went, and I remember saying to Mike that if I thought that all this healing stuff was a bit weird, then this was out of this world. But I do not think poor Mike was in any mood for my jokes, as he said he did not know if it was a cure or a kill.

"Don't ask me," I said, "I don't think I'm in the driver's seat at the moment."

Mike's seven-year-old daughter, Mia, who had been in bed when I arrived, must have been awakened by all the commotion, because she came out into the living room to see what was going on. As she came through the door she stopped dead and stood there staring at her father's leg.

"What's the matter, Mia?" asked her mother. Both Mike and I looked up at Mia and seeing a look of amazement on her face I asked, "What can you see?"

"Red and green and lots of other colors sort of glowing and moving around your hands and Dad's leg."

"Come and point to where you see them," I said and Mia came across the room and placed her finger right between my hands and her Father's leg.

"Right here, all glowing and moving," she said. I looked over at her mother and said, "Blimey, she can see the energy." Then more to myself than anybody else I said, "This energy thing might be real after all." Mike and I just looked at each other, no words necessary. Wow, I thought, I think I just passed the point of no return. It was going to be difficult to deny this healing thing from now on.

Face it, seven-year-old kids do not get a look on their face like that unless they really see something they have not seen before. And Mia could place her finger exactly where the energy was flowing. Yep, this young lady was really seeing the energy, seeing it with her open eyes. This was not wacky-wacky, this was real. And what was more, Mike could certainly feel something happening in his leg. Maybe it was only myself who had doubts, but after all this, I had better think again.

Almost an hour after I had started the healing Mike's discomfort had reduced somewhat, although he would still flinch as pulses of energy shot from my hands through his leg. But most of the time, a steady flow was being transmitted.

I was quite calm again and my body had cooled somewhat when I had an urge to sort of scoop up some imaginary something from around Mike's leg and get up and walk to the outside door. As I moved towards the door my hands were being pulled back toward Mike like a tug of war. I was really pulling by the time I got to the door. I was using all my strength to keep moving and my hands were stretched out toward Mike, pulled by some invisible thread. Mike was almost ready to shoot me because of the pain, but my body kept moving away from him. My arms felt as though they were about to come out of their sockets, the pull was so strong.

What the hell was happening I had no idea, but I got to the door and kicked it open with my foot and almost fell over as I moved out of the house. The resistance or pull on my hands stopped. It was like somebody had cut the thread.

At precisely that moment, Mike let out a yell. As he told us afterwards, it was like a big piece of gunk was getting pulled harder and harder, and as I went out the door it sort of felt like it came out of his leg all at once. When that happened the pain was atrocious, but after that the leg felt much better. He said it felt like I was trying to pull something out of his leg through a small hole and I was pulling harder and harder and then it squeezed through and was gone. His leg looked no different, but he said it really felt much softer and much more comfortable.

Well! That was all a very new experience, even for me. Sue had not talked about anything like that. I did not really know what to think, and I remember telling Mike about how I got guided and had no control over what I did, even to the point of my body doing things like pulling stuff from his leg. I then did a bit more energy healing to the leg until I felt that it had enough. This time Mike felt no pain, only a nice tingling. The whole time I was at the house working on his leg lasted no more than an hour or an hour and a quarter. I left his house with the understanding that he would phone me in a couple of days to let me know how things were going.

While driving home that night I started to connect the energy surges I had felt and the other things that had happened. When I worked on Mike, the energy that came into me was like the energy I had felt for years, but it was the first time in my life I had been able to turn it on or plug it in when I wanted to. I felt like singing and yelling at the top of my voice.

At last I was starting to understand, starting to put years of strange experiences into an understandable pattern. Maybe, just maybe, the energies I had felt all my life would be able to be used for healing. At last, I might be able to have some control over when and how I used it.

Maybe the clairvoyant, Patrick and others were right, after all. Maybe I did have some gift or ability to heal. It is hard to recall how I was feeling emotionally while I was thinking all these things. One part of me was still in denial, while another side was ready to heal the world. Well, I thought, the next few days will give me lots of answers. I did not know it then, but I would not have to wait that long.

CHAPTER 9
QUESTIONS ANSWERED

It was about seven the next morning when Karen, our daughter, came over to the milking shed to tell me that Mike's wife was on the phone and that she urgently wanted to talk to me.

Running to the house, I was almost in a panic thinking that something had happened to Mike. When I picked up the phone I almost died, because she was crying and begging me to come up and see Mike straight away.

"What's wrong, what happened?" 1 asked.

"You've got to come now, you've got to see this," she begged.

"Is Mike all right?"

"Yes, yes, but come now, you must see it." I could not get any more information from her, she was too emotional and could hardly speak. I did not feel her crying was in anger or panic, only very emotional.

I did not wait any longer. I asked the kids to tell Denise where I was going, then jumped into the car and was away. Arriving at Mike's place, I rushed straight in through the back door and into the living room. Mike was sitting up on a chair, wearing shorts again, and as I focused my eyes on his leg, my heart stopped.

There, before my eyes, was this leg that less than ten hours before was black as the ace of spades, and now it was nearly normal in color. I just stared at it. All the black bruising was gone and around it were just a few red blotches. It was a different leg, and if it had not been for the red blotches it would have been hard for me to accept that I had seen any bruising at all the night before.

I looked up at Mike, "Bloody hell, looks like it worked," I spluttered.

"Sure does, and the leg feels much better. I can even move it," Mike replied.

I think I sat down as it sank in. I knew bruising like that did not just disappear overnight. It usually takes weeks! Mike's bruise was black, and now it was gone. It just did not exist. If anybody had tried to tell me that such a thing could happen, there was no way I would have believed them. Yet here before my eyes was a physical body that had changed dramatically overnight in a way that was medically inexplicable.

Mike's wife came into the room with coffee for us and I stood up. We gave each other a big hug. I did not know whether to cry or laugh, it was all a bit much for our emotions. The three of us sat there for a long time in silence, just coming to terms with what seemed to be a miracle.

Feeling the need to be alone, I said I would be back that night to do a bit more energy healing on his leg and excusing myself, slowly drove home. I remember feeling rather shaky, but there was also a tremendous humbleness. No turning back now; I would have to accept this healing thing. The change in Mike's leg was too real to be passed off as mumbo jumbo.

I think I had at last given up fighting myself that morning and started to accept that I had the ability to use this energy to help people. I visited Mike twice more that week. By then he was back at work on the farm, with only a slight stiffness in the leg.

Word quickly got around the district, and soon I was seeing quite a few people at home who had physical injuries, from football players to truck drivers with sore backs and farmers who could hardly walk due to pulled muscles. I was doing more and more electrical balances on people. The healing work certainly gave me a reason to be much happier, and as a result my emotions were settling down.

I was introduced to some self-improvement techniques that included chanting mantras and other meditations, which I found improved my emotional state quite dramatically. I became so busy working on people at home that the kids got sick of not being able to watch the TV, as I was doing the healing in the lounge, so I opened a small clinic in the nearby town and was soon busy most days working from there.

The farm was just holding its own and I was able to get a little money from the clinic, so it was not too bad financially. I would still go away on retreat every so often, and more and more I was getting in touch with emotional shit I had buried long ago.

This was not a pleasant experience; the anger that would surface was quite frightening. It got to the stage where I was starting to get angry at my anger as I struggled to find a way to change myself. Energy would often flow into my body, activating my emotions, and I would become like my old self as I released old shit.

Of course, at the time I did not realize that this was happening, only that I was extremely angry and going into denial about my ability to heal. At times it was pure hell, and the more I felt like that, the more I blamed myself and got angry at myself for getting angry. I was living two lives, one a gentle, kind man in the clinic and the other, a raving, angry bull up in the mountains.

It was some months after Mike's healing when Sue and I spent another weekend away in the mountains that I had my most startling physical proof of the power of the spiritual, or maybe even the existence of God.

At the time I was extremely reactive and still struggling with the idea that the energy I used had something to do with the spiritual realm, or even that there was such a thing as a spiritual realm. I was desperately seeking answers, and every book seemed to suggest a different truth. I was becoming hostile to the continual pushing from Sue; I really needed some proof, some sign that there was really an existence beyond this earthly plane.

To me, my reasoning was sound; if the energy came from another dimension, then it had to be controlled or at least guided, and something or someone had to be able to do this. On the other hand, maybe it was just cosmic energy that was available to us humans to use as and when we learned how. There just had to be some way to find out.

Sue and I had argued, (again), and by late evening it had developed into a full-scale row. The energy was extremely high in both of us. I remember my body almost at meltdown. I was using the energy with all the negativity and anger that I had learned over a lifetime of reactive living.

Sue was one of the few people in the world I knew who could be in my company without feeling afraid or threatened by this kind of emotional outburst, but even she could not take the sheer power of this lot and left the room in tears.

Remarkable as it may seem, I was furious. Damn it, the woman had run out on me, could not take the heat. She had helped start the bloody fight, so what right did she have to leave just because it got too hard to handle?

Typical woman, I thought as I tried to maintain my arrogant, righteous attitude in a vain attempt to blame someone beside myself. There was no way I would admit to being a right asshole; hell no, my ego was too worked up with sheer dominating power for that. The male control mechanisms were turned full on. I was at my absolute worst, hating myself, Sue and the whole bloody world. Fuck the lot, fuck the whole spiritual thing and all this healing shit, just fuck everything! I had had enough.

Why the bloody hell was it so difficult for people to understand just how much built up hurt and anger I was feeling and that it had to come out somehow? Why did everybody always think it was directed at them, just because I was verbalizing my frustration and anger? Why did Sue leave when I needed her more now than ever?

The raw power of my anger, fuelled by a deep inner fear of not being good enough and stoked by an intense struggle with my spirituality, was accumulating in an emotional fireball rapidly going out of control. I remember looking around the room, and everywhere I looked was black. God damn the whole room was black, but the lights were on.

A sudden fear overtook me and I ran blindly outside. As I ran down the road, the fear gripped me even tighter, until I was going like a bolting horse and my only feeling was of pure terror. Terror of what, I did not know, but I was not stopping to find out.

Gasping, my lungs burning, my chest heaving in desperate attempts to get air, I finally slumped over the side of a bridge and vomited my guts out. I was there for what seemed like an eternity. Painfully dry retching as the last drop of gastric fluid burnt its way up my throat, I finally opened my eyes and stared down into the dark, cold water below. Why not, I thought, at least it would put an end to this bloody crazy, emotionally painful asshole life.

As my upper body started to lean farther over the side of the bridge, slowly, ever so slowly, as if in slow motion, I could visualize the water coming up to meet me. I felt my feet leave the road. This was it, I thought, as relief flooded my consciousness, the end, the blissful end ... I felt my body transfer its weight to my hands holding the bottom railing as my feet came up over the side.

At that moment my body froze. Keep going, I yelled, end it now! I really wanted to, but my body would not budge. Suspended, more over the side than not, gravity should have done the job, but I felt my body being slowly lifted back over the concrete edge.

My mind was numb, I could not think, or even yell out, nothing worked. My feet again made contact with the road, and as I tried to push myself off again, my legs gave way and I slumped down onto the roadway in a daze. There I sat, oblivious to the subzero temperature as powerful emotions welled up and uncontrollable sobbing overwhelmed me.

I have no way of knowing how long I was there, but I remember walking aimlessly around the village and arriving at the door of a magic little church overlooking the alpine lake.

Still in a daze, I walked up the stone steps and entered the dark interior.

Taking a seat in the back pew, I was surprised to see Sue near the front, silhouetted by the moonlight shining through the large windows overlooking the lake. Hearing movement behind her, Sue turned and saw me. I watched with water-filled eyes as she slowly came down the narrow aisle towards me.

Reaching out and taking me gently by the hand, Sue led me to the alter rail where we knelt down. Sue put her arm around me and within a short time I was crying softly. I did not want to be alive, let alone crying in a church. Soon Sue was crying as well, and we held each other in the moonlight, in the little church overlooking the lake, the high mountains forming a guard of honor. We sought and received tenderness and forgiveness in each other.

We stayed quietly in that little church a large part of the night. I slowly went over my life and all its torments, frustrations and fears. Feeling a sense of peace gradually percolate through me, I asked Sue, "How does a person ever really know about spiritual things? How can I really believe all the things that have happened to me were promptings from the spiritual world?"

"Denie," she said, "that's what faith is. You have had many signs and many experiences, and now it's time to let go and just believe."

"Faith? Believe?" I jumped up out of my seat, instant anger pulsing through every fiber of my being, "Faith - bullshit, believe - bullshit, believe in what?" I yelled, "Everything that has happened could be all my crazy imagination, just me going nuts or something. I've had enough, I want proof, damn it, I demand proof!"

By this time I was standing in the front of the church yelling at some unseen God.

"If you are up there, God, if you exist or if some other spook exists in spirit land, and if you want me to believe in all this healing stuff and believe in your existence, you can damn well prove it! No more driving vans around the country or energy surges through my body I can't explain, but some real, *physical* proof. Something that Sue and I can't deny, something private and physical so it can't affect anybody else, but can be seen by us, felt by us. If you want me to do this work, that's what I demand. I'm sick of all the confusion. I demand facts, real proof. I want to know!"

I fell to my knees, drained physically as well as emotionally, sobbing, from the very depths of my being.

I had had enough torment, enough financial hassles, enough of not knowing. There was no reason for living; what was the point? Sue came over to me and wrapped her arms around my body. There we stayed, on the floor of that little church on the shore of the lake, guarded by the high mountains. I was waiting for my world to end, and Sue was just being there for me.

Dawn was lazily drifting her light and energy down the face of the hazy mountains across the dark waters of the lake as Sue and I, immersed in our own thoughts, slowly walked away from the little church. Entering our cabin, we silently pulled the bedding over our drained bodies and dead emotions as sleep cast its welcome spell.

The warmth of the sun, shining through the undraped windows, willingly gave its life-giving rays to our two bodies as we awakened, stiff and tender from the cold night in the church.

Our bodies, now so warm and close, moved in total oneness in response to being alive, feeling, searching, the sweet smell of warm breath, the softness of tousled hair on the bedding, of lips on erect nipples, tongues moving, ever moving, seeking the depths of open mouths, hands, warm, soft, tender feminine hands, moving, squeezing, stroking the erection, eager, almost demanding, but now gently seduced into slowness by the movement of those feminine fingers, sweet moistened quivering lips, opening with eagerness as legs part, ready, wanting, oh so wanting to receive, but hands holding hardened member, higher ... higher.

She releases, and bodies come together, the groans of pleasure about to explode from gasping breath... "Aahhhhhh!"... Sue screamed in agony, twisting her body away from mine. I lurched back in shock and pain from my penis almost being bent in half.

Sue sat bolt upright, eyes wide with pain and terror, her hands clutching her crotch. Shaking, I looked down at my rapidly reducing member, the pain of the bending now dissipating - "Jesus, what the hell was that?" I said, fear resonating in my voice. Sue doubled over in pain, shock emanating from terrified eyes, said, "What happened? Why can't you take me - it can't get in! What happened? God, what's going on?"

I waited for the pain in Sue's body to subside so she at least could lie flat back on the bed. She was white as the sheets and still in shock as I took a close look at her vaginal opening.

There was a membrane, it was across the vagina about a half an inch in from the opening. It was tender to the touch and looking closely, I could see it was live tissue with blood vessels running through it. There was a small opening at the bottom no more than three-eighths of an inch long for her urine to pass through. Other than that, her entire vagina was sealed off.

To say we were in shock would be quite the understatement. Face it, only a few hours before I had stood in a church demanding that God, or whoever, give me a physical sign that Sue and I could not reject, or pass off as coincidence. Well, this sure was physical, and it concerned only Sue and myself. There was no way we could pretend that it was caused by some natural phenomenon. Hell, Sue was a mother and we had made fabulous love not twelve hours earlier and all had been fine.

For hours afterward, we were too scared even to talk about God or what to expect next. We just sat on the bed trying to come to terms with what happened. I had read about all sorts of things that were said to have happened to people, but nothing like this. Things like this only happened in the Bible and the like. To put it mildly, we were two terrified people.

As the day wore on we frequently tried to rationalize Sue's "condition." I gave her vaginal opening repeated close inspection, hoping that what we had found had been just a dream. But no, it was for real. In fact, as the day drifted into evening the membrane seemed to become thicker, stronger and did not even look like new skin.

I went on a long walk late in the evening just to be alone. Sitting on a rock looking across the lake and feeling insignificant in comparison to the high mountains around me, I tried to allow myself to accept the significance of the changes in Sue's body.

What was I to do now that I had my proof? I had no more escape routes left open. I could not deny the existence of the spiritual world now; there was no way out. I started to shake as my body reacted to the undeniable amazing truth. Yes, God or some powerful invisible being had been able to create a change in Sue's body that had to be discovered by both of us simultaneously. The new tissue had grown within just a few hours. I felt so overwhelmed that my mind was numb. Every time I thought about it I started shaking. Poor Sue was too shocked to say much at all. She must have wondered if it would go away and when.

That day will forever be with me; I will always remember it as the day God answered me. I had asked the question and gotten my answer. I learned that if you are not willing to accept the answer, do not ask the question. I had demanded proof, never believing in a million years that I would get it. When I did, I was forced to accept the reality of the invisible realm and power of spirit. Even more frightening, I came face to face with having to accept my own spirituality.

During the next few days we talked about lots of things - accepting God, love, healing, ourselves, what was going to become of us, what we should do and (God forbid) what if the membrane would not go away.

We burst into laughter at the thought of Sue trying to explain to a doctor what the problem was. "Well, doc., it's like this...." Face it, it was going to be rather difficult for the medical profession to understand how a woman who was sexually active and who had children by vaginal delivery could now have a vaginal hymen. The thought of explaining that one was just too much!

In rejecting church and religion - and by default, spirituality - I had thrown out the baby with the bath water. This had now been turned on its head, and I was facing everything I had put down. I had backed myself into a corner and some invisible intelligence had taken advantage of my stupidity. Yeah, I got caught real good.

When something dramatic like this happens, it becomes amazingly easy to change your reality. There was no other logical way to explain it. There had to be an invisible, spiritual reality that had the ability to form physical tissue at will. There was nothing on this plane that could do this. When you eliminate all other possibilities - or cannot even imagine any other answer - you have to accept the only possibility staring you in the face.

Mountains, lakes, rivers - all the spectacular scenery that is the Southern Alps - was ignored as I slowly started to put everything I had experienced together. I was now able to see that I had some help years ago when I had been able to see through steel and brick walls of furnaces, when the camper van had turned itself into Stu's driveway and when something led me through an unknown city to Father Sherry's residence. I had to have gotten help from an invisible source - call it a guardian angel, guides, or God, or whatever. Maybe - just maybe, mind you - the basic teaching of the world's religions and wise men from ancient times had a thread of truth after all.

Sue and I did a lot of analyzing over the next two days, and when it was time to leave our mountain retreat the membrane was still intact. Sue was less worried about it by this time, somehow feeling that everything would work out. She had to catch a plane home, so on Monday we drove to Christchurch and she booked her flight for late that day.

By this stage I fully accepted a spiritual connection for all that had happened, so while we waited for her flight we found a nice, quiet place to spend the afternoon. We did not talk much, but found comfort in being close and knowing that we had been part of a very special spiritual experience neither of us would forget.

As the time came for Sue to leave for the airport, our emotions overtook us and our passion once again became very physical. We would not be seeing each other for some months due to work pressures, so the urge to join our bodies became overbearing.

Sue felt the membrane was starting to weaken and open more, then almost without realizing it we began experiencing a heightened level of sensation, and as our bodies came together, the membrane parted and we were lovers once more.

We were gentle and slow, as Sue was still in some pain. Her vagina was very tight, and I remember saying that she had been rebuilt into a virgin state.

Glorious waves of emotion pushed me to heights of feeling and love that seemed to take me beyond the earth. Spent, I lay cradled in Sue's arms, a feeling of humility rolling over me. It felt like I had been party to an awesome spiritual revelation.

Sue twisted her wet body to look at my face and asked me if I realized it was exactly three days since her "condition" had happened and now, on the third day, it was gone. Instantly the biblical story of the resurrection three days after the crucifixion flooded my mind. My body relaxed sobbing into Sue's arms.

We lay there, each in our own thoughts, for what seemed an eternity. When it was time to get going we parted reluctantly. I could not understand the feeling I had, especially about what the resurrection story had to do with our strange experience, but I could not stop thinking about it. Sue also sensed some connection because on the drive to the airport she wondered why it was exactly three days. "God, it's getting more weird every time we meet," she said.

Our parting at the airport was our most difficult - neither of us wanted to be alone. We knew we had experienced something very spiritual, a realization, a new understanding that neither of us could ever forget, yet we knew we could not share it with anybody else.

Delaying boarding the plane until the last minute, Sue, tears streaming down her cheeks, took hold of my hands and looked deeply into my eyes. "You are a very special person," she said, "more special than anybody knows." Then kissing me lightly on the lips, she was down the air bridge, leaving me to my thoughts and very mixed emotions.

I sat at the airport for a long time, not really knowing what to do, afraid even to think, let alone face the other world of farming and living and all the things that now seemed so utterly unimportant.

Driving slowly back to the farm I felt emotionally dulled, unable to concentrate. But I also felt a deep stillness, a closeness with my spiritual self, almost an acceptance of everything. Arriving in darkness, I went straight to bed.

In the following weeks, I experienced a distinct double personality in myself, one dominated by thoughts about my spirituality, the other the old reactive self. It was extremely uncomfortable at times, because I never knew what phase I would be in. I was becoming like a Jekyll and Hyde, with two very different energies living in the same body, and I did not know which one would gain control and express itself.

Even with what had happened with Sue, there were times I still tried to deny the reality of spirit and believe it was my ego pulling the strings. At one time, desperately wanting more answers, I visited a doctor who was skilled at reading the higher frequencies of the human aura and also getting readings from the subconscious with a Vega machine.

Because the cost was very high for this consultation, I was hoping for some good, understandable answers about what was going on in me. After wires were connected to my head, hands and body, the machines were turned on.

All went well while the doctor was getting readings from my physical body, but when he started to move into questions about my subconscious and spiritual self, the machine malfunctioned.

Now, this was a machine and thus had no mind of its own. Yet each time the doctor tried to get a reading from the spiritual part of my subconscious the machine would go haywire. After nearly two hours of trying he finally gave up, saying to me that there was no way he was allowed to access my higher self, which I took to mean the information contained within my outer energies that made up my aura.

I was frustrated, really pissed. It cost me heaps to fly from one end of the country to the other, plus the cost of the consultation, and here he was telling me something was not allowing the information to be accessed.

What was I to do now? Who could I go to? This doctor was said to be the best in the country for this type of thing, and in fact he was operating way outside the norm for most doctors. He was at the leading edge in understanding the functions of the body's aura and using different high-tech machines to read these frequencies. Now he was telling me that somehow the machine did not work for me, that out of the thousands of people he had read with his setup, this was the first time it had not worked.

The doctor told me that the frequency range he had started to pick up was way outside the norm and that I had a "very different" energy around the outer edge of my aura. He then told me that perhaps I had better go home and be a farmer, because I apparently was not ready to make contact with that energy.

"Wasn't ready?" I argued. "Hell, what was I doing here if I wasn't ready?"

But he insisted, saying the frequency of energy in my outer aura was very strong and different from most people's. He said I would not want to be influenced by or have this energy come through and affect my physical body until I was ready for it.

"How will I know when I'm ready?" I asked.

"Just be patient. It will happen bit by bit as you understand more."

"Understand more what?"

"Understand and accept yourself," he answered. I burst out, "Can't anybody give me a straight answer?" With that I got up and walked out of his office.

I had really had enough of this. I had been working in my own healing clinic using energy healing and even doing a lot of emotional counselling and getting some amazing results. I had a long and thorough training, and there were not many emotional outpourings I had not experienced. So I knew all the tricks and pitfalls of how to survive and overcome most things.

But now I wanted to know more about me, to really understand what made me tick. What was happening that caused me to change my personality so quickly? Was I two souls sharing the same body? Was this unusual frequency that everybody from the English clairvoyant to this doctor had picked up on really so powerful that sometimes its power would seep through my aura and energize my endocrine lands with a surge of power that would send them into chaotic function and throw my emotions into a reactive state?

I was getting desperate to find some answers. I needed to find out how to stabilize my emotions to accommodate the energy changes that were occurring. I was living two very different lives, alternately helping people in the clinic and struggling to keep the farm going.

The different frequencies of energy I was trying to function in were at opposite ends of the scale. I was making a lot of judgments about my behavior and enduring gnawing doubts about my healing because I had so many other problems.

How could I be helping and healing others and at the same time be so messed up myself? That was what I was thinking anyhow. Of course, when I was at the clinic and "plugged in," I certainly was not the same person I was elsewhere. Which was the real me, I did not really know.

When I was in healing mode, that was my reality, and I had no perception of the material world - and vice versa. Most people have trouble dealing with one reality, one life, one dimension, and I was struggling with two very different lives. What was even worse, I was trying to marry the two together so that I could live both on the same day, a bit like trying to push water uphill with a garden rake. The frustration was getting to me, but in a sense it was this frustration that was forcing me to find out what was going on and try and alleviate the misery that it was causing.

Life was not any easier, even though I accepted that the spiritual world existed and studied many aspects of religion and many forms of natural healing. I still wanted to know more. I had to keep on searching - for what I did not really know. I felt that when I found it, I would at last be able to put to rest my inner (and not so inner) struggle. I guess lots of people have these struggles.

I started studying Alice Bailey's writings, and this helped me to understand much more about spiritual things. The more I read, the more knowledge I wanted, so I sought out books from libraries and friends, and purchased as many as I could afford. The insatiable urge to know more became overwhelming. I devoured books morning, noon and night.

Sue had wanted me to follow a path that was rather dogmatic, one where there was lots of chanting of mantras. But somehow that did not feel comfortable to me, and I was starting to go my own way. I had a deep knowing that kept me from getting caught up in some religion or cult, and if anybody tried to tell me their way was the best or only way, I would backpedal fast.

To me this spiritual thing must also have logic; it must be able to be explained through an understanding of the full energy spectrum. If our bodies registered many more frequencies of energy than the ones that made up the physical aspect, then these frequencies must be somehow connected to, or have something to do with, what most people called the spiritual world.

If that were the case, religious dogma could be unmasked as propaganda. During my search for this energy connection, Bailey's writings seemed to be the most probing. Of course, most Eastern philosophy pointed toward some overall energy connection.

When we reflect that our bodies are made up of cells, the cells of atoms, and atoms of electrical charges or impulses of energy, then we begin to catch on. Physicists maintain that everything in the universe is made of atoms; therefore everything must be energy. And Jesus has told us that God is everywhere, right? Maybe he defined the God force as the interconnectedness of all energy.

Maybe science and true spiritual understanding are on the same path. Just maybe, energy is the guiding or God force that all else revolves round. Put another way, the interconnectedness of all energy, the way energy can communicate, gives energy a certain intelligence, an overall knowingness and maybe this consciousness of energy is God, the guiding light.

I was starting to put things together, and this was something my logical brain could understand. Instead of struggling to understand spirituality, I felt that I could concentrate on understanding energy, which would lead me to the logical, natural understanding of spiritual things.

For the first time in my life, I could see that what was spiritual, was not of another world, but was a perfectly natural part of me and everything else. I realized that there was no separation, that what was termed spiritual was in fact just a higher frequency of the energy that was also myself.

From there it was easy to put all the things that had happened to me into place. Even the existence of guides and guardian angels and others out there seemed perfectly natural.

If we can think of our physical world as the world of ice and water and the spirit world as that of steam, we can see that it is only a frequency difference. Water turned into steam has not gone anywhere, it is still H_2O molecules, but the vibration rate of the steam molecules are at a frequency that we often cannot perceive.

We are spirits and spirits are us. We humans, in physical bodies, live in a world of slower frequency and spirits inhabit a higher-frequency mode (world). But we are of the same stuff. And like water that can be raised to the frequency of steam, so too can we raise our vibration to get closer to spirit.

If we are the same energy, then it is easy to understand and accept that we can communicate from this dimension or frequency to theirs and vice versa.

That put a heap of mysteries like channeling, clairvoyance and energy healing into a frame of reference that was quite natural and even scientific. I came to the understanding that there were many dimensions of existence other than ours and those other dimensions were only different frequencies of the same energy.

On this frequency that we call earth, we are human; on some other, we call spirit; on some other, we call extraterrestrial and so it goes. But really we are all the same stuff, all the same heritage, from the same place. We are all related, we are all energy. There is no separation.

Understanding this, I was much more able to control my emotions. Even though I was still searching, I was starting to fit more and more pieces into place. Even so, I would still get grumpy at times, and it was during one of these moods that my next insight came.

The struggle with the farm had left me wanting to get rid of it, but due to the continuing low prices for milk we could not sell it and recover our debt. The continual seesaw between my healing work and the farm was getting me down. This often led to arguments with Denise; well me arguing and getting bitchy was more like it; and one night I was feeling really bad.

Denise had gone to bed and left me in the lounge with my bad mood. I can remember lying on the couch and thinking that I would teach her a lesson and not go to bed - that would make her worry about me, or so I thought.

As I tried to convince myself that I had reason to be angry (in fact, working hard to remain in that state) there came from nowhere a loud voice saying, "Denie, Denie."

I froze. What was that? I tried to think; the voice did not come from outside my body, but it was so clear. I really had heard it. It was so loud and demanding that I knew I was being growled at, being told to get to bed and not be so stupid by staying angry. I heard it so clearly that I knew it was not my imagination. It was definitely a male voice, using perfect English.

Feeling a bit guilty, I got up and went to bed. Denise asked me what had changed my mind, so I said, "Nothing," trying to make my voice sound angry.

Then she poked me in the ribs and asked if I got lonely out in the lounge, and I said, "No. I was not getting lonely." Then, unable to keep from laughing, told her what had happened.

"There you are. You see, even your guides could see you were acting and pouting over nothing."

"Just leave me alone," I told her, as I heard her chuckling to herself. (Bloody women, how come they're always right?)

I lay on my back, still trying to feel angry at myself when I became aware of an extremely bright shaft of light coming at me. It was not visible to my eyes, but I could see it clearly. It was way out in space, but it was coming at me at a trillion miles an hour.

I was spellbound. I could not move. My eyes were wide open and I stared at the ceiling as this beam of light kept on coming. As it neared, I could sense how fast it was going, and there was no doubt it was coming at me.

My body stiffened and I tried to push myself down into the bed and let out a yell, but in the next split second it hit my body and a charge of energy shot through me.

I felt myself sort of glow and instantly all the anger left me. A feeling of tremendous love came over, within and around me. I felt a joy, a deep feeling of relief; I was happy. There is no other way to describe it: I was incredibly happy.

My body was tingling all over, and I just lay there in this charge of energy from the spirit world. Why me? Well, I did not really care. I was more than happy to receive that sort of energy anytime, thanks.

Amazingly, even after ten minutes or so I still felt the same. In my mind I could still recall the energy coming at me. I could not feel one ounce of negativity or anger within me, that was the really incredible thing.

Even now, I can recall how I felt as the energy was about to hit me - sort of afraid, but unable to do a thing. It was the most uncanny experience. But how was I able to see it? It must have been at least eleven thirty or close to midnight. The bedroom was dark, and as the energy sped toward me, it appeared to fill the room with light. It all happened so quickly that it must have taken a split second. Denise, who was almost asleep, never saw a thing.

When the energy hit me, my body jumped and instantly it was quite hot, a bit like when the energy would come into me when I was healing. But this was more like a tremendous, sharp (but very short) pulse that hit me at a million miles an hour. I remember just lying there almost floating. My body's frequency was so high that I am sure gravity had much less effect on me than usual.

The incredible peace and pure love I felt is indescribable. I remember telling Denise that she would not believe what happened. And when I explained it to her, she said she felt me get suddenly very hot and that she was glad that somebody out there was helping me.

I had not thought of it like that. (Women are so knowing, why is it that us men are always the last to understand?) After that I think I said thanks to whoever it was that sent the love shot (as I have since called it). I had never experienced anything like it in a physical sense. If this was cosmic sex, I was all for it.

Later, some clairvoyant friends said that I had an energy connection with a master on a high spiritual level who had somehow opened my crown chakra and aligned all my chakras in that split second. Christians would call this the incoming of the Holy Spirit.

That got me thinking and recalling the stories in the Bible. I could see some similarity to what I had experienced, so the next time I went to the city I called on a Catholic priest I knew and told him about it.

He did not pooh-pooh my story. He said that there was evidence of the Holy Spirit (or Holy Ghost, as the Catholics call it) having a marked influence on some people. He even said that there were stories of people being hit with the Holy Ghost like I had described it, and it had changed their lives.

After visiting with him for over two hours, he blessed me and I left, not knowing whether he believed me or not. In fact, I was not even sure that he believed his own teaching; perhaps he thought these things only happened thousands of years ago. Well, I knew what I had felt, although I could not fully comprehend the why or even the how. Whatever or whoever it had been, it sure had been real. It had a marked effect on my emotions, as well as my physical body.

For the first time in years I could go for long periods without feeling any anger at all. Instead, I had incredible feelings of love within me and loved and appreciated everything around me. I had never, ever experienced this kind of peace within myself, and my work at the clinic took on another dimension.

It was as if my healing ability had changed gear. My body was now able to be a transformer for much higher frequencies of cosmic and/or spiritual energies than before. Another thing I noticed was that my body never seemed to get tired from the healing work in the clinic. Some days I would be so busy that I would work twelve hours without a break. One person after another with only a quick drink once or twice during the day and many times without food, and yet at the end of it I would not be tired or hungry.

My body would be so charged with energy that it would be hard to think about things like driving home and other normal, earthly things. I still needed to rest and my physical body would become tired, but the other inside me was not tired, and after days like that I often felt that I was almost floating around the building - a real space cadet at times.

The hardest thing was getting myself down to earth so I could think about the things on the farm when I got home. That was always difficult; it was very hard to change frequencies. But all in all, I was a much better person as a result of my love shot.

Upon reflection I realized it was the "experience" with Sue that weekend in the mountains, followed by this experience that allowed me to accept over time that maybe this energy phenomenon that had been bugging me for years was meant to bring me to this point, so I could realize that this was the work I was meant to do. I had fought my spiritual awareness for a long time and searched and searched until I found logical concepts I could accept.

Energy was the common denominator, and when I understood that, then all other dimensions of reality, including spiritual phenomena, were totally understandable and perfectly natural. I had a lot more to learn, but for now I had satisfying answers - answers that would allow me to proceed with a degree of confidence I had never felt before.

There really was more to this life than just the daily struggle, and I began to actually feel good about myself. The emptiness deep inside was starting to be filled. I was starting to have, for the first time, love and acceptance for me. To totally feel that I was important, not to anybody else, but to me.

When we find our truth, life can be an explosion of understanding and awareness. Searching for our truth can be a real bitch, but there are answers. Like Shirley MacLaine, I had gone out on my limb, and many times I was sure that I was so far out that it would break off and I would fall flat on my face.

But I did not - it only felt like it. I actually got through many layers of self-doubt and patterning instilled by this crazy western society. I was starting to feel, to be free to experience a much greater reality than I ever thought possible. If this was what awareness is, what all the great teachers called enlightenment and what the Christian church taught as experiencing heaven, I was all for it!

When we allow ourselves to completely accept that we are part of a much greater whole, then and only then can we start to understand the real reason for being. Our cosmic connections are as real and as natural as day following night.

CHAPTER 10
ACCEPTANCE

Due to my work (or stirring, as some people would call it) in farm politics, I was invited to lead a grassroots group of farmers to look at agriculture in a Third World socialist country. This was the first time a group of normal, everyday farmers had been invited to visit Cuba from this part of the world.

Cuba is so totally different from what most people believe. Without doubt, Cuban society is (or perhaps was, when I was there) one of the best in supplying the necessities of life, including one of the best education systems and total medical care for everybody. The people are the most emotionally secure I have seen in any country I have visited. This was interesting to me.

Talking at length to a parish priest of a large Catholic church in Havana (yes, religion was very much alive and well in Cuba), I found that the people felt secure because they believed in what they were doing - that is, running their country their way, even with the most severe and long-term illegal economic and trade suppression any country has had to endure this century.

A country where your food, clothing, schooling, medical care, housing and child care is a natural right, a right granted by the fact you are a human being, is rather unique in this world.

To my surprise, Cuba had all this and more. In fact, a large portion of its fast-growing tourist industry included people coming from Western Europe for high-tech medical and surgical work. I was able to experience firsthand its largely drug-free medical care during my treatment for an illness I had developed in Mexico on my way to Cuba.

This highly developed and practical "green" medicine, based on herbal and, to my amazement, energy healing, developed because the U.S.-initiated embargo of thirty years had largely denied the Cubans the ability to purchase drugs.

Even in animal care, their non-drug treatment is startling - more so to us Kiwi dairy farmers, because we were aware that the extreme heat would make dairying very difficult. I was quite aware that drugs cost New Zealand farmers tens of thousands of dollars to control calves' diarrhea. In Cuba they had researched the Chinese understanding of the body's electrical system and knew what pressure point (acupuncture) to rub to stop a calf scouring without drugs.

The truly incredible thing is that the doctors are trained in all fields of medicine, not just drug-based allopathic medicine. Due to their experience, drug treatment is used only for very advanced and specific problems, because they have found that other forms of medicine or energy healing are much more effective and have the added advantage of being less invasive and largely free of side effects.

The result is that as a society, the Cubans were physically, emotionally and mentally more healthy and lived their lives with more joy and harmony than people in the U.S. or even New Zealand.

They did not have the access to consumer goods that the Western world had, but that is not their fault. Cut off from trade with the rest of the world, Cuba had to develop their own independent way of life. From what I could see, this may be a blessing in disguise. Another thing we noticed was that

Denise and the women on the trip, could walk alone around the cities at night in total safety, something that is not done in many cities in the Western world.

I was amazed to discover that Cuba had taken in over ten thousand children from the U.S.S.R. to treat for radiation illness caused by of the Chernobyl accident. Using alternative forms of treatment, the Cuban doctors had much success in alleviating the problems caused by radiation. This got me thinking about how much there was to know about energy healing in all its forms.

What I saw on that little island in the Caribbean could close down the drug companies overnight and free us all from the stranglehold of drug medicine most of us are subjected to. If people in the U.S. realized that the Cubans had education, medical and childcare as a right, and most of it more effective than theirs, then they might start to question their own society and its way of doing things.

Cuba has some difficult problems, but my trip through that country really brought home to me the reality of my own life. Also, I thought about the way the people in the U.S. are driven and motivated by fear. This fear develops a dog-eat-dog attitude and forces people to become locked into a debt-driven existence to the point that most people are just one sickness or layoff away from being unable to support their family and losing their home.

What a contrast to the people of Cuba, who have none of this fear, due to the way they run their society. I was able to see parallels in my own life, with all the hassles that money (or the lack of it) caused. I reflected on how impossible it was to pay the bank's interest rate and then struggle with exchange rates and dollar value changes, not to mention product price fluctuations that were manipulated by the big Western power players.

All this had put my life under increasing, indescribable oppression. I could see that the mental health of the Cuban people, visible through their happiness and joy in being alive, their acceptance of life's lot and their willingness to run their country their way and not be dictated to by their overbearing neighbor, had direct parallels with my own disillusionment when struggling to keep my farm going. By looking at the Cuban people, I could see that my own happiness was more important than the material things I had aspired to for so long.

I realized that following my inner urges, staying in my truth and letting go of my struggle would free me to become the person I really was. From halfway around the world, I could see that harmony existed in a society because the people were living their truth. I realized that one's inner happiness was not about what went on in the world, or what we achieved materialistically. If we followed our inner truth, we could live more in harmony with ourselves.

It became clear to me that trying to hold on to my farm and to resist my spiritual awakening (and in the process trying to live two lives) was slowly destroying me. I had found a new reality and direction, but I had been resisting making the changes that would allow my life to go forward along this new path. This resistance was based in the fear of not being accepted and of being different.

If the Cuban people could find such peace and inner contentment by following their truth and running their society for their own benefit, then surely I might be able to find my long sought-after harmony if I followed my truth. I knew then that I would have to find a way to free myself from my economic jail and let go of the farm so I could devote myself to helping people.

The urge to serve humanity, to find my place on this earth, to really be me, to let go of my anger and find my inner peace was becoming paramount. I knew deep down that I would not be able to find this space and endure the hassles of the farm as well. I had been trying to change the world using the big stick method. But the only way to change the world was to change people's consciousness, and the only way to start that process was to accept and to change my own, if necessary.

I remembered another verse in the Bible that went something like, he who fights by the sword, shall die by the sword and he who uses love, shall find love. It is pretty hard to change, but a darn sight harder to accept that we have been doing it all ass-backwards. I could see a lot of things I did not like about this world and myself in particular.

I had been beating myself to death by using a method that could never work - anger and ego. Only by achieving my own inner harmony and truth and the strength to live by it, could I effect outer change.

With this latest experience very much on my mind, stopping off on our way home for four days in Los Angeles really brought home to me how crazy this world really is. Sitting on the sidewalk on a busy street in L.A. I took a good look at people who walked by, and it told all. With all the so-called wealth there, the people seemed sad and lifeless. Nobody talked or even smiled at anybody else, in contrast to the happy outgoing people of Cuba.

Surely the people of L.A. cannot be free, because free people do not look like that. But people who are weighed down and imprisoned by economic and social pressure, who are struggling daily with life sure can.

It was strange how I was putting it all through my mind, looking over all my perceptions, starting to feel my beliefs change and transform into a new understanding.

It was during one of these moments of deep soul-searching that I picked up a phone book and found myself looking through the yellow pages for psychic readers. Once again, I was doing something I had not planned to do, acting almost by instinct, but by now I knew it was my spirit guides (an aspect of my higher frequency) who were supplying that instinct.

My eyes settled on a listing, and even though I looked at all the listings I kept coming back to this one name. To double-check I got out my pendulum, and without looking I slowly slid my finger down the page. When the pendulum went into a strong swing I looked beneath my finger and the same name that had grabbed my attention was there. "Good enough for me," I said, and phoned the number.

Rose could see me that evening and during the fifteen minute cab ride I tried not to feel like a fool. What would I say to her? Worse, what would she say to me? I had seen a few psychics over the years, some very good and others not at all specific. This time I was hoping for a good detailed reading. At least, I thought, there was no way this lady could know anything about me.

Rose turned out to be a big woman who was pastor of a Spiritualist church in Anaheim, and I had to wait until she had finished talking to some other people. I was asked if I wanted an open reading or a longer private session. I opted for the private one.

The first thing Rose did was to ask me if she could hold something that had been on my body for a few days. I gave her my watch. Almost immediately she started talking and the first thing she said was that I was to be working as a healer much more in the future than I was at present, and that my life, as a farmer, was to end. I did not need it anymore.

Also, my life with my wife was also over, even though we were still together; the emotional and energy connection was gone. We had been through too much pain and stress together for too long. She said I needed to be able to take a complete break from the farm and that environment so I could really come to terms with who I am.

I just sat there shaking my head in disbelief. How in hell did she know all this? I could not believe it, she was right about most things, but the bit about our marriage was a first. To be frank, I had felt trapped for a long time, but my responsibility was with my kids and there was no way I was going to walk out on them and Denise.

Rose was insistent when I questioned her about it, saying that I would be on my own for quite a while, and even though I would have many friends around me, I would have no partner as such. She also told me that I would find it quite hard to find total peace and direction, but over the course of nine to ten years I would grow in awareness, and by the end of that time my real identity and purpose in life would be very clear.

I pushed this last point to get more information, but she said only that I would be the kind of healer the world has not seen for a long while and that I would be a much-traveled teacher. She went on to say that I would not be deserting

Denise and the kids, that my work was out in the world and the job of being a father was largely complete anyhow. Now I was to start the training and the performing of what I had come to do.

She also told me that the kids would always understand and would know that I would never stop loving them, even when I was on the other side of the world. She said that they would be given the knowing and understanding, and that I was not to worry about it.

When I asked her about Denise, she said that was not my concern; she had earned many blessings and her life would be very happy. She would be fine and well taken care of.

Not knowing what else to ask, I just sat there letting it all sink in. The really weird thing about it all was that I knew she was completely right. All the things she said about my marriage were right on. I had felt totally frustrated by the pull to go out into the world and learn more - or was that an excuse? Hell, I did not know. I did not want to leave the kids and Denise, yet the ever-increasing feeling of being trapped was so strong that at times I would erupt.

I could now see that a lot of my anger and emotional outburst were caused by trying to be a happy farmer when my higher self had another agenda. It was time to move on; my life had changed but I was still trying to hold on to my old world. It seemed that the harder I tried to hold on, the more I got knocked around.

Rose asked me as she looked right into my eyes, "do you think all the droughts, money problems, pesticides in your soil and the things that happened to you were all flukes?" (my God, this was a rerun of what I had been told in New Zealand). "No, my friend, you had better start to take notice of what is going on around you. The more you resist the changes, the harder you will get kicked. Young man, there are those that think you are too important to be a farmer any longer, so you had better start to follow your heart. You know as well as I do that farming is not in your heart anymore."

Well, she was right about that, she was spot on, there were no secrets with her. But I still wanted to know who the hell I was supposed to be, what I was supposed to do. Just being told that I was a healer and teacher was not good enough. I wanted to know more. I wanted to know what the hell was so special about me, because I did not think I was very special. In fact, I usually felt the opposite.

What I wanted to know was, what was so different about my energy that caused Rose and other psychics to get so excited when they saw me? It did not add up when they kept telling me that I was this great healer, while I could see that I was completely fouled up most of the time. I seemed to always come away from these people with more questions than answers.

After I pressed Rose to keep answering my questions, especially about my relationships with other people who were close to me, she said that I would always have special friends, and that I was not to push them to change their lives because they were there to help me understand more about my life, not be long-term partners.

This pissed me off, because I had a strong connection with Georgina, who worked with me in the clinic and who had sort of taken over from the point where Sue had taken me to. Georgie had a unique ability to act as an intermediary when I was working on young children or doing absent healing. She was able to let her body connect totally with the person I was working on; then I was able to receive and send information to the other person.

Because we could work together to such a high level and if I was going to commit my life to healing, I wanted to have somebody like Georgie sharing it with me. I could see no joy in the world by being alone. At the time, I needed to share my feelings and have someone around who was on the same wavelength and pushing awareness to the extreme that I was - someone to talk to about what was going on inside of me.

I liked Georgie to just be there and understand - rather, just be there and let me talk and understand my own reality.

Now this Los Angeles psychic was telling me not to put pressure on Georgie, as she had her own life, and that I would meet others. Rose was adamant that I would always have a close special friend and that I was not to worry about it.

It was easy for her to say that, I thought, but she had hit the nail on the head and had gotten me to accept a lot of things I had been holding in. How she could be so right amazed me. There was no way she could have known anything about me, and here she was, telling me all about my innermost secrets.

Finishing my session with her, which had lasted well over one-and-a-half hours, I taxied back to our hotel, but instead of going in, I went for a long walk. I had a lot of things to think about, most of all, how to tell Denise about what I had been told. It was well after dark when I made my way back to the hotel through the fumes, smog and endless traffic.

Finding Denise in our room, I sat down and told her everything. I never held back a thing; I bared my soul to her - Sue, how important Georgie was to me at the time, the lot - all the frustrations, urges and pain I had battled over the years. I told her I did not know how long we would be together, that I had no idea where my life was headed, that I just had to follow the overpowering urge within to break free from the materialistic world, and that I was scared as all hell.

Above all else, I told her I could never stop loving her. I said that I would understand if she got angry at me and kicked me out there and then, but as we had been through thick and thin and to hell and back together, I never wanted us to regret loving each other. To me, the most important thing in my life was family; she was a part of me that could never be put aside, never be downgraded.

I wanted so much, yet I knew I was going to lose even more, a loving home that had always been there for me. Walking away from her would mean leaving the most loving and gentle person a man could ever want.

I think at that point we were holding each other very close and crying. For the first time in my life, I was opening up, really opening up, and this time it was with Denise. I had never been able to do this before, and that had always bothered me. I think I was afraid of losing her, afraid of being rejected. Now the floodgates were open and there was no holding back. All the years of withdrawal into myself, holding in all my thoughts and anxieties and the fear of accepting myself as spirit ended then and there.

We spent the night talking, crying and laughing as I realized how stupid I had been by not confiding in her. She had known years ago how much of an inner struggle I was going through. Many times she had wanted to just put her arms around me to comfort me, but because I had shut myself off to such an extent, I had also shut her out. I had never even realized how much pain she had felt as a result, and as I withdrew even further, communication became hopeless.

It was that night in a hotel room far away from home that we both realized we were going down different paths and there was nothing either of us could do about it. After eighteen years of marriage we would not be spending our old age together. I tried to be strong and told Denise that she would be better off without me and that she would be looked after and would not have to be alone.

As could be expected, she could not see how she would ever meet anyone that would ease the sense of loss she was then feeling. We talked about the children, how it would affect them, what would they think, why this was happening to us, but underneath it all, we both knew that it had to happen.

Facing it was hard. I think we both realized that night that there was a tremendous amount of love between us, a love that would never die. Perhaps underneath we were able to find an even greater love, an unconditional love, a love so strong that we could let each other be free to follow our own paths, wherever they led.

The pain of letting go would take some getting used to and we would each grieve our loss in our own way. I told Denise that there was no way I would leave until she was able to feel secure.

"What about your work?" She asked. I told her, to hell with my work, that can wait for however long it took for her to find her way again.

I remember telling my guides and God that if he or she was listening, I would not be going anywhere until Denise was looked after, and I felt it was up to them to help make that happen so that she would always be happy.

It is very difficult for me to describe my emotions that night. I felt a sort of relief mixed with excitement and sorrow. Mainly I felt a great weight lifting off my shoulders because now I would never have to keep things to myself. I could at last, after all these years, talk to Denise.

I also knew that I could now let go of the farm. When and how that would happen I did not know, but I knew it would happen.

Denise said she wanted to talk to Rose, so the next day I phoned and we agreed to meet her at her house later that day. I think Denise found some comfort in hearing what Rose said to her, and she had a good long session.

We both had a lot to think about on the long flight home. The best thing about it was that now we were able to talk to each other about our innermost feelings. It was a trip each of us would never forget, and looking back, it was a real turning point for both of us, a realization and gradual acceptance of what we really wanted out of life.

Of course, the actual changes resulting from that realization were harder to achieve. For me, the months ahead were very different emotionally, because I knew we would have to wait a while before we sold the farm, and I had to come to terms with the connection Georgie and I had.

Georgie and Denise had known each other and, as a result of my telling Denise how I felt, she and Georgie spent a lot of time together and became very good friends, largely because they both knew how difficult it was for all of us to accept the changes we were facing.

Denise was only too happy that Georgie was able to help me. I had always found I could talk to Georgie, better than I ever could with Sue. We had an almost total mind connection, like we had known each other for tens of thousands of years - and we probably had.

I can remember our first meeting, how I felt instantly comfortable in her company. Georgie could read me like a book.

If there is one person other than Denise who understood me, it was she. We spent as much time together as we could, and she assisted me in the clinic at every opportunity. At other times she worked on me, trying to get me to get in touch with my childhood.

For me that was a no-no, but she had other ideas. It is really strange how she came into my life at that time, because without her unconditional love, I would not have had the strength to go into my past and dig up all the too-hard-to-deal-with stuff. It is only possible to expose yourself to that level when you have the utmost trust and a very special connection with someone; I was extremely fortunate to have this with Georgie.

It was a strange time and I seemed to be on hold spiritually, almost like I had to take time out to get my act together. Even though I'd had many emotional times with Sue, they were about my acceptance of myself and spiritual things, but with Georgie it was very different. This time I was forced to dig deep into myself and drag up and expose all my behavior patterns and the reasons for them.

Georgie was ruthlessly efficient at pushing all my buttons. She had an incredible skill of doing this in a gentle, loving way, so that I was unaware of it until it hit me. Every time I got really defensive and agitated, she would know when to hold up a mirror by bringing out my inner fear, and I would be faced with looking slap-bang into a side of myself that I hated. The woman was good; she could get right inside me and just keep on working at me until it felt like my entire consciousness had been turned inside out and beaten like a rug on a clothesline, until the last bit of trauma I had stuffed in as a child was knocked out.

You can imagine what this was doing to my emotions. I was going through hell, and it was during this time that I must have cried all the tears I had held back for many lifetimes. The pain of having to look at your own stupidity is greater than all the physical pain in the world.

If I had to pick out the hardest thing to accept, it would probably be admitting how painful it had been for my kids to be on the receiving end of my anger and uncompromising attitudes. I must have cried a million tears coming to terms with that one.

Georgie just kept on digging. Out came all my anger at Dad, my perception of his rejection, my feelings of not being good enough, my need to succeed, the drive I developed as a young man - everything. It was awful! I would never have gotten through it if it had not been for Georgie.

Of course, all this did not happen overnight; in fact, it took a year or more, and Georgie and Denise used to meet and compare notes about my reactions and emotional state, no doubt having a good laugh at my expense. Those two incredible women sure had the measure of me. Big old macho Denie, falling apart all over the place, was sure getting his comeuppance. If this was my karma, then Georgie and Denise were going to make darn sure I got the lot. Not one drop was going to get past these two.

During the ups and downs at this time I found myself becoming aware of feeling more - feeling more for people, being aware of how my behavior and actions could affect and hurt others, and how easy it was to do this. I was also able to feel for the animals. I guess I always could, but now it was more enhanced. I could not even shoot a rabbit on the farm. I found myself slowing down on the farm motorbike so that the mother duck had time to get all her ducklings hidden away from her perceived danger.

I was starting to smell the roses that Denise had grown like an Amazon rain forest. I was enjoying the kids much, much more, and I could feel my whole level of enjoyment lift. In the clinic, I found a new awareness in being able to feel people's hurt to a much greater degree. I was actually becoming a much more sensitive human being. As I unloaded my garbage, I was coming more alive. I was coming back to life.

Denise and I were now getting along better than we had for years. We were able to talk about everything, and because I was able to look at myself more and more, I was able to tell her things that I had kept secret for years. I guess we were enjoying each other's company more completely than we ever had. I was becoming a much more caring person and as a result, we did not have reasons to argue. Since we both knew where we were at, there was no emotional tension between us.

To anyone outside it would have seemed to be the perfect marriage. I guess that is what real friendship is, a total acceptance of each other, and we had that and more.

After returning from our trip we both started to go to the spiritualist meetings in our local town. This was the first time I had attended anything that resembled a church since I had left home, but this was not like a normal church.

It was much more informal and not at all pushy, just a few hymns and a prayer or two, then about a half hour or more of clairvoyant readings. Because I had come to accept and, more importantly, respect the gift or learned art of clairvoyance, I found these sessions really interesting. I was always amazed at the accuracy of some of the clairvoyants.

In fact, at our first meeting, a visiting clairvoyant gave me a reading. The first thing she said to me was "did I know that I was a healer and that I had tremendous ability to channel healing energy through my hands?" She also told me that I had many guides around me and that soon my inner struggle of acceptance would be over. She finished my reading with the advice to hang in there and not be afraid to follow my inner guidance, as that would eventually lead me to my total fulfilment. This from a person who had never seen me before that night.

Another time, I had arrived late and was standing at the back of the church when the clairvoyant came to me. As she started to speak she stopped herself and gave me a long, hard, but surprised look. She then said, "I just have to tell you what I can see. I have seen this only once before in all my years of readings. Do you know you have a very powerful presence with you?" I sort of looked around a bit self-consciously. What was she on about? I thought.

"You have what I can only describe as the presence of the Christ standing completely in your aura, a little to the back of you, with his hands on your shoulders. I call this presence the Christ because that is what I understand it to be. The power, the stature, the incredible energy of this presence is like nothing else; it is a mass of translucent golden white, all-powerful energy, and as I focus on you both, I feel throughout my body the most amazing feeling of love."

You could have knocked me over with a feather. I could only stand there looking blankly back at her. There was utter silence in the church; then I became aware that every single face in the building had turned and was looking at me. I could not move, and my face probably had a more disbelieving look than anybody else's. I stared back at her in disbelief.

Then she said, "You are blessed; this has been a great honor for me." I was so stunned that I do not think I even said thank you. Without another word to me, she calmly called on somebody else and proceeded to give them their message.

Feeling my legs about to collapse under me, I moved to the table on the other side of the door where my dear friend and clinic receptionist Kath was sitting. She had a grin from ear to ear, and she took my hand and held it tight. I just did not know what to think, and to make matters worse, people were still turning around and staring at me. I felt like sinking through a hole in the floor.

The reaction I got after the service ended was rather strange. Everybody stayed for tea and nibbles and lots of small talk, but I felt like an outcast - this among a group of people where a good number were clients at the clinic and many were well-known to me. I felt that everybody was avoiding me.

It was all a bit hard to take, but this clairvoyant was regarded as very good and had been doing this for years. However, it was hard for me to believe the boss made house calls, so as the weeks went by, I dismissed that reading and just carried on with my life.

That incident was not the first time a clairvoyant had seen a Christ-like energy around me. In fact, it was only a few months earlier that a young lady I had never met before had made an appointment to visit the clinic. When she walked into my room, she stopped and stared in amazement. She said she could see my complete aura, and superimposed on my physical body was the image of Christ.

She was so shocked that she could hardly stand, and as we talked she was able to give me very explicit and graphic explanations of what she saw. It turned out that she had never before seen a person's aura and by coming into my presence, her vision was suddenly turned on so that she could see the higher energy frequency. Rosie (not the L.A. Rose) and I became very good friends, and as a result of the energy work I did with her, her psychic abilities became so skilled that she became a highly regarded and sought-after clairvoyant.

I will always remember that day, because I had had a very full booking and had been working for over ten hours without a break. Rosie had come in late in the day. In fact, I think she was my last client, and what happened blew us both away. I had done some high-energy healing with earlier clients, and my body was operating at a very high frequency.

I had said to Kath, my receptionist, that there were some powerful spirits coming through that day, but I had never even contemplated that the boss might be lending a hand with his energy. But Rosie was adamant that she saw him completely merged with my energy and the details she gave me sent shivers down my spine. We spent hours talking into the late evening about the connections we can have with the spirit world and she could understand it all. To her it was perfectly normal, as she had a deep and natural connection with her spiritual self.

In the following months Rosie, Georgie and I did a lot of work getting instructions on how I could use my "friend's" energy to help me when I was working on ill people.

Soon after that, I met a six-year-old whose mother brought her in to see me because the child could see everybody's aura and the mother, who was freaking out, was wanting to know more about what was going on. As a result I arranged for us all, including the six-year-old, to meet weekly on Friday nights at the clinic and we would have what you could call a meeting of worlds.

Rosie, with her clairvoyant ability now fully working, could communicate with our friends from the other side. I would be able to use her like a telephone to get instructions about where to place my hands for different effects on people's bodies. Georgie's body was used for these experiments and the young girl was able to see clearly the energy coming into my body from the spirits in the room and out into Georgie's body. As a result, she was able to give me a blow-by-blow account of what was happening, while I followed Rosie's instructions, which she was relaying to me from our helpers.

It was amazing stuff, and our young friend would climb all over the table, pointing out where the energy was flowing and what color she was seeing. As the frequency changed, so would the color. When the child described the color change, I related it to what I was feeling in my body. At times we would ask our spirit friends to channel energy through me that could heal different diseases. By this method we were able to see what frequency and what parts of my body would be used.

In other words, we were able to see that not only my hands but other parts of my body would be used to channel the healing energy into whoever I was working on. Sometimes up to five or more spirit entities would be inputting energy into my body using different chakra centers, and then the corrected frequency would flow from my eyes, hands and other areas into the client.

Our young friend could see all this energy clearly, and she would be excited when she put her hands into the energy flow to show us where it was going and what color it was. Through Rosie, we found out that the spirits could not channel their high-frequency energy directly into lower-frequency humans without first having a human they could work through as a sort of transformer. The transformer's body was used to correct or change their energy to a frequency that the human body could handle.

If you can imagine that the spirit guides operated at a frequency of a house plug (110 volts), I would be the transformer or the battery charger and the person on the table a flat 12 volt battery.

You can see that if the energy were fed directly from the 110 volt plug into the flat battery, the battery would be damaged, so transformers (that is what battery chargers are) are used to cut down or lower (change) the frequency to that which the battery can handle. That is, from 110 volts to 12 volts. The battery (ill person) can be energized with the correct energy frequency and it (their cells) will be charged and start to work properly. This is really what happens with energy healing, regardless of what and how some people like to dress it up and call it as a result of misinformation or religious belief structures. (That is the kindergarten way of understanding energy healing, anyway.)

With all the information coming through I was able to start to understand why my body got so hot when I was healing or when my friends from the other side were working through me. Battery chargers and other transformers that are used to lower voltage (change frequency) all get hot due to the need to dissipate the heat that occurs as a result of this energy transformation (change). In my case, my body's heating and subsequent sweating acted as this heat-dissipating function.

The changes of frequency that my body has been required to accommodate has, at times, generated so much heat that I thought I would have a meltdown. There have been times when I have finished working on serious illnesses like cancers that I could literally ring the sweat out of my clothes.

This was simply a result of changing the high-frequency cosmic (spirit) energy into a form acceptable to a human body, and that is all an energy channeler/healer does. We are just walking transformers - nothing special, nothing occult, but just people who our friends on the other side can use as intermediaries so they can be of help to us, their brothers and sisters in this dimension.

Why me? I do not know. I guess if you can answer why Elton John can sing or Carl Lewis can run, you will find the answer to why some of us can be used as energy transformers for healing. As for asking our spirit friends, all they said was that it was my choice, and that this is what I came to this dimension to do.

Apparently, I had soul energy at a frequency that, when embodied on this earth, would affect my body in such a way that the physical cells would be able to handle the high-frequency energy from their side. This is all fine and dandy and understandable, but I wish somebody had given me an instruction manual or a copy of my contract to bring with me so I would not have had to go through all I did to accept this.

We had lots of interesting times, always learning and, I think most importantly, expanding our belief systems to fully embrace the reality that there really is a dimension of life that we call the spirit world. To all of us during these nights of learning, their presence was so real, their energy would be so strong in the room, that we could feel it with our physical senses - even the air was different.

Sometimes the room felt like it was crowded with people, although there were only five or six of us there. When I asked our young friend how many spirit people she could see, she would slowly look around the room and count them off with her fingers. One night she went over both hands twice. It was crowded in there at times, all right.

As I learned, I was able to help them use my body and to assist in the inputting of the energy into the client. I was able to lift my awareness and my ability to feel so that I could recognize the different frequencies that were working with me. I was able to ask for a specific frequency from a specific spirit, but of course I always said that if they thought I was not asking for the correct frequency they should make the correction. I could feel the change in my body.

Sometimes when I was working, I would feel a change, so I would ask, why now, as I did not think a change was necessary at the time. They would say, just testing, just testing - the cheeky sods were having me on - and then I would feel the frequency change back again.

One thing I learned quickly is that a sense of humor is very high on their list of priorities, and they love to mentally spar with us. In fact, I think they have one heck of a celebration when another of us dense humans finally realizes that we are not alone in the cosmos and that we can learn to communicate and interact with them.

Another point is that this had nothing to do with religion whatsoever; in fact, most religions in the Western world have got it so wrong (or are deliberately suppressing the truth) that they make it harder for their followers to find their spiritual connections and thereby grow in awareness.

There is nothing in the cosmos that is "supernatural," or whatever name we choose to use. Everything is perfectly natural; it is just that we have not allowed ourselves to accept certain realities. We tend to get locked into a very narrow perception of reality. We think we are so bloody good, so advanced and educated, yet dolphins have a much greater awareness and perception of energy than we do.

Even our pet dog is more aware of some things than we are. A dog can perceive infinitely more frequencies of energy called sound than we can. Its ability to smell (also an energy frequency) is about five thousand times more enhanced than ours; therefore a dog lives in a very different or broader world than us.

If we think the cosmos is made up of only what we can perceive, we are living an illusion. There is much more going on around us than we think. The ability to first realize, then to accept, then to become part of a much greater whole is what awareness or enlightenment is all about.

For me, now, my playground is not limited to this earthy dimension; rather, the cosmos has become an unlimited, multidimensional, many-faceted but perfectly natural, normal, safe but exciting adventure park. I have friends, some personal and some not quite so personal, on all sorts of dimensions, from all different realities. Some have rather dense frequencies like me and others have frequencies way beyond our earthly plane. But they are not so different from us. We are all related, all connected, all made of the same stuff (energy), and all perfectly natural.

CHAPTER 11
LETTING GO

Returning from our Caribbean trip, both Denise and I had lots of things to think about and together we had to find a way to get off the farm without going broke. Because product prices were starting to creep up after a couple of very low years, we decided to hang in there in the hope we would be able to pay off some more bills.

My emotions at this time were real good. I was excited and invigorated by what was happening at the clinic, and somehow I did not fear losing the farm, as I had a year earlier. To take the pressure off, we were employing labor on the farm, and as my time at the clinic was increasing, I decided not to do any contracting with the machinery that the farm had left after the contracting company had gone belly-up. I still had one big tractor that the farm owned, so I hired it out to a friend for the harvesting season, and that allowed a bit more cash to come in.

The milk prices for the year kept on going up, and for a change we were paid at a level that we actually made a profit. As you can imagine, with four hundred cows when you make money, you really make money, but when you lose, you lose heaps. But this time, we paid off most of our short-term debts, and the industry leaders said that the world market looked good for the next three years and that prices should hold at this level.

With this good outlook we put our farm on the market and listed it with the realtors. Not needing a quick sale, we were prepared to wait for our price to be met (which we thought would not be too long). We had high hopes, and if nothing else the reason I would not let the farm go at a low price was that after twenty years of bloody hard work I felt I was deserving of a bit of payback, and I also wanted Denise to have enough so she could be comfortable. God only knew she had done enough work for two lifetimes, so why should she have to struggle now? No, it was one of the bargains I had made, that Denise would be taken care of.

However, at times, my emotional nakedness was so real that I felt very exposed and alone. I was going through a period of incredible change and adjustment, and of course this cannot happen without first stripping away all the old coverings and masks we have used to hide our fears and other stuff, and when that goes, we feel very vulnerable.

It is this vulnerability that brings on more fear about the future, all the "what's going to happen to me, how am I going to live, what am I going to do" thoughts that fill our minds. The uncertainty is very real and has the effect of making us emotionally unstable. It did to me, at any rate.

Georgie and I would talk for hours, Georgie trying to get me to accept that I needed to go on alone, so that I would find peace within. She knew in her heart that if we were together, I would rely on her for my happiness, and that I now would have to find this for myself.

Georgie could see this. But I was trying to deny it. I was about to lose everything - Denise, the farm, my kids, my way of life, even the me I knew. Georgie had been there for me, and as a result I had been able to look at most of my too-hard-to-deal-with issues. We had been brought together for a purpose, and now it was time for me to go on alone. I would be much stronger and more in control of my life as a result of our connection, but each of us had our own path to follow. I was being stripped bare.

There comes a time in our lives when many of us face similar changes; we are torn between this place or that, this job or moving on, and, heaven forbid, this husband or wife or finding our true happiness. It is actually a hard one to deal with. Change is always hard, even one change at a time, but I was looking at changes that usually occurred over many years all happening at once.

Many times, I felt like I just wanted to run away, just disappear, forget all about everything and go off to some island somewhere where nobody knew me. I desperately needed to make the final break, to learn to be me, to learn to not be dependent on anybody else, to completely face myself.

It was as if I knew that the new me, the really changed me, would not be able to fully manifest until I made a complete break with the life I had known. The incredible urge that would well up inside would tug at the very roots of my being. I would be tormented for days on end with feelings of desperately wanting to leave, alternating with the fear of leaving.

Feelings of guilt, anger and out-of-control emotions would haunt me and tear at my sanity, and it was Georgie who would help me get through these periods. I think I was subconsciously distancing myself from Denise, not really wanting to let her know how much I was hurting inside. I was trying to be as calm as I could at home, but I was not exactly achieving any prolonged period of calmness, and my old angry defensiveness started to rear its ugly head again.

I felt like I was drifting, almost like a sailboat, waiting for the next fickle breeze to come along, from which direction I was not to know.

Denise was starting to find herself more. She was getting off the farm, doing things for herself and meeting different people, so I was alone with my thoughts a lot. I had always found it difficult to meditate, and that was one of the things Georgie had always said I must practice. I seemed to have a built-in resistance to it, but with lots of time alone now I decided to try and get to the bottom of this meditation problem.

I enrolled in the meditation workshop of any seminar I went to. One of them was being conducted by a visiting teacher from England who was billed as the featured speaker for the event, so I went along with high hopes of getting some insight into this meditation thing. After a thorough introduction into her technique, she started the class in slow, deep breathing while she talked us through a series of mind exercises that were intended to deeply relax us.

I had been to many similar classes before and always my phobia (pig-headedness) had stopped anything from happening, so I was surprised when I felt the frequency of my body change. I had plenty of experiences with energy changes and different energies over the years, so I was aware when even very small changes occurred. This time, the change was from within my own cellular structure and not from any outside influence.

I slowly felt myself relaxing until I was aware of almost no sensation of my body. For a brief moment my mind started to take control, but I convinced myself that it was okay and the panic attack passed. I felt myself sort of slip out of my body - that is the only way to describe it. It was not like my body taking on another frequency so as to be able to receive another energy such as in healing, but this time it was as if a part of me was going some place.

I can remember the instructor guiding the group to climb the rungs of an imaginary ladder, and each time that was exactly what was happening for me. I could feel the increase in frequency and the change in my reality, which felt like a great veil was been pulled back as each step was reached. Up and up I went, and the universe kept on opening. I lost the awareness of my physical body completely for the first time in my life. My only sensation was a feeling of ever greater expansion, an expansion of self. I could vividly hear the instructor slowly counting out the steps, higher and higher. I could hear her telling us not to be afraid, but to seek our higher selves, to look for the highest frequency of existence that our evolution had taken us to, and to see our guide(s) and to ask for and accept that guide's help on this path of discovery.

I'd had some experiences, but this one got exciting. At about the eighth step, I became aware of two large beings - my protectors, my guides. I could see them quite clearly from where I was (wherever that was). I asked them to be with me and help me to find my highest evolutionary state.

It was at that point that it happened. It was as if I stepped into the breach of a torpedo tube and was propelled outward and upward at a speed that would make light appear to be going backwards. My only sensation was that I was reaching out toward the most incredible energy I could imagine.

This appeared to me as an all-encompassing ball of golden light that completely merged with my reality. As I reached it, one great final expansion of awareness poured into my consciousness. I felt what can only be described as a state of heaven, a state of absolute total peace and harmony.

The amazing thing was that I not only felt this for myself, but I sensed that all atoms in the universe felt my harmony and I felt theirs. It was a feeling of true oneness, a total awareness and acceptance of all by all. Words cannot describe the feeling. I do not really know how to describe the reality I was in or the level of expansion I was aware of, other than to say it was everything, just everything.

I felt reluctant to leave this place, state, level of consciousness or whatever it was, but way in the distance I could see those two entities, and I felt a need to go toward them. Immediately after that thought passed through my mind, I was back with them and we nodded out of respect toward each other and I felt the most tremendous joy and love coming from them.

Falling back from the guides, I became aware of my body again and the instructor talking us down the ladder. I think she was down to about forth or fifth rung when I became conscious of the physical plane once again. As the count came down I tried to stay focused on my feelings and to hold on to the memory of what I had experienced. I tried to analyze the changes that had occurred and to separate the wishful thinking (if there was any) from the real experience, which was not an easy task.

I think the instructor had finished the count back before I was willing to let go of the focus of the trip, and as I did I became aware of my body (rather, the physical state I was in). The physical state it was not in, would be more to the point, because I could not move a muscle. I could only sit there like a blob of jelly, and there was not a dry piece of clothing on me.

I turned and looked at the woman sitting next to me, half hoping to get assurance that I did not do anything wacky, but all I got was her staring at me with wide-open eyes. By now the instructor was getting people to explain their meditation experiences, and one by one the group said the usual things, such as becoming very relaxed or drifting around the fringe of a higher dimension or meeting the guides on one of the spiritual planes. Many explained in detail what their guides looked like, and many felt lots of love and peace out there.

As usual for me, I was sitting in the back row, so nearly all the participants had given the group their experiences, and none had been anything like mine. So when it came to my turn I just waved it on by saying I was still trying to understand it. Up until that point the instructor had not allowed the others to chicken out of sharing their experiences with the group, but with the faintest smile on her face that only a handful of very perceptive people in the room noticed, she moved on to the others waiting to share their story.

Struggling for the remainder of the class to get my body's energy back to normal and my temperature down, I was largely unaware of what the instructor had to say. It was with some relief that I greeted the class ending, because quite a few people were turning around and staring at me.

As the class left the room, the woman sitting next to me turned and asked me where the energy I was radiating came from. I just shrugged my shoulders without saying a word, but on my way out of the room the instructor cut me off and asked me to wait until she was finished with everybody else. Then she came over and said,

"Well!" I said, "Well what?" But there was no fooling this lady because she then told me what I found during my trip.

She was a darn good clairvoyant and could see most people's energy, so she could easily plug into mine.

Since she knew what I had experienced, I asked her to explain what happened because I did not really understand it. To cut a long story short, when people meditate they usually slow down or lower their vibration rate (frequency), and that is a form of self hypnosis and not meditation. That is why I had problems trying to meditate: my frequency would not come down. But true meditation is getting in touch with higher energies or dimensions, so it is all about raising one's vibration rate. With this method, I had made contact with the overall energy that could be called the God force or the pure love frequency. She said that some Eastern teachers would say I had found my real self.

"How many people can find this?" I asked.

"Oh, about one or two a year in my classes," she said. I just looked at her in disbelief. She smiled and gave me a big hug and said I would be okay because I knew what was going on and I had no need to worry. I wished I did know, but at that time, I was so out of it that I just wandered around the gardens for the rest of the afternoon.

Going out to meet this energy - or the highest aspect of myself - was a bit like the time that the energy spike hit me when I was lying in bed trying to be mad at Denise. This was the first time I had been able to control my state of consciousness, however slightly, and move it into or out of different levels of reality. It is really quite a frightening experience to consciously, in a fully awakened state, experience other realities like this.

Through my studies since then I have learned that there are many levels of frequencies with their own conscious reality that stretch between our earthly level and that of the pure energy state that I experienced. It is apparently due to the frequency at which my body resonates that as soon as I allow it, my consciousness moves straight to the pure energy frequency, bypassing all other levels. With practice, I have been able to move my awareness to this level at will, and as a result I now live totally without fear and with complete knowing that life never ends, it just changes frequency.

Many psychics are able to plug into many of the frequencies between the latter two levels, and that is where they get brain waves or other inspirational thoughts. Many musicians and artists also receive their inspiration from these outer levels of existence. That is because we are all connected to the All That Is.

Western culture developed an almost totally closed mind to anything other than the physical frequency because of the entrenched attitudes imposed upon us by the western churches and lodges to keep us from knowing the truth and thus undermine their control over us as a society. If we really understood what is out there, we would start to enjoy this earth a lot more and be a darn sight more caring about it. Of course, that would not suit the industrialist or the world's money barons, to say nothing of the oil and chemical conglomerates.

You see, our system has conned us all into going hell-for-leather down this materialistic path which can never give us any lasting fulfilment, as I discovered the hard way. If all of us understood what really existed out there, and that each of us can be part of and fully experience it and use that knowledge for each other's benefit, there would be no need for the economic slavery that has overtaken this world.

Of course, this could lead to a very different system of government and way of doing things; we would not need to burn polluting oil to power our transport because there is more than enough energy contained in our own reality to transport ourselves anywhere at any time. This has been demonstrated by many races in published, independent literature, and was also amply shown to us two thousand years ago by Jesus, who is reported as saying that we all could do all that he had done and more.

I personally have experienced some of the things he was talking about, and hardly a week goes by without my understanding increasing (and probably more importantly my acceptance increasing, which has the effect of leapfrogging great gains in what I know and can do). The most thrilling thing for me is that we all can do these things, we can all know the reality of our higher levels, and we can all play in the cosmos - at will. It is all there for us, every God-created bit of it. We just have to let go of our preconceived and ingrained attitudes and concepts.

Abilities and power like this are not beyond scientific possibility, and even now we can measure such things as ultrahigh frequencies. Perhaps complex physical talents that we may have believed to be a bit occult may someday be as definable as electricity or microwaves are today. Science already knows that every object in existence, every definable bit of matter - is energy, and that energy is a measurable field.

The excitement comes when we realize that we are made of the same stuff, and that leads us to the realization that we must be able to communicate with all that there is. And we jolly well can; just believe it. It is your reality, your right, your cosmos. But of course, it is not that easy to believe all this, and at that time, my beliefs were not much different from anybody else's. Besides having rather strange things happen to me, I had come to the conclusion that I was being helped along a path of learning, and I had accepted that, even if I had no idea where it was taking me.

I had made a decision not to leave the farm and Denise until she had her life sorted out, and I believed that she would find somebody and fall in love again. I had made an agreement with my guides that they would help her - well it was more like an ultimatum, really (I do that and get away with it most of the time, but then I have always been told I am a stubborn so-and-so).

Well, it happened! Denise had started to go to dance classes and had met this really nice man who had become her dance partner. Soon she started to have an incredibly powerful feeling for him. I laughed and gave her a big hug when she told me how she felt and told her to go for it and not to deny her feelings. Poor Denise, she never thought that she could fall in love again, but here she was, all smitten and forgetful. It was so good to see. She was having fun and enjoying herself and falling in love more each day.

I remember the day very clearly; I had been out on the farm working. It was late summer, but the evenings were still long. I had come in at about 9 p.m., just at dark. Denise and her man were sitting at the kitchen table holding hands, the kids were in the lounge, absorbed by the TV, and as I came in I said, "Hi, you two."

Denise looked around, her face aglow like only those who are in love, and Murray got up and gave me a big hug. Then he said,

"I am here to look after Denise and the kids. You go and do what you have to out in the world."

We looked long and deep at each other and each of us knew there was nothing more to be said. There was complete understanding at a soul level, even if neither of us knew what was going to happen to our lives on a physical level.

Spring arrived with farm product prices looking good, so we decided to put more effort into the farm sale. We received a very good offer on all the cows, so we sold the lot, put all the remaining machinery up for auction and hoped like hell we would sell the farm before too long. I moved out into the second house on the farm to give Denise and Murray some space, and as there were no cows to milk, I really concentrated on working at the clinic.

It was during a rare break between clients that I picked up a magazine and was drawn to an ad (rather, the ad popped right out and hit me in the eyes) about a trip to the U.S. with stops in L.A. and then a week in Sedona, Arizona. A rush of energy went up my back, my neck hairs stood up and I tingled all over.

As I reached forward to pick up the phone to call the number on the ad, I remember thinking, here we go again, doing things without conscious choice. Somebody wants me to go to Sedona, wherever that is.

A female voice answered the phone and I said I wanted to book a place on the trip to the U.S. that was advertised. "Fine," she said, and proceeded to take my name etc. She said she would send me the itinerary, and to secure my place I would need to send her a deposit for the airfare. I said that my mind was already made up and I would send her the check that night.

Putting down the phone, I went into see Kath, my receptionist, "I'm off to the U.S." Her typewriter fell silent and she looked up at me.

"When?" she asked.

"Oops" I replied, "I wonder if it's on the ad?" I ran back to my office and got the magazine. "Here, that's where I'm going, to Sedona. Blimey the tour leaves next month!"

"And what about the clinic?" Kath asked.

"I guess we'll have to close it," I replied.

"Why, how long will you be away?" Her voice trailed off as she read the ad, "Oh it's only for three-and-a-half weeks. You'll be back."

"No," I replied, "I think, my dear Kath, I won't be back. I don't know why or how, but I feel that I will be spending some time in the U.S."

Poor old Kath, her one joy in life was the feeling of self-worth that she gained by being at the clinic. I had given her a set of keys so she could come in before I arrived and get everything tidy and ready. She took tremendous pride in the way everything looked. The dear old soul had a heart of gold and just lived for her "job" with me at the clinic.

I could see the tears well up in her eyes as the realization of the clinic closing hit her. Then she said something rather strange.

"I always knew that you would be going overseas. You have such a gift to share with people all over the world. The clinic here has only been training for you. Soon, you will be working and teaching many people in lots of countries." She came around from her desk and gave me a big hug. By now tears were running down her face.

"Don't be afraid, you have been chosen to do God's work. Just follow your guidance wherever it leads you. You are blessed more than you'll ever know."

With that, she, left me standing there not knowing what to say. Even Kath seemed to know more about me than I did, I thought as I slowly walked back to my office. I sat for a long time just staring into space, needing to be alone. Jolted back into reality (whatever that is) by hearing Kath talking to my next appointment, I somehow got through the rest of the day.

I remember driving home to the farm that night with feelings of deep contentment. This was the right thing to do, I just knew it. There was no logic in it, because the farm was not sold and I would lose money by walking out on the clinic lease. Would Denise and the kids be okay? Even with all that, it felt like this was what I just had to do. Was this what all the events over the last few years, all the trauma, droughts, money problems, the healing and energy experiences were all about, just to get me to let go of the farm and my life, so I could fully commit to my path of - I still did not really know what? This was really an act of faith for me.

Dining alone that night in the worker's cottage on the farm, I had the time and space to be very quiet within, to really listen and feel what I needed to do. You know, it is incredible how little time we, and men especially, take just to be quiet and give honor to ourselves by actually listening within (some would say to our guides). We tend to get so caught up and absorbed by what we perceive as our world, our life.

This expanded reality of going in to find my truth and essence was starting to be a very real and accepted part of my life (compared to a few years back, I am now starting to sound like a "sensitive new-age guy" - scary, eh?). But it is true, the world that most of us live in is such a small part of a much bigger whole, and it seems to me that very few men are able to allow themselves to stretch just a little bit and accept that there is more, much more to his earthly existence than work and controlling everything and everybody.

I hope and pray that not every man will be so thickheaded and stubborn as I was and have to go through all the trauma I did, before waking up to this fact. I would not wish that on my worst enemy. But then again, maybe that is the only way we can break out of our past patterns and grow. One thing is for sure, the shit just keeps on coming until we change.

Talking to Denise later that evening, I shared with her how good I felt about going to the U.S. In fact, it was more like a pull. How it would help me in my process I did not know. I had no idea where I would end up, but I knew I just had to go.

One or two people were looking at the farm, so we felt confident we would sell it fairly soon. The weeks leading up to my departure were rather hectic, with tidying up the clinic for its closing and spending hours talking with prospective buyers for the farm and generally sorting everything out.

After the years of struggle to save the farm, we were now negotiating to sell it, and there was almost a feeling of relief. It was as if the time was right; I had no further attachment to it. I needed to be free - free of debt, free of worry and hassle, no more worldly holds on me. That was really it: I did not or could not have anything that would hold me.

Once I made the decision to go to the U.S., it was as if I had turned a corner in my life and all that was important to me was to be free. I wanted to sell or dispose of every bit of the "things" that had cluttered up my life until now. It was like a great spring cleaning of myself and everything around me. It was as if I were clearing out my entire consciousness, from my soul out. I was letting go of everything that was me up to that point in my life.

As if on cue, we received a meaningful offer on the farm, and everything looked good for the sale to go through. Here was twenty years of my life, and I was giving it away. Giving it away was truer than I wanted to admit. Because of the pesticides in the soil and the general condition of the agricultural sector after the change in economic policies, we were getting only as much for the farm as we paid for it.

In effect, all the money we had spent developing it into a high-producing dairy farm went down the drain. The cows were the only thing we made money on, but that profit only helped clear our high debt. But - and it was a big but - we came out of it with all debts paid and a modest amount of cash. We had survived the biggest economic crisis since the Great Depression without going totally belly-up.

It was hard to be aware of my feelings at the time; I think I was more numb than anything. There was no great feeling of loss or sadness, rather quite a sense of relief. Face it, that farm had nearly killed me and Denise with the amount of work and worry we had put into it, and now we were selling it - yes, that was the difference. This was a conscious decision, nobody was forcing us into it. This was our choice, as far as the so-called normal world was concerned. Who knew what or who was pulling the strings from up there somewhere.

The day the big trucks came to collect the cows was by far the most difficult emotionally. These cows were our friends - well, Denise's more than mine. They had been through the whole thing with us, droughts with its lack of feed, and we had asked them to still keep milking, so they gave the flesh off their backs.

In the big drought some of the old girls got so skinny you could almost see through them, and still they would make the twice daily walk to the milking shed and give every thing they could. And for what? You know, in our entire farming life, the biggest single expense in dollars those poor old cows gave the meat off their backs for was interest, yes, to pay the banks their usury tax called interest.

When I look back over my farming years, the thing that caused us the most strife was the interest payments. All the other hassles pale into insignificance when compared to what the banks did to us - no, to the entire country. Loading those cows onto the trucks was hard; in many ways the cows were closer to us than the land was. That certainly was the case for Denise. A tear or two found their way down a weather-beaten face that day, that is for sure.

The cows were gone, the equipment sold, the clinic closed and we had a contract to sell the farm, which would leave Denise with a small nest egg to get herself, Murray and the kids a good house without too much debt.

I was ready to put my backpack on. As I had given Denise all the proceeds from the farm and kept only enough money to last me for the trip, I was for the first time in my life alone, broke and homeless. I had to let go of everything. Inside, I felt good, quite calm, maybe a bit apprehensive, but not at all grief-stricken or in mourning. My life had finished going down one road and now I was turning down a new one. I did not know the road's name, or where it would lead me, but I knew I just had to take it.

For the first time in my life I was running purely on instinct, just following my guidance and going with the flow. It was a hell of a risk for me, but it felt so right that I was almost excited.

The trip to the U.S. was only meant to last for a matter of weeks, but as I boarded the plane on a fine late summer's morning, I had the distinct feeling I would not be seeing these beautiful green islands tucked away in the South Pacific for a much, much longer period of time.

CHAPTER 12
SEDONA, THE FIRST TWO WEEKS

Leaving New Zealand, and all the experiences I had on the plane and in Hawaii, then LA and Bill, I finally arrived at my destination - Sedona.

Having met up with the rest of the tour group at Los Angeles airport, we landed in Flagstaff and were greeted with subzero temperatures and pine trees out of picture post cards, their deep green needles sprinkled with lily-white snow.

Driving down into Oak Creek Canyon with darkness casting its magical shade on the tall pines and towering red rock cliffs, my tiredness was swept aside by my expectation and excitement. Sedona, the name that had ignited a compulsion within me all those weeks ago back in New Zealand.

I could not find Sedona on my map, yet its power called me. From halfway around the world it called, and now we were to meet. What have you in store for me, dear Sedona?

Jolted back to reality as the minibus stopped outside our hotel, I realized I had arrived in a place whose energy was vaguely familiar. As night hid the surrounding beauty, the town itself looked very much out of place in relationship to what I was feeling.

Not wanting to miss any of the daylight the next day, I was soon in bed. My stay in Sedona was meant to last for seven days, and as sleep overtook my fatigued body I had an uncanny feeling that the next week would be rather long.

Awaking to a brilliantly clear day, I was immediately in awe of the magnificence of the surrounding view. This place was grandiose. Rim country at its best, with towering buttes, canyons, pines and colors to inspire the most feeble hearts.

As our little group had a busy schedule, we were soon out exploring the sites. First, was tour of the energy vortices that the area is famous for. Arriving at Bell Rock, some of the ladies in our group were excited and discussing how the energies felt.

What energy? I thought to myself, I do not feel a thing. Okay, I thought, I guess I must not be centered. So I climbed up to what I thought would be a good place, sat down and meditated. Nothing. Not a bloody thing, no feeling, no energy, no change in my body's frequency, just a big fat zero. Blimey, I thought, I must be a bit thick, because people all around me were dancing, moving, swaying and singing, supposedly in response to the so-called energy. Here I was, dead as a dodo.

I guess I felt a bit self-conscious and did not want to let on that I could not feel anything, because when some wide-eyed ecstatic-faced woman said to me,

"Isn't it just *so* wonderful," I answered with a fake smile and a "Yes, just wonderful." As she passed I thought, this place is full of weirdos.

Our next stop was at a medicine wheel that people had built back in a canyon. Now, this medicine wheel was quite an impressive structure. It was about twenty-five yards across with foot-high stone walls on the perimeter and smaller stone walls forming the cross. In the middle, there was a large stone structure about a yard and a half in diameter and about three feet high.

There were about twenty or thirty people there when our small group arrived, and again many of the people were going nuts about the energy they were feeling as they climbed all over it. I walked over to a large rock about ten yards away from the wheel and sat down with a feeling of great sadness.

I just sat there looking at all those tourists who did not have a clue what a medicine wheel was all about. Instead of taking a moment to reflect on the meaning of the shape and form of the structure to understand why the old cultures built things like this, they were too busy clambering over it, "oohing" and "aahing" over some energy they said they were feeling.

They were completely self-absorbed in their own reality, treating the wheel as a plaything, a toy, an object of curiosity, another interesting thing to talk about back home. And let's not forget the million and one photos. O Lord (great spirit), forgive those who know not what they do. My cynicism and slight anger at the goings-on at the medicine wheel came from deep within, a knowing that was easy to access.

You see, a medicine wheel is not just a circle of well placed rocks. It is a physical mark of honor, a recognition of the connectedness of this physical world to the unseen worlds, in many ways not unlike our churches. I wonder how we would react if a crowd of Native Americans came into one of our churches, climbed all over the place, moved things around, went up to the altar and touched everything, made lots of noise and generally behaved in a manner that we would not normally associate with being in a church.

Somebody would very soon call the cops, perhaps the swat team as well. I can just imagine the headlines the next day. "Native protesters hijack church," etc. And yet that is what the people were doing at the medicine wheel, not because of any intention to be disrespectful, but being disrespectful nonetheless because of their ignorance about the meaning of the wheel and lack of natural respect for the powers it represents.

Just like our churches, the medicine wheel is a place of honor, a place for quiet reflection and communication with the spirit world. Being joyful and filled with love and the vitality of our connection with the rest of creation is fine, but honor the structure and the reason it was built.

That was my first day in Sedona, a total let down. Nothing happened to me except becoming quite irritated. I had come all this way, and I had not had any great amazing revelation or insight into the meaning of life.

Climbing into bed that night with a heavy heart and a sadness I did not understand, I prayed that sleep would wipe away my depression. That was about it for the rest of the week, other than one afternoon when our little group hired a mini van and journeyed to the Hopi reservation.

There we observed one of their spring ceremonies, and once again the majority of the visitors had no idea what the Hopi were doing or why (more on this later). Probably the highlight, if you can call it that, was during the drive back to Sedona, when our young driver drove so dangerously that he scared the heck out of us.

Awaking to another cloudless Arizona day, I immediately noticed a difference in my body's energy. Just my bloody luck, I thought. The day I am leaving, things start to happen. As my group was to bus to Las Vegas and then fly back to New Zealand, bag-packing was first on the list, and getting all my things into my backpack was no easy task.

Mission accomplished, I helped some of the others with their bags, and when all were safely stowed on the waiting bus I went up to my room, hoisted my 100 pound plus (well, it felt like it) pack on my back and headed back down.

Down the stairs I went and out through the lobby with every intention of following the others onto the bus. Two steps from the bus, I felt my body stiffen, turn left and walk on up the street. Lord, I thought, not now. I will miss the bus! I tried to turn, but no way. Damn, it is happening again, just like years ago.

I was talking to myself, telling myself to turn around and go back to the bus. With a superhuman effort I sort of half swung myself around just far enough to see the bus pull out onto the street and head up Oak Creek Canyon toward Interstate 40 and Vegas.

"F—," I said out loud. Now what? My body just kept walking past all the tourist shops and headed for the Y (Sedona's main crossroads).

"Okay," I said out loud as I looked skywards, "you guys are obviously in charge, but I will tell you this. I am not going to carry this pack very far, so you had better organize something real quick." At times like that, I always found myself talking out loud. Thank goodness most people drive cars everywhere in the States; I would have been locked up in the loony bin if people heard me.

Down past the post office I went, and as I started up the long hill toward West Sedona the weight of my pack really started to take its toll. Stopping to take off my shirt, I cursed myself for bringing so much stuff with me. It must have been about mid-morning, because the day was starting to get darn hot. As I struggled on up the never-ending hill, I started to talk to whoever would listen.

"Look," I said, "what's with you guys? Is it give-Denie-a-hard-time-day or what? If you don't give me a break soon, I'm going to turn around and head back down this bloody hill."

I almost had to smile, because I had the distinct feeling that my guides answered me back. I heard a voice deep within my consciousness say, "Try it if you want, try it if you want," as if to say to me, "Yeah, sure."

So I said out loud, "Assholes!" and kept walking.

I remember chuckling to myself (I do that when things get serious, and it gets me into heaps of trouble because people always take it the wrong way) as I thought about the predicament I was in. It is one thing to be driven around my own country by some spook with the farm check book in my back pocket, people I knew and places to stay, but this was something else. I did not have a clue where I was going (except up this bloody hill), did not know a soul and had darn little money. I remember thinking it would be a great "once upon a time" story for my grand-kids one day.

With legs about to turn to jelly and shoulders screaming with pain, any humor I might have had about my situation was rapidly leaving home. My God, is that car stopping? Yes, it really is. Thanks guys, I thought as I caught up to where the car had stopped.

A middle-aged woman got out and, talking across the top of the car, said, "You look like you could do with some help."

I am not sure what I said in return, but I am sure that the biggest smile I ever had said it all. Moving off with me blissfully sunk into the seat beside her, she introduced her self as Margaret. I returned the nicety and then she asked me where I had come from. (These Americans must think I talk funny - they always ask me that.)

"New Zealand," I said.

She lit up like a light.

"I've got a son who is in New Zealand right at this moment," she said, "in Opunku..... Opunauk.... oh, it's a such a difficult name to say."

"Opunake," I said.

"Yes, yes that's it," she answered, "do you know it?

I started to chuckle,

"I should," I said, "that's where I was born."

Margaret looked across at me with a half-disbelieving but amazed look. I laughed out loud and said, "True story." I think at that point we both reached out and clasped each others hands. Margaret then reached over into the back seat, picked up a parcel and placed it in my lap.

"Open this for me," she said with a big smile. "It's from Roger, my son. I have just been to the post office to collect it."

I looked closely at the parcel and noticed the New Zealand stamps and a shiver went up my spine as my eyes stopped on the post mark, Opunake. I remember thinking, something is going on here, this is no coincidence. Little did I know, just how much effect this lovely lady, in whose car I was riding, would have on my life. (To those of you who are really observant, you will recall a Margaret in the credits in the front of the book. Yep, that's her, first draft editor.)

A connection was made that hot Arizona day, or rather a reconnection would be more precise. You know, one of those people you meet every so often that you just know you knew, a past-life connection maybe? Well, that is how this felt.

Margaret asked me where I was going, and not wanting to sound stupid by telling her I did not have a clue, I did some quick thinking and said, "The Eye of the Vortex book shop."

I had been told earlier that it was the best metaphysical book shop in town. "Okay," she said, "that is not too far along the road." Arriving at the Eye of the Vortex, I struggled with my pack and finally got it out of Margaret's small car and thanked her profusely.

As she drove off, I paused for a moment as my awareness followed her up the road, then bringing myself back to my predicament, I sat down on the seat outside the shop. There was a packet of smokes sitting there, so I helped myself to one and lit up. I think the last one I'd had was with the young sheep shearer on the plane out of Auckland, so this one really hit the spot.

"Who said you could have one of those?" a female voice said about an inch away from my ear. I jerked away sideways with a hell of a fright.

"Jesus," I said, "don't scare me like that."

"Don't take my smokes then," she said.

I looked up ready to apologize but was met with a grin from ear to ear.

"Have as many as you want," she said before I could get a word out. "You look like you need some. Hi, I'm Jane," she said as she sat down beside me. "Can I have one of those?"

I passed her the packet. "Thanks," she said.

"You're welcome," I answered.

"Cheeky with it, too," she ribbed me.

I let that one go as my mind drifted away into nothingness, enjoying the Camel.

"Talkative today, aren't we?" she said after a long pause. I did not answer.

"I'm a good listener," she went on.

"That's good," I said, "but I'm not talking."

"But you want to."

"How do you know that?"

"People come here for two reasons, to buy books and to talk."

"How do you know I don't want to buy books?"

"Because it's real hard to find the ones you want from outside the shop."

I chuckled to myself and said, "Good point, but I still don't want to talk."

Jane looked at me the way only a woman can, with a "don't give me that shit" look and just waited for me.

"I don't know where to start," I finally said.

"At the beginning is usually a good place," she said as she passed me another smoke and placed her arm around my shoulders.

So I told her my story, what had happened to me over the years, some of the strange things I had experienced, Hawaii, Bill, Margaret etc., how I had been drawn to Sedona and now, being here, how totally lost and alone I felt.

"Hey," she said, "you are not alone, you have already made two friends. That's pretty good for Sedona in one day. Look," she said, "this place is like no other. It either supports you or spits you out in little pieces. When it supports you, you'll find that things fall into place good and quick, but if it doesn't, then the more you try to stay, the more knocked around you get. From what you've said and what I feel, I think you'll be here for longer than you think."

"But I haven't even got anywhere to stay and I can't afford a hotel anymore. I like my creature comforts too much to spend too many nights sleeping under the stars without washing."

"So what can you afford?" Jane asked.

"I don't know, to share a house or apartment, something like that."

"Okay, put that out to the universe and see what your guides and Sedona think about it."

"But how long will that take?"

"Look, you dumb Kiwi, if it's meant to happen, it will. Just have some faith."

We talked for about another half hour or so and then Jane went in and made us both a cup of coffee. While she was in the shop I heard the phone ring and when she came out with the coffees she handed me a piece of paper and said I should check it out when I finished my drink.

"What's this?" I asked, as I took the note from her and read it. It was an address, so I asked Jane what the address was for.

"That phone call was from a lady who lives on the next street. She asked me to put a room-to-let notice on my bulletin board, so I told her that I could do better than that. I would send around a homeless Kiwi."

"You're kidding me. Does this happen often?"

"No to both. It's the first room I've had for the board in about a month. Go on, get going, it's only about five minutes walk up the next street. I'll look after your pack while you check it out."

By nightfall I was settled into a furnished room in a very comfortable home, with two dogs and a wonderful landlady. Fed, watered and tucked up in a good bed, I took time out to thank my guides for the amazing organizing they did that day. The way things had worked out was mind-boggling, and boy, was I grateful. I went to sleep wondering what was in store for me next, but knowing Sedona had accepted me.

Climbing around the buttes and canyons that surround the town, I spent the next day in total bliss. At last I was starting to feel good about being here. The higher I climbed, the more at home I felt. I spent the late afternoon sunning myself on a rock outcrop high above the town.

Arriving back at the house just after dark tired but happy, I treated myself to a long hot bath (the hotel had only showers, which I hate). Just as I was about to fix myself something to eat, there was a knock on the door. Opening it I was confronted by a large, dark-skinned stranger.

He thrust out a massive hand in greeting and said, "I'm Domingo, who are you?"

You do not waste words on niceties, I thought to myself as I hurriedly tried to sum him up. I felt quite okay with his energy, so I said, "I'm Denie. I'm new here and the landlady is not in. How can I help you?"

"You're in the wrong place. You should be in the apartment I'm in and I should be here."

"What do you mean? What's wrong with me being here?" I said, taken aback.

He must have detected a bit of anxiety in my voice, because he said, "Sorry about being abrupt. I'm in a bit of a hurry, I have spoken to your landlady and she doesn't mind if we swap. I'm in a place just the other side of the highway. It's perfect for you. Celia is a good woman and a darn good cook, but it's not for me. She's too young and the little one (Celia had a small child) is always into my paints. I need somewhere quiet with no kids."

"What do you do?" I asked, starting to feel quite comfortable with this upfront dude.

"I'm an artist," he said, "I paint designer clothes."

I found out later that Domingo had had a meal at the diner where Donna (my landlady) worked, and that is where this apartment swap had been sorted out. Domingo had rushed around to see if I would go along with it.

He then asked me if he could take me and introduce me to Celia, so I said, "Okay."

Arriving at Celia's, we had an instant rapport with each other. Her place was every bit as nice as Donna's and the rent was the same, so I decided to the swap there and then. On the drive back, I asked Domingo how he knew I would feel happy to move in with Celia.

"Oh," he said, "I just know these things. I knew when I moved in that it wasn't right, so I asked my guides to help me sort something else out. Today when I was having a meal, I knew I had to ask Donna if she knew of any rooms to let. She said that I was one day too late, because she'd just rented hers out. Then I asked her if she would mind if you and I swapped. It was okay by her, so I came around to see you."

Well, I thought, this is a guy I could get along with. There is obviously a lot more to him than meets the eye.

Arriving back at Donna's place, Domingo asked me what I was doing for the next few days.

"Nothing much," I said, "just a bit of climbing and exploring the area."

He paused as if in deep thought for a moment, then said, "I'm driving down to Texas tomorrow to pick up some more clothes from the manufacturers. Why don't you come with me?"

"God, I'd love to," I said, "but I haven't the money for a trip like that."

"That's okay," he said, "it won't cost much more for you to come. I'll pay and it will be good to have some company. Anyhow, you need to see a bit more of the country while you're here."

Blimey, I thought, I am not one to look a gift horse in the mouth. So I said I would go.

"Good," he said, "I'll pick you up at 8:30. Be ready."

"Yes sir," I answered as I got out of his van.

Feeling extremely famished, I realized I still had not eaten, so I rummaged around in Donna's fridge, found some bread and cheese and made myself a cup of coffee.

Stretching out on the carpet, I went over the events of the last couple of days. Bloody hell, I thought, talk about jumping out of the frying pan and into the fire. I must be nuts going on a big trip with a black artist dude I did not know from a bar of soap.

Then I ran my mind over the events since my guides made sure I did not leave Sedona: being unable to get on the bus; nearly dying walking up that bloody hill on a hot morning with my heavy pack; getting a lift from Margaret; then meeting Jane and having my head straightened out; being offered a place to stay, and now this trip.

"Well," I said to myself, "I do not know where all this is leading me, but you know the rules. Keep following the synchronicities and you might find out. Go with the flow, this is how life is meant to be lived. Yeah," I said jokingly to myself, "this is how you can bloody well get yourself killed too."

"Oh well," I said out loud, "if you guys upstairs are preparing me for something, it's your job to keep me alive, so I'm not going to worry about it." Finishing off the last bite of bread, I felt glad about not staying at Donna's house.

She was such a health nut. I hate that whole bran bread. I got up and went to bed.

Hearing a horn blast, I looked at my watch, 8:31. Late, I chuckled to myself as I closed the house door behind me.

"G'day mate, how's it today?" I asked as I clambered into Domingo's van.

"Great," he answered. "This is Iris," motioning to the van.

"Good morning, Iris," I said, patting the dashboard.

"She's a good van. She takes me all over the country, never lets me down," Domingo said with obvious feeling. "People think cars are just things. They're not, they are alive, just like us. Treat them right and they will treat you right."

"Got no argument with me on that one," I said as I pulled both arm rests down and settled into the big, comfy seat. This is going to be interesting, I thought to myself as we headed south out of Sedona. Other than small talk nothing much was said for about the next two hours or so, and then Domingo started to tell me about his life.

He was an interesting character, incredibly spiritual. He had a wide understanding of the way things worked metaphysically. He told me that his young years were spent with his aunt, a Navaho wise one, as he put it, and that he tried to live his life by obeying the laws of the universe that she had taught him.

Many of the things he said corresponded with what Bill had told me in L.A., and made lots of sense. He told me that for the last 20 years he had traveled to every city and most towns in the country. He had no permanent home other than his van and stayed nearly every night in a different motel.

Every three months or so he would head back to some friends in Texas who had a clothes manufacturing business. There he would stock up on fancy designer jean jackets and skirts, then spend the rest of the time decorating them with his painted designs and selling them to high-priced boutiques and the like all round the country.

He did not know how long he was going to stay in Sedona, but he had many friends there and sold lots of his jackets in the tourist shops. I had the feeling as we drove south into the desert that I was going to find out lots about Domingo and learn even more for myself over the next few days.

Approaching nightfall on the second day, we arrived at our destination, and Domingo spent the evening on the phone talking business.

The next day, loaded with jackets and skirts, we headed back north. As we approached a town, Domingo asked me if I had a pair of cowboy boots. I did not, and Domingo said, "every man needed a pair," so he pulled into a factory shop and got me fitted with a pair. He would not let me help pay for them.

"This is my gift to you," he said when I offered to pay for them.

Next he told me that I needed some better jeans and some real American shirts. By the end of the day I was looking like a real cool dude. He was amazing; he would not take no for an answer, insisting on paying for the lot.

"Look," he said, "I got what I wanted at less cost than I'd figured, so I'm not really spending anything on you; you're just getting what I didn't spend on my own stuff. This way you get some cool gear and I haven't spent any more than I had expected."

I gave up arguing after that and just asked that he be blessed. I was coming to the conclusion that if there ever was a saint in disguise, then Domingo must be it. As I bedded down in a Motel Six that night, there was no way I could have known just how big this man's heart really was. I was in for some surprises very soon.

Domingo spent a good part of the night painting his designs on the clothes he had gotten in Texas, so it was well into the morning before we were on the road heading north again. Neither of us seemed to be talkative, so the day passed with each of us in our own thoughts. It was after dark when Domingo finally pulled Iris into a motel deep in the heart of a big city.

At the time I thought it a bit strange, because we usually stayed close to the freeway. Finishing our meal at a nearby restaurant, it must have been all of 11:00 p.m. and instead of driving back to the motel, Domingo wheeled Iris deeper into the bowels of the city. As Iris was gently brought to a stop, I realized we were in the midst of a railway marshaling yard.

"You keep an eye on Iris," Domingo said as he climbed out.

"Where are you going?" I asked.

"You'll see," he said as he disappeared into the darkness.

About fifteen to twenty minutes went by, then the side door of the van was suddenly slid open.

To my astonishment there stood two scruffy, dirty young girls, whose age could not have been more than eleven or twelve. Domingo said only one word, "In," and the two of them shot onto the floor of the van and Domingo disappeared into the darkness again.

Another five minutes and he arrived with someone else, this time a boy of similar age. Not a word was spoken by anybody as we traveled back to the motel. I looked around at our strange cargo. In all my life I had never seen such a scared looking group of kids.

Arriving back at the motel Domingo had the kids shower, girls first. As each one finished he handed them a large clean T-shirt to put on. After they were cleaned up, he made them wash their underwear and hung them up to dry.

The only words spoken were the one- or two-word instructions that Domingo gave. He then got a piece of paper and asked each one their name, where they came from and their parents' phone number. He then bundled up all their dirty clothes and left the unit.

I did not know what to do, so I tried some small talk, which was not very successful. I think the kids were still in shock from having Domingo pull them out of the freight wagons they were sleeping in (I am damn sure I would have been if a big black guy like him had grabbed me in the middle of the night).

It was about half an hour before Domingo returned. He said to the kids, "Okay you lot, your parents know that you are here and that you are safe and well. We will talk about what you want to do in the morning. Now get some sleep."

Awakened by hushed voices I saw Domingo sitting on the floor with the three kids. The hard, overpowering manner he had the night before was gone, and in its place was this gentle, kind, loving man. I have never seen anything like it. I sat there listening to him give those kids a talking to that they would never forget.

He spoke with so much love, so much gentleness, that they all had tears in their eyes. He was telling them about love, how important they were, how important they were to God, how much they were loved, how this was no way to live their lives. You could see that he was touching them with his heart, with his love - and boy, those kids responded.

He must have talked to them for at least an hour, and when he finished he asked each one what they wanted to do. One by one they said they wanted to go home.

Domingo left the unit, and while he was gone the motel owner's wife delivered their now-clean clothes to our room. I figured that this was not the first time Domingo had collected up a bunch of runaways and brought them back to this motel, cleaned them up and sent them home.

Domingo arrived back soon after with pizzas all round and we all ate our fill. The change in the kids was dramatic. Now they were talkative and behaving like normal kids. The girls even cried while they talked about the things that were important to them at home, things and friends that soon they would be reunited with.

Talking with them, I found out that one of them had been away from home for nine months without any contact and the others three to five months.

Leaving the motel, Domingo drove us all to the airport and bought them tickets home, leaving them in the care of the airline staff as unaccompanied minors.

We resumed our journey, not talking much for awhile. What was there to say? That was what the guy did; he found runaway kids, gave them some love, shared his heart with them and sent them on their way.

I had witnessed something very special, I learned the meaning of what Native American elders would call honor. Treat everybody and everything without judgment and with love - that is honor. Domingo had shared everything he had with those kids - his home, his food, his clothes, his money - all totally without judgment. He never once asked them why they had run away. He just gave them love and hope, and he honored them as a part of himself. In their time of need, he shared of himself.

What happened next brought home to me what Domingo and Bill had told me about the meaning of honor. When you come from a position of honor, the universe will honor you by abundantly supplying all your needs.

Later that day, we reached Phoenix and Domingo left the interstate to head for Scottsdale, a very wealthy area. Driving deep into real money country, we stopped outside what looked like a mansion. Domingo selected three of his painted garments from the back of the van and disappeared into the house. I had not even finished my first smoke when he appeared at the front door accompanied by the most impeccably dressed woman, in her mid-thirties.

They talked as dear friends do, and then she gave Domingo the most sensuous, loving hug you could imagine and waved him farewell. As we drove off, I said, "You sold all three of them." He nodded.

"How much?" I asked. "A couple of hundred each?"

He shook his head.

"What, more?"

He nodded.

"Still in three figures?"

He shook his head.

"You're kidding me!"

He shook his head again. "Four figures, each" I gasped.

Domingo looked across at me and said, "She's a good person. She likes to wear things that nobody else has, I see her maybe once a year, a good heart."

And that was it.

When Domingo did not want to talk any more, he didn't, so we drove on in silence. But I had lots to think about, what he had done for those kids and how much money and time he had spent, and how less than a day later he had been repaid many, many times over.

I remember Domingo saying to me that the more you try to own and control things in life, the harder life becomes. The secret is to treat everything with honor, and the universe will treat you the same. He said that you can have anything you want as long as you are prepared to give it all back. As soon as you think you own it, you are heading for problems. To live life the Native American way is to be free, to neither own any part of life or have life own you.

When I look around at our society, I see everybody trapped in work, the money game, possessions. Face it, everybody is out there working their butts off to own things, then working even harder to keep them. Are they free? No way. The more they try to own and control, the more owned and controlled they become.

Most of our society is in a straitjacket of work, money and a closed mentality with no place to go. Very few people have learned the secret of freedom. You see, being free comes from the heart; you put heart energy into everything you do and remain nonjudgmental in all things.

If you try to own and control things, that is the energy you put out. Since you are transmitting that frequency, that is what must manifest for you. You will become owned and controlled. That is the law of karma; or, in Christian terms, what you sow, so shall you reap. It is a basic law of the cosmos, the law of energy. All energy comes back to its point of generation; the circuit must be complete. That is natural law.

Therefore, what you transmit is what you experience. Think about that the next time you want to "own" something, or else do not bitch about life owning you. Being with Domingo that week taught me a good lesson, the lesson of honor, and when you share yourself with the universe in heartfelt love, the universe will share itself with you in abundance.

Domingo was the freest man I had ever met. Nobody ever told him what to do, when to do it or how. If he wanted to sit in the mountains for a week, he did it; if he wanted to go some place, he went, and the whole time he was treating everybody and everything with honor, living in his heart and transmitting unconditional love. And, of course, that is the only thing that came back to him, in many, many ways.

During the drive back to Sedona we covered lots of topics and several times Domingo gave me an insight into my life. He told me that I was being readied for the time when I would use all the wisdom I had gained in teaching many, many others the importance of honor.

It was during one of his rather deep, thought-provoking monologues that he suddenly pulled Iris over to the side of the road and stopped. He clambered into the back, located a much-traveled bag and rummaged through it, muttering to himself as he looked for something.

I thought it was quite amusing that one minute he was driving down the highway at seventy miles an hour and giving me profound insights into spirit, and the next minute he had stopped dead and there was only muttering to be heard as he rummaged around.

It is a crazy world, I thought. I did not have a clue what he was after, or why it was so important at this very minute, but I had learned not to question Domingo. The things he did usually had a darn good reason that sooner or later I would see.

"Good, it's still here," I heard him say as he clambered out from under the racks of clothing hanging across the back of the van. Settling down into the driver's seat, he held up a small hide bag that was tied at the top with colorful braided cotton twine, with a small feather held by the knot. "I have to give you this," he said.

"Why?"

"Because it's yours, that's why." He held up his hand to stop me from saying more, and muttered something about me always asking questions and talking too much instead of listening.

Undoing the knot, he tipped the bag upside down and I gave a low whistle as the most magnificent silver ring fell out onto his hand.

Domingo picked it up with slow deliberate movements, paused and spoke a small Indian ceremony over it, then reached over and grasped my right hand, still softly speaking the ceremonial words as he slid it onto my ring finger. When it got to my knuckle it stuck. Domingo's voice increased in intensity and he gave the ring a slight twist - on it slipped, a perfect fit.

I sat there spellbound. The hairs on my back and neck bristled as an energy flooded into my body and filled my chest and heart with a wonderful, gentle love. No, it was more than that: I felt deeply honored. I looked at Domingo, unable to say a word. Tears of gratitude crept from my damp eyes and inched slowly down my face. We sat there, each of us feeling the sacredness of that special moment.

Domingo held my hand and said,

"Brother, thank you." I knew enough this time to keep silent, so I just sat there and cried.

As we began travelling again and would soon be back in Sedona, I asked him to tell me about the ring.

"Many years ago - it must have been seven or eight - I went back to the place where I was taught as a boy for the funeral of my Auntie. There, during one of the ceremonies held to ensure that the old knowledge was not lost, I was presented with that ring. I was told I had to be its guardian, for the time would come when I would meet the person it belonged to. When this happened, I would be informed by the old ones, and through me, they would present the ring to the honored one, one of our white brothers. So I only did what I was told. It is yours, it always has been, but only now have you come to collect it, only now do you have the wisdom that entitles you to wear it. You have been blessed."

That was it. He never said another word during the rest of the drive into Sedona. I, on the other hand, had millions of questions but knew not to ask, so I looked over my new piece of jewelry. Most rings are made with a round band, but my fingers are not round and rings have never felt right on me. But this felt right. Its solid silver double band was exactly the shape of my finger; the fit was unbelievable.

Truly, had it been custom-made in a silversmith's shop, it could not have fit more perfectly. It was uncanny. I looked at it for a very long time, and to this day it has been off my finger only five or six times, and then only for short moments.

We arrived back in Sedona on the anniversary of the second week of my arrival. After switching apartments, I only saw Domingo periodically. In the years since then, whenever I am in the States, I sometimes catch up on his whereabouts, and still find him painting incredible things on clothes for those who want that little bit extra - and no doubt still rescuing runaway kids.

As for me, well, I am still wearing the ring, and as each year goes by, I realize even more the gift he shared with me - the gift of love, the gift of understanding and the gift of showing me what honor really is. With the passing of each year, I have gained ever more insights from his words of wisdom, and I hope and pray that maybe one day I will be able to pass on to others that very same gift.

CHAPTER 13
SEDONA, THE FOLLOWING MONTHS

Settling into Celia's place was easy, and for the next couple of weeks I spent a lot of time walking, climbing and just generally being alone. My days spent up in the hills were very special to me, because for the first time in my life I did not have anything that needed my attention. No cows to milk, no farm to worry about, no bills to pay, nothing, just glorious nothing.

I allowed my mind to go over my experiences with Bill and Domingo, sorting out everything that had happened, and letting things cook a while. I was able to get my head together and convince myself that all the things that were happening to me were quite all right. They were in my highest and best interest and that the best thing I could do was learn as much as I could, gain as much insight and understanding of everything I came into contact with, no matter how bizarre it might seem at the time.

I also had to convince myself that it was all right to stay, because it was hard to get over the reminder that my airline ticket said I was not meant to be there. I kept telling myself that there was nothing back in New Zealand that I was needed for. I had closed the clinic, sold the farm, Denise and the kids were with Murray, so why not stay?

It was a chance that might never come again. I was finding it hard to change the pattern of a lifetime and feel comfortable at having no responsibilities.

It was a weird feeling to go through that sort of change, a lot of strong feelings one way, then the other. Change is hard to experience in the best of times, and I was being forced to accept change on many different fronts and levels all at the same time. If I could get used to this, I would never again be concerned about any change that happened my life, or, in fact, any change that occurred around me. I felt like I was being conditioned to become bombproof.

Everything that had been important to me was gone from my life - everything. I was on my own and learning to be comfortable with myself. I knew that not many people have the ability to feel comfortable when they are truly alone, but I had not realized how difficult it would be until I went through it myself. All sorts of alarming thoughts went through my mind and it took a bit of time to sort out my true feelings from the ones that ego used to trick me into believing: I cannot survive without money; I am a failure if I cannot afford a good car, etc.

I thought I had long since dealt with a lot of it, but being really alone for the first time made it seem almost like I had to start over. This letting go of everything was happening at the same time as all these new events were adding some spiritual or energy activation into my life. I was getting a double whammy.

The hardest thing to come to terms with was my constant feeling that I had let my three kids down, that I had been a failure. Not returning from what was supposed to be a three-week trip was bad enough, but to add that to their having to leave the farm where they had spent their lives really got to me. How can you take away a kid's home?

The farm was as much theirs as it was mine. They had invested their work, emotion, love and heartbreak as much as any of us, and now it was gone because of me. I had taken their home away, I had taken their Dad away. I must be a selfish, low-down, asshole - and for what? I was not out there saving the world or doing something important.

The love I felt for my kids, the pain of not being able to be there for them, or share my love with them would at times overwhelm me. Tears of utter despair and loneliness would consume me. What the hell was I doing here, why was I here? There were no answers, only emptiness, only tears and more tears.

How would my kids ever understand? Would I ever understand? Where were the deep urges that controlled me coming from? Why couldn't I just have a normal life with my kids like everybody else? What was the purpose of all the things that were happening to me? I had no idea.

The only thing that I knew for sure was that I was powerless to stop the process. I was on a trip and there was no way off. Alone, scared and on an emotional roller coaster, I knew I had to go through this by myself; there was no other way. Domingo was there to rescue runaway kids, but who was there to rescue runaway Dads?

Days turned into weeks and weeks into months as I struggled with my pain and self-worthlessness. Some days I would feel good and others I spent in the pits of despair. Sedona was cleaning me out and putting me through the wringer. I hoped and prayed that I would come through in one piece.

Running low on money, I was having to face the prospect of going back to New Zealand, but something, some urge or guidance had other ideas. I had seen a sign that was advertising a lecture by a well-known Indian speaker and writer that I just had to attend.

Arriving at the lecture hall after having spent the day climbing, and not really being able to afford the admission, I begged the door lady to let me in for half price. The lecture was a bit boring and not hearing anything I had not heard before, I was wondering why I had felt the need to be there when who should I run into during a drink break, but Margaret, the one who had rescued me walking up that hill.

"Hi, you still in town?"

"Not for long, I'm all but out of money."

"Would you like to earn some?"

"Sure, but how?"

"Wait here," and she disappeared for a minute or two.

"It's all organized," she said on her return. "I have rung my boss and she said you can work all weekend as we are snowed under and could do with the help."

"Great! Where do I go?" I asked. Margaret gave the address and explained what I was to do.

The next morning I arrived at the building and was shown the job and left to it. Apparently, they had been so busy that everybody had worked many weekends and this was their first weekend off, so I had the place to myself.

The task was not too difficult, and I soon got into a rhythm and just kept going. I worked late into the night and the next day I did the same. I started early the next morning, Monday, and by the time the boss arrived I had finished the job. She took one look at how much I had achieved and said, "You're hired!"

That was it. I had a job, and more importantly, money. Sedona was not finished with me yet. Able to keep body and soul together with a little left over, I attended many workshops, channelings and lectures that Sedona OD's on. I was not learning anything new, but the continual reinforcement of what I did know was helping me to put everything into perspective.

Slowly, I was able to smooth out the crazy emotional swings and accept everything that was happening. I had not done any healing since I had closed down the clinic back in New Zealand as I was too occupied in sorting myself out. Anyway, I did not want to work on somebody else's energy system until I felt centered in my own, and there was no chance of that while I was going through my emotional mine field. I just left it to my guides to start the healings when I was ready. (That was the theory, anyhow, and like all theories, things often happen to shoot holes in them.)

Arriving at work one Monday morning the boss came rushing out back to where I was working and said, "Quick, come with me. You're needed."

"Okay," I said, "what do you want me to do?"

"No, no, not here. You have to go and help Elsa [Elsa was one of my coworkers]. She has injured her back and hasn't been able to move for two days."

"That sounds serious. Why don't you call a doctor?" She swung around and gave me a frustrated look.

"The poor girl needs help, not a week in hospital. You're the healer; just go and fix her. Here," she said as she thrust some keys and a piece of paper into my hand. "Take my car to this address."

There was no arguing with the woman, so I took the car keys and left. Driving over to Elsa's place I thought, I will have a look at her, she has probably slipped a disk or something. I can help her into the car and take her to a doctor.

I was in total denial of my own ability. I had fixed dozens of backs at home; in fact, I had quite a reputation in the farming community for getting them right. But I was a failure, remember, so how could I help anybody?

Pulling the car to a stop outside Elsa's house, I felt a wave of anxiety ripple through me. Hell, I thought, somebody is turning me on already. "Scram, you guys," I said out loud, "I don't want this. I'm not ready."

Letting myself into Elsa's apartment, I found her lying on her back in a jumble of bedding and pillows.

"You look a mess," I said. (Charming farm boy bedside manner, eh?)

The poor girl tried to laugh but winced in pain instead.

"Don't make me laugh," she said, "it hurts too much." (Elsa always knew how to take my sick humor.)

"Sorry," I said, chuckling, "but a bedroom looks a lot tidier if the bed is made at least once a week."

"Asshole," she said as she struggled to throw a pillow at me. "You going to help me, or stand there all day and give me a hard time?"

"Well, at least you can't hit me when you're like that."

"You'll keep."

"Promises, promises."

By this time I had knelt down beside her and was allowing my energy to focus in on her back. As I did I felt my frequency change, and it was as if another part of my beingness was manifesting. For the first time in a long while, I started to feel centered and alive. I felt my body rapidly increase in heat and felt the familiar tingling develop in my hands.

As I moved my hands into Elsa's aura, her entire energy matrix became visible to my consciousness, and I brought my awareness to her spine, each vertebra in turn showed itself to my vision with total clarity as I passed my hand down the length of her body. I remember thinking, this is better than a MRI scan. By this time my hands were on fire, like the time Bill had turned my body on.

I told Elsa that there was not a thing wrong with any of the mechanical parts of her spine, but I could see very clearly that the energy in the muscles was extremely congested and that the muscles had gone into spasm due to a chronic lack of energy flow. I told her to hang in there, because there might be a bit of pain. I brought my focus onto the energy fields around those muscles and let the energy flow out of my hands.

Looking at her face to see if she was okay, I noticed that she had her teeth clenched and an I-cannot-take-much more look about her, so I said.

"Hang in there, girl, you can do this." The energy was pulsing through my body so intensely that my arms shook.

"Jesus," Elsa said in pain, "this is incredible, I can feel every muscle. They are moving and twitching and jerking into place." She shook her head in disbelief, "I can feel everything. This is weird."

I just chuckled and said that if she thought the feeling was incredible for her, she should be in my body and then she would know what incredible really was. My hands, only inches above her body slowly moved downwards, over her pelvis to her legs. As they hovered over the muscles in the upper legs, her legs gave a jerk and a few twitches, then her body let go and relaxed.

It was an amazing thing to watch. I could see every cell liven up and glow as the energy circuits were reconnected and the energy started to flow.

"Wow," she exclaimed, "that's amazing. The pain has just gone; my back feels free. Hey, I can move!" She tried to sit up.

"No!" I yelled, "not yet."

"But it doesn't hurt," she protested, and sat bolt upright with a big smile on her face. "See, I can move, and it doesn't hurt anymore."

I just shook my head and said, "Bloody woman, you can never be told!"

After that I got behind her to feed energy directly into her back and then went around to her legs, sending energy right up through her body to make sure all the circuits were working. As I did this, she sat there wide-eyed looking at her legs in astonishment.

"I can feel a river of energy flowing right up through my body," she said as she fell back on the bed in total bliss, the energy now flowing unhindered through her body.

I have always been able to tell when a person's body is fully charged, because the energy would stop flowing through me. So I kept my hands at her feet until that happened. When I felt my body shut down, I thankfully sank down beside her on the bed with sweat dripping off me.

"That was intense," I said.

We looked at each other and burst out laughing.

"Nobody will believe this; hell I don't even believe it. I could feel everything! The muscles were just letting go, and I could feel the bones moving. There was so much movement. And now my body feels loose, alive," Elsa said as she stretched her hands up in joy.

I got up off the bed and Elsa rolled over, got to her knees, stretched, and stood up. She moved her body back and forth and then bent over and touched her toes. She looked at me and said.

"Do you realize this is the first time I've been able to get up off this bed for two days and two nights? And now I can move every part of my body! And you've been here only about half an hour. I don't believe this is happening!"

Then she came over to me and gave me a great big hug and kiss.

"Yep," I said, "pretty weird stuff, eh? The Indians call it powerful medicine."

We burst out laughing again. I took one last scan of her energy and said that a bit of leg massage would help to make sure the muscle cells kept working, and that she should take it easy because there might be a little tenderness, but that usually went away in about twelve hours or so. I looked at my watch and said.

"I'd better get back to work." We squeezed each other's hands in knowing thanks and I left.

Driving back to work I could not help thinking that the emotional cleansing I had been going through, plus all the things that Bill had done to my body, plus the insights and wisdom Domingo had shared with me, must have made a big difference. I had never been able to see the energy so clearly or had such third-eye clarity of the inside of the body.

My body was still buzzing when I arrived back at work so I sat in the car for a few minutes. I offered a wee prayer of thanks and honored the understanding of the purpose of why I had been guided to come on this trip. I had taken a quantum leap in my ability to perceive energy, and was starting to accept that nothing happens by chance. I figured I had better stop fighting myself and accept a few things. Yep, Sedona was doing her thing on me, whether I liked it or not.

I remember laughing at myself later that day when I thought about how I went to Elsa's place, totally believing that I was not going to do a thing to her, and then remembered how my body had moved into healing mode as if it were the most natural thing in the world. I was sure the real problem had been my two completely different realities and personalities and the continual switching between them.

The resulting changes in my body's frequency had apparently been causing my emotional upheavals. When I was in one reality, I did not want to accept the other, for whatever reason, and vice versa. I was always trying to keep the two parts of me separate. On one hand I wanted all the things that made me feel successful - lots of money, nice house and a flashy car - and I did not want people to think I was weird. On the other hand, when I was healing, all those things became totally unimportant and were, in fact, a hindrance. Part of me was saying, "I want, I want", the other, "I don't want, I don't want." No wonder I was a blathering idiot emotionally.

I could see the thing I had to do was accept that having lots of money, a nice house and car etc., did not have to impinge on my spirituality. I could feel good about working in the healing arts. I did not have a problem knowing what made me happy, because I was totally happy when I was healing or teaching. I just had to find a way to feel good about me when I was *not* doing it.

The life that I used to live was so far removed from what I wanted to do now and what made me most happy, that finding a way to feel good and to accept all parts of myself as one person, and not trying to separate them, was the thing I had to achieve. I could hear old Bill telling me,

"You have the knowledge, all you need is the time to get some wisdom." Old buddy, I think you might be right, as usual.

With some money coming in, I was able to find myself a used motorbike and on the weekends I would head into the mountains and spend lots of time thinking about all the things that had happened and about where my life was going. I also made friends with an old lady on the Hopi reservation and spent many hours talking with her, learning as much as I could about their understanding of the cosmos and different ceremonies and how that fitted in with my understanding about energy. I was pulling a lot of information together.

On one glorious, hot day I went through an Indian sun ceremony with my Hopi friend, where I was able to perceive a lift in my body's frequency. My ability to perceive and communicate with the unseen world was slowly increasing and my acceptance of its reality was total, even though I never talked about these things to many of my friends. I guess I still wanted people to think I was normal. The trouble was, I had difficulty knowing what normal was - the old me or the new me. I still had trouble fitting that together.

A short time after I had worked on Elsa, I was asked to write a monthly column for a magazine that had a metaphysical leaning, and that was a new experience, as I then had to put some of my understanding of the way the body worked electrically onto paper in a simple, logical manner.

Because Margaret was the editor of the magazine and liked my writing, she encouraged me to put my life story into words (if you find this boring or too far-out, she is the culprit, because without her this would never have been written, bless her soul).

I often think about the amazing synchronicities that shape our lives. If Margaret had not been driving towards West Sedona the very day and minute that I had been walking up that hill, so many things might not have happened. Looking back now, I can see a whole train of events that took place from the time I first met Sue all those years ago back in New Zealand.

What would seem on the surface to be a string of unrelated coincidences was, in fact, a very coordinated series of events, and without them all happening in their precise time frame, and in their precise sequence, none of what you have read would have been possible. I could start at any point in my life and see the logical and planned synchronicities, but let's look at one moment that accelerated my change of direction.

Sitting in my Natural Health clinic and leafing through a small freebie magazine, something or somebody made me focus on the ad for Sedona. The immediate overpowering urge to go on the trip had to come from somewhere, certainly not from my conscious brain; I had no prior thoughts of going on a trip.

And why close the clinic? God forbid, I was only meant to be going for three weeks, and the clinic was a perfectly good, profitable business. So what or who put the "close it" signal in my brain? The decision was so easy that I did not even have to think about it, I just knew that was what I had to do.

Then on the plane across the Pacific, where did the message to go down the back and have a smoke come from? I had not smoked in weeks, and out of three hundred people, how did I end up sitting beside the one person who had the ability to talk (channel) to his long-dead relatives - when he did not even know he could?

I could have picked any of about a dozen empty seats, and the one that I did pick was not even in my aisle, but on the other side of the plane. What or who made me walk around a jumbo 747 in the middle of the night believing I wanted a smoke, when that desire had been gone for weeks, just to sit me next to some young dude so that some spooks could talk to me? Coincidence? I do not think so.

Next was the Whole Life Expo in L.A. There were in excess of ten thousand people who went through the place over the four days. What was it that made Bill run after me, scaring the shit out of me? Bill had told me why he wanted to talk to me, but who put him up to it? One thing I am sure of is that he never would have stood at his stand for four days waiting for some Kiwi farm boy to walk by so he could grab him by the scruff of the neck. Coincidence? No way.

Then Domingo and the way we met, the trip down to Texas and the insights I had on that trip. It would appear that the trip had been in the planning for over seven years so that someone could make sure I would get a silver ring, for what and why? And do not forget Margaret. She told me she never picks up hitchhikers or anybody else, for that matter, yet she was almost forced to stop for me.

Talking about forcing, when I had wanted to get on the bus with the rest of the group "they" (whoever they are) did not even give me a chance to say my good-bye's to the group I had spent two weeks with. My body had been completely taken control of; there was no free will in that incident. A figment of my imagination? I think not. The fact that I ended up in Sedona for the next eight months is living, breathing proof, that is for sure. Someone out there made darn sure I was going to be there and nowhere else.

Was all this just a bunch of coincidences, an overactive imagination? That is a possibility, but I think that I am a reasonably rational sort of person (though there may be those who wonder - poor souls, I forgive you). No, there was something definitely going on here. There were too many synchronicities, a whole series of insights strung together. And I think I know the answer.

CHAPTER 14
PUTTING IT ALL TOGETHER

Finally feeling not guilty about needing to go home, I stayed where I was, not knowing what other insights I would find or when. In fact, life was rather boring in a way. I was saving as much money as possible because my ticket home had expired, and to get home I needed to purchase another one. But, for the time being, I was content to sit it out.

One of the bonuses of having been to nearly every conference and seminar on the new age circuit was that I had sorted out who knew what they were talking about and who did not. When you can have a good look at a person's energy field, it makes it so much easier to sort the chaff from the seed - and believe me, there is a lot of chaff out there. Some of it is quite entertaining and good for a laugh, and some had some relevance.

One of the most knowledgeable people and (to me) one of the few who really knew what he was talking about was Dr. Robert Jaffe. I had first met him in New Zealand when I attended his presentation at the Healers for Peace conference in Hamilton. At the time he was the only person I had met who had an understanding of the body's energy system as I understood and could see it.

During his presentation, he explained the energy he was seeing and it corresponded with what I was seeing. This was a great help because it validated the accuracy of my vision and boosted my confidence.

At the time I left New Zealand I had no idea that Dr. Robert lived and worked out of Sedona. In fact, I only found it out after Margaret had go me the temporary job. It transpired that the place where I was working was where Robert had his printing done. Another coincidence, maybe?

Well, Robert had started a school in energy healing that I would have loved to attend, but the cost was way out of my budget. As it happened, Robert needed some printing done just prior to the school starting, and as we were running way behind, I worked all weekend to finish Robert's job. When he came in on Monday morning to pick up what he thought would be a small part of the job, I presented him with the finished article.

This was the first time I had talked to him since seeing him in New Zealand, so he asked what I was doing working there instead of running a healing clinic or teaching. I told him that I was doing some work on myself and learning a bit more. He then said that I should be attending his school. I told him that I would love to, but there was no way I could afford the cost.

He left, and I thought nothing more about it until on the following Wednesday when he came to the back of the print shop where I was working. He said that his guides had told him to make sure that I came to his school, so he had decided to grant me a full scholarship.

Needless to say, I was flabbergasted. There was no one I would rather train under.

"What about my job?" I asked. "What would the boss say about me leaving so suddenly?"

"That's all taken care of," he answered. "I've just spoken with her and she agrees that you have more important things to do than work here."

Well that was it! I worked out the week and started Dr. Robert's school on the following Monday. There was only one problem with this unexpected turn of events. My income earning came to an abrupt halt. Normally I would have been extremely worried about this but I did not let it concern me at all. I decided to follow the synchronicity and see where it would take me. I was finally learning to go with the flow and not swim against the tide.

The school was brilliant, just what I needed, even though much of the material was rather old hat to me. I was able to see beyond the words and pick up on the understanding behind them. It was as if an avalanche of awareness was taking place and the pennies were finally dropping.

One word, one sentence would trigger a whole series of perceptions and realities for me. Everything was coming together - understanding my life, its why's and how's, my acceptance of who I am, what I was doing here, and most importantly, what I wanted to do with my life. It all became clear.

The struggle I had been having between the two sides of myself became almost laughable. I realized I had been trying to hold onto my past reality. I had thought being in control of things around me was what life was all about, that was the real part of being here on this plane, and that the new part of my life meant that I was going soft or losing control.

I somehow thought that thinking about spiritual things and learning about guides and other dimensions of existence was not really me. It was all right to learn about these things, but they were something else other than me. I was *me*, the man, and these other things were separate. This other reality was too foreign. I could learn to use some of their methods, to totally accept their existence, but that world was still separate from me.

Bulls-eye, I had hit it. ***That was where I was wrong!*** I was them, *we* are them, there is no separation, we are the same beings. Well, different sparks, but of the same energy. What I had thought was the real me, struggling to make my life work on earth was not the real me ***at all***. The real me, the *"I,"* was just having an earthly ***experience***.

The experience became so real, I thought it was everything that I was. As I started to learn that there was more out there, I became frightened of how easily I could be part of that more. I thought I was losing myself into a strange reality. It was easy to become this other reality, and it made me totally happy.

It was the **only** thing that made me happy, because that is who I **was.** It was like going home. It felt good because it **was** good. It was who I was; I was being who I was, a cosmic being, and using and doing what was perfectly natural to me. That is why when my body made an energy shift at the start of a healing it felt so good. The rest of my worries just disappeared. I became who I really was, and the illusion of who I was and anything that was important within that illusion became totally unimportant.

I was not a human struggling for my spirituality, I was a spirit *having a human experience.*

I had been like a yo-yo, forever swinging between two realities, like being between heaven and earth. All I had to do was stop in the middle and let each half of myself merge into one glorious whole. All I had to do was accept and honor the fact that I was part of each reality and each was a part of me, and that it was me and only me that could allow the connection to be made. I would become one. That is the natural state of beingness. Separation was the big illusion and I had fallen for it too long.

The time I spent at the school allowed me the space to put all my experiences together, to look back over my life, and to finally accept, from the core of my beingness, the truth that there is much more going on than I had allowed myself to believe. I was finally coming to the conclusion that it was all right to follow the urges and promptings from within, and that I did not need to fight with life. In fact if I allowed life to unfold around me and went with the flow, I could experience absolute joy and the thrill of living without having to be concerned about where the next dollar would come from.

The less I put my judgments and perceptions on what my life should be like, the better my life became. I realized I had been trying to create my life using only a small part of myself, and that there was a much bigger, a much more powerful part of myself that I was only now starting to accept.

For the first time in my life, I was truly starting to understand the power of energy, the amazing diverse frequencies of energy that make up this cosmos, energy that *I* was.

The concepts that would shape and transform the rest of my life flooded into my mind. For days I was delirious with bliss and happiness to levels that were previously unknown to me. Being part of the group energy of the school helped me to spiral upwards and outwards.

There did not seem to be any limit to the heights of bliss I felt as the keys of life dropped into place in my consciousness. All the years of struggle and trauma, all the weird, wacky and crazy things that had happened to me started to make sense.

The emptiness and loneliness that had consumed me over the years was being replaced with a deep love and feeling of honor for myself. I was starting to feel a part of this cosmos, not just knowing it from an intellectual perspective, but actually feeling it. As I allowed the feeling to grow in intensity, to manifest in every cell of my body, my ability to perceive, visibly see and understand the energy in and around the bodies of those around me developed to a stage of total clarity.

It was as if a switch had been activated, a switch that had sent me from AM to FM, to short wave and on up to cosmic frequency all at once. But in truth I knew it had taken me more than ten years to move that switch. The rise in frequency in my cells was an incredible feeling, like being lit up from the inside out. I really felt that I was translucent.

There were times I could hardly walk, due to the feeling of not being physical. I had to really focus on my body to make sure it was still there. If you can imagine a piece of ice, a group of really slow vibrating H_2O molecules, then increase their frequency to that of water, and then to that of steam, you can understand how I was feeling. It was such utter lightness, expansion and totally multidimensional.

From this reality I could tune into any frequency or dimension I desired. I only had to look at a person and instantly I was tuned to their energy, their auric field visible around them. Focusing on their body was like looking at a three dimensional, full-color MRI scan.

Bringing my awareness to a smaller and smaller field of vision I could get down to being aware of the electrical function of an individual cell. No, I was not on the latest whiz bang drug, or smoking wacky backy. This was walking, talking, breathing me, but vibrating at a frequency that allowed my consciousness to be aware of frequencies of energy that are not normally perceivable.

I realized this is where I had been guided to, not to this school, but to this level of awareness. This is what all the events in my life had been leading up to. I had been shown, forced into understanding bit by bit that there did indeed exist a reality outside of what we called normal.

I had been given time to get my logic around each bit, to let the knowledge slowly become my truth, my reality. And what a reality! Sure, I had glimpses of tuning into frequencies of energy when I tuned into people during healing sessions, but this was very different. I was finally becoming that higher frequency, there was no "plugging in" required. It was what I was.

The enormity of the cascade of knowledge and the power of being at this frequency almost overwhelmed me. I realized why I had been knocked down physically, emotionally and mentally all those years ago, why I had been stripped of all my earthly wealth, why I had to leave my family, why I had to be completely broken. So that I would know, really **know** what it was like to **hurt.** To hurt so deep that every fiber of my being cried out in desperation, so that regardless of who I became, regardless of what power I became, I could never **ever** use any of it to hurt another being. Ever.

And what power. To become the frequency of the cosmos is truly awesome. To have the ability to be consciously aware of the frequency of all that is around you allows you to become that. And when you can operate at that level, kill or cure is only a matter of conscious choice.

It is just as easy to turn off an electrically perfect cell as it is to turn on an electrically malfunctioning one, which is what disease is. The responsibility that comes with this reality can only be described as awesome. As I had found out over the years, there was nothing new about this knowledge, or this ability.

Most of the ancient cultures knew or had some understanding of the power of energy, and knew how to use it. We know this by the different labels and processes that are part of the folklore, and so called "religious" ceremonies, that to this day are practiced by many cultures.

Acupuncture, which most people are aware of, is the label given to the ability to work with the body's electrical circuits called meridians. The body's aura is part of this system. This subtle electromagnetic field can now be recorded and measured in and around everything that is know to exist.

Before the period of our present Christian era, the use of energy was practiced by the leaders and the wise of their cultures, not to mention the medicine man/woman, for the health care of their village.

The power of using energy, even if those using it did not know it as energy, has always been with us. The reality that was known, as evidenced by ancient ceremonies, healing practices and esoteric knowledge that has survived to this day, suggests that we are only now regaining some of this ability.

To understand and to work with the unseen has always been a difficult path to follow. **It requires a degree of self knowledge and discipline that few are prepared to work for or accept.**

The knowledge of the power of energy and its use, by us, normal humans, is often referred to as the "esoteric" knowledge, or in more modern times, the sacred knowledge, and is the basis of all known religious practices. Of course this is the very reason why so few of us know the enormity of the power of this knowledge.

Religion in its wisdom made darn sure we do not know. It was not so very long ago that psychics and people who could see these fields of energy were labelled as witches and anybody who worked with the unseen were called occultists who practiced voodoo, black magic, superstition etc. and were burned at the stake, fed to the lions or simply beheaded.

In fact, a good portion of the population of medieval Europe was suitably silenced, the monasteries where much of this knowledge was studied were ransacked, libraries that held the books were burned to the ground and any cultures that the New World explorers came across were soon destroyed along with their understanding, all in the name of "religion." The church of Rome, the basis of modern western society, has been the worst offender. (And the Vatican in its "Forbidden Works" archives, holds the world's largest collection of such knowledge.)

Those cultures that were not conquered (converted) were labelled as pagan, and cultures that could not be destroyed were classed as uncivilized natives with primitive over-active beliefs based on superstition.

Our society became one of total control based on fear, we became pawns in a gigantic power struggle where we were denied the truth and lost our connection with the God that we are all a part of. Of course, if we went to church and paid our dues (taxes), we were told that we did not have to worry as we would be saved.

Looking around the world as I knew it, I did not see many people behaving as if they were about to be saved. Quite the contrary, most people in the western world lived in a state of despair and emptiness, devoid of even the most basic sense of self-worth. Living a reality that was controlled by the experience of life, always reacting to life, never *being* life. Everybody seemed to be experiencing life from outside of themselves, the real being that they are was completely divorced from their experience. There was total separation.

And of course the church in its wisdom taught us just that. In fact, we were so separate from all other realities that we were told that if we did not do this or that, or even more insidiously, did this or that, we would be cast into damnation and hell forevermore. For the life of me, I could never put that concept and the biblical - "judge ye not" - into any sort of acceptable logic.

My mind was going a million miles an hour, concepts were taking shape and my logic was being expanded in parallel with my increasing ability to be aware of the energy in and around people. I could clearly see the seven chakras within the energy system of the body. When a person spoke, I could distinguish which chakra was being activated and see the frequency of that chakra being transmitted.

Years before, when studying Cell-Electrology, I had been shown depictions of the different wave patterns, and now I was seeing them. When one talks, the frequency that is transmitted depends on which chakra is being activated, and each chakra has a very different wave pattern (frequency), so not only could I hear the sound of the words, I could see the frequency of the energy that was being transmitted as well.

There are many times when the energy that is being transmitted is no way on key with the words that are being spoken. We have all experienced that situation, when somebody says something to us and we just know that their worlds are false, or the words sound fine but you know that is not what they are really thinking. What you are picking up is that the words are different from the energy that is being transmitted.

It is this energy transmission that is the most important aspect of communication; in fact, it is the real power behind all communication, and when the frequency of the words gets out of sync with the frequency of the chakra's energy transmission, a very disharmonic energy matrix is sent forth.

As it is said many times in the Bible, "what you sow, so shall you reap," the basic law of karma. So if we are not breathing, walking, and talking our truth, we will be sending out into the cosmos a very disharmonious energy that will create for us, as it returns, that same disharmony. Our lives, ourselves, become disharmonious.

Each chakra has a very different frequency, and by allowing ourselves to be in different moods, to feel differently, different chakras are activated, and once activated, that chakra amplifies the energy of the feeling.

As my awareness of energy increased I was able to distinguish which chakras were activated by which feelings and emotions. I was making tremendous strides in my ability to see and understand, but I still had a nagging feeling that something was missing, some factor that would help me put everything together in an even more profound way. I knew I was being led towards something even bigger, but at the time I did not know what it was.

CHAPTER 15
BECOMING ONE

During the school I met Zara. I think it was on the second or third day that we realized there was something, some connection, some magic, between us. Zara, who was feeling some powerful energy, asked her guides where it was coming from. Ask Denie, ask Denie, was all she got. Not understanding the answer, she had enough awareness to follow her promptings and asked me at the morning break if I had something to tell her. This was news to me, as this was the first time we had talked, but following my intuition I suggested we meet for lunch. As they say in the movies, the rest was history.

The next day during the midday break, we were clowning around and having fun in the gorgeous afternoon sun, with the red rocks in their brilliance towering all around us. Zara and I were holding hands and swinging each other around. Then, gathering her up in my arms from behind, I started to tell her about a sacred sun ceremony that I had learned from my Indian friends that could be used to raise one's vibrational rate. A part of it was to stare into the midday sun.

Zara thought I was loony and that if anybody did that they would be blind as well as crazy. So I calmly lifted my head and stared into the sun. As I brought my full focus onto the sun I immediately felt my body respond. A surge of energy pulsed through me and I felt my body lighten up, my awareness went right into the sun and I lost all feeling of my physical presence and seemed to have completely left my body. It was like going towards the sun and then into it.

The only conscious reality was of becoming one with the sun's energy, then I felt myself moving beyond the sun into a space of total oneness with everything. At that point there was not the slightest feeling of glare of the sun's rays but only a total coming together of all that I was. A feeling of being one with God, totally transcending any physicality, of being - no - knowing that I was everything.

When I finally broke contact with the sun I remember just standing looking at Zara with my face aglow and vibrating profoundly in every cell in my body.

Zara was stunned, and said that she now knew I was crazy and that she would never do such a thing. But what a high I had. I think we lay down and I immersed myself in that incredible feeling until it was time to go back to class.

By the second to last day of the school most of those present were at a level of consciousness that would allow the body's vibration rate to go beyond anything they had ever experienced. In the morning lecture, the class was talked through a process that has been known by many different names in most cultures and is commonly called a soul merge by today's aware new age seekers.

In Christ's time it was described as "tongues of fire entering the hearts of the disciples," and when you can see the energy, that is exactly how it looks. The latter Christian era refers to the process as the incoming of the holy spirit, not a bad description and when you take out the religious labels and replace them with what is actually happening, the incoming of energy, more energy than you have ever, ever experienced, it truly is an awesomely profound life changing, mind blowing, awareness expanding, beyond words "experience."

Anyhow, by using music and movement most of the class was able to increase their vibration rate to start the process off. I am not going to go into great detail here about how the process takes place, as I believe that it should only be experienced as a result of the correct build up.

We are dealing with a vibration rate at a cellular level that most people's cells have never experienced, and unless the preparation, awareness and mastership of one's energy has been learned correctly, real physical and psychological damage can occur.

This is why I am extremely fussy in the way I prepare and teach those that attend our International Academy of Vibrational Medical Science schools. The preparation for this "soul merge" - one of the greatest initiations - has to be darn good.

Zara and many in the class had very powerful soul merge experiences, but my body never went to a vibration that was above some of my previous experiences. I had done a lot of energy work with Bill and others, so it took a lot to impress me. In fact, I was a bit disappointed, nah - quite pissed with myself really. Some people in the class also did not get to a high enough level, and some had real traumatic experiences as their undealt with emotional frequencies got blasted out of their cellular storage and into their very sensitized emotional bodies.

So I spent the latter part of the afternoon assisting those who were having difficulty with their emotions and one lady in particular who was too afraid to allow herself any expansion at all.

I guess everything is perfect, it's just that we cannot see the perfection in its outplaying, as maybe I was needed to assist those with emotional blocks that afternoon, because the next morning my body started to go ballistic. It was during morning dynamic meditation, without a conscious thought on my part about achieving any great happening, that I felt my energy change.

Continuing to move with the music and holding my focus on myself I felt a expansion start to take place on a physical level. Zara who was next to me saw what was happening and went outside to get away from the intensity of the energy and allow me my space.

My body got hot, but not as hot as it had at other times, but the expansion got to a point that I was having difficulty standing up, let alone moving in time to the music that was playing. To stop being noticeable, I sat down and just let the energy "a keep on coming."

It was just so wonderful, wave after wave of the most wonderful energy rolled through my body. I sat there feeling my body come alive, being exquisitely aware of every cell as they were caressed and expanded into a oneness of total love, harmony and peace with a knowing that you and God are being introduced to each other, that you and God are each other.

It was like being bathed in a bubble of embryonic fluid that was the heart of God. There is no other way to describe it, it is beyond words, it is like the feeling that would put a smile on your face for the next thousand years. There is nothing other than you and love - no, nothing other than love, just total love, just ... love.

Yes, I achieved my soul merge, not with any great emotional outpouring, or other theatricals that usually signifies an unprepared state, but a beautiful, harmonious, and deeply loving experience with which I floated through the remainder of the week.

We had graduated from the school, and Zara and I were spending a few days together in the northern Arizona mountains around Flagstaff. Zara had gone through a pretty amazing transformational experience during the course and was having to deal with some very different outlooks on life as well as coming to terms with a greatly enhanced energy awareness. Her body had become super-sensitive to the frequency of everything around her. This super-sensitivity is quite normal for a time after high-powered energy work and usually settles down as the body adjusts to the new frequency that it is vibrating at.

In a way Zara was fortunate to be with me at this time as I had been through many energy processes before and knew what to expect. I could explain to her that some of the things she could perceive and feel was not her going nuts, but in fact were very real feelings and realities that she could now perceive.

To be on an accelerated learning trip can be a very frightening experience if you have not got someone you can talk to who knows what is going on. Sadly, in the ensuing years as I have worked with people in the energy medicine field, I have had on many occasions the job of putting people back together emotionally as a result of unscrupulous teachings. I have come to the conclusion that there are very few people who actually know what they are doing, and even fewer who know and understand energy.

There are hundreds of processes and modalities out there, but the large majority of them are only fluffing around the tips of the iceberg in their understanding of energy and what they are doing. Even some of the well-known and widely-used natural health modalities are woefully deficient in the basic understanding of the energy system that is the human body.

Nobody in their right mind would let somebody cut their body open and perform an operation without being pretty sure that person had some darn good training and knew what they were doing. Yet how many so-called practitioners are out there working on people's electrical systems, who have no idea of how it works.

How many are using a modality that uses words and labels from another language and do not even know what they mean in English - and even if they did, they would not be much the wiser as they probably only had two or three weekend experiences called training. To me this has got to be nuts; your body can be harmed just as easily by working with the electrical circuits as it can be by the knife.

Think about it, there is not a pain, symptom or disease that manifests in the body without there first being an electrical malfunction and many of these "diseases" only manifest years after the original electrical malfunction. It often takes that long before the cells finally give up under the stress of a damaged energy system.

The energy system *is* what the body is, and Vibrational Medicine demands the professionalism and expertise that any other health care system requires. In my opinion this professionalism and *expertise* cannot be achieved with two or three weekends' training.

There are also many meditations and other forms of energy-enhancing processes that can cause all sorts of problems for the eager seeker. Unless there is adequate training and on going back-up it is all too easy to have people spin out of control.

I have come across many teachings and processes that have packaged a small part of the available knowledge and created a fixed structure and labelled or named it this or that. To have fixed attitudes or perceptions is dangerous at the best of times, and so very much more when dealing with energy.

There is not one group or body who has the mortgage on energy understanding, and those who think they have all the answers are usually the ones who teach the narrowest perception. Most of the time, those with the most controls and "have to do it this way" or "this is the only way" or "this is the way it works" know the least about energy and sadly do not even fully understand the power they may be releasing within their students. Certainly, the student has no idea what Pandora's box of realities and emotions are about to be brought to the surface. A very dangerous state of affairs, indeed.

Without a very full understanding of energy devoid of dogma, it is almost impossible to traverse the tightrope to enlightenment without many nasty falls. And believe me, there are times when all the king's horses and all the king's men have difficulty putting Humpty Dumpty back together again.

Zara and I spent the next few days in bliss up in the pine forests. We talked about all the things that were happening to us, and that we would like to work in the healing arts and that we liked Flagstaff.

I was surfing the energy, going with the flow, allowing life to unfold around me, making no plans, no judgments, expecting nothing, yet accepting everything. I was starting to use the wisdom and life was working for me, I was learning to become the energy.

The next few days were hot and clear and after spending an early afternoon in blissful exuberance and sun bathing at Slide Rock in Oak Creek canyon, just outside Sedona, Zara suggested that we spend the rest of the day in Flag.

As soon as she mentioned that we should go to Flagstaff, I felt what was by now a familiar feeling come over my body. I meditated for a while as the feeling evolved into a course of action I was to take. I knew this was going to be something big, as the anxiety level I was feeling went way above what I usually experienced.

An urge manifested within me to go to the Hopi sacred mountain, the San Francisco peaks which tower above Flagstaff.

Taking the driver's seat I told Zara to belt in real tight as this was going to be some trip. Leaving Slide Rock we headed towards Flagstaff and then on out towards the mountain. I could feel the energy rise in my body as we got closer to the sacred area. Turning onto the road that heads up to the ski field, I pulled a lower gear in the white Porsche (Zara has good taste in cars).

One of the world's finest sports cars responded with a deep throbbing growl as the revs built and the Pirelli tires got the message as we drifted through the first corner. I felt myself slip into the groove and become one with the car.

Responding to the energy, I gripped the taut pulsing gear shift, moving it through the gears in harmony with the revs as they moved to, and at times beyond, the red line. Pushing the Porsche to its limits was pure poetry.

To become one with a good fast car in a wild drive up a mountain with a beautiful wild woman, who had a gorgeous stunning body and blue eyes to die for, has to be heaven, and is still one of my most pleasurable experiences.

I am sure Zara thought her most prized possession was about to become a crumpled heap of scrap metal at any moment but she kept her cool, her mouth shut and held on.

Arriving at the top of the road I pulled the Porsche to a stop just above an open field and we sat motionless while our bodies normalized from the adrenaline rush and we drank in the wonderment of our find.

Laid out before us was this incredibly beautiful panorama. A field with tall grass gently waving in the breeze and in the distance rolling away for mile upon mile, pine covered mountains. I just sat there, spellbound, what a drive, what a car, what a woman and what a view.

This surely is a sacred mountain. My body was tingling from head to toe, and I knew that something very special was about to happen. It felt as if I was about to awaken to a very profound truth about myself. I sort of felt at a deep level of my knowingness that I had experienced this all before.

Leaving the Porsche, we walked down into the field for about seventy yards and, drawn to a large flat rock, I sat down. Zara moved down a little more to meditate on her own, leaving me to my thoughts. To the right of me was a lone pine tree, but other than that the field was bare.

I had experienced my soul merge, the merging of the soul energy with the physical, one of the most profound experiences one can have on this earthly plane and now within days of that I was being prepared for the next initiation, something even I thought was not possible at this stage, the merging of my higher self or Christed energy with my physicality. Ascension. This is the biggie, this is what the years of training had been all about, the years or more like hundreds of lifetimes.

The amount of beings that were around me was incredible. I knew that this process would be amazing to the extreme and I had a fear that my body would not be able to take what was about to come. But the presence of so many from the higher realms gave me confidence to go through with it. The frequency that my body was at by now made it hard to feel and control.

The stimulation from the very fast drive up the mountain and the work my guides were doing had prepared me well. From deep within my being I felt and knew that this was my path, the only reality that was now open to me.

This would finally be the end of my searching for myself, because I was about to become myself, all of me, body, soul and spirit, as one, on this earth.

The next hour or so of my life was an experience that to this day I still have difficulty talking about. Not because the reality has faded, but because of what actually happened. How can words describe an experience that has relevance only to that which we would normally have no perception of?

From a purely spiritual aspect, we can read about things like the incoming of the holy spirit, we can hear things like the word "ascension," but do we have any concept of what it actually is, what it means or what takes place.

Of course we don't, how can we, these things do not happen to us....well that is what I used to think. What do I think now? I do not think, I know, my experience was real, more real than anything I have ever experienced.

It was as if all the lights in the cosmos had been turned on. It was if I became the cosmos, I became connected with everything and everything became connected with me. I could see the whole picture, the whole truth.

It started slowly; the energy came into my body in gentle waves and built into ever increasing pulses of light that seemed to emanate from deep in the cosmos. I could feel each pulse hit me and my body responded to the increase in energy by heating and vibrating all over.

I think at this stage I stood up and surrendered to the process by opening my arms and heart to the pulse of God. I remember my body getting lighter and lighter as the frequency built in my cells until I had no conscious knowing of my feet touching the ground.

More and more energy poured in. I was unable to do anything other than allow. The feeling of expansion was tremendous, I was barely able to feel any physicalness. I was on the crystal mountain and I was on fire.

The energy just kept on entering me, I was becoming the energy. There was such brilliance, and it was not separate from me. My body felt like it was being blown up like a balloon with even more expansion. The heat in my body was phenomenal. I could feel every cell, yet was unable to consciously move any part of my body.

Then it happened. A great shaft of energy hit and entered my beingness - light and more light.

Layer after layer of illusion fell away and my being kept expanding. I could see a shaft of light opening in the heavens and the heavens came unto me. My body was on fire, my skin barely able to hold the pressure of the expansion, more and more light poured in, more layers of dross and conditioning fell away, my hands reached up, accepting the light, honoring the light, becoming the light. The light becoming me, merging into total oneness. I was the light, the light was me, completion, Christed, ONE...

CHAPTER 16
AFTER ASCENSION

I have no idea how long I was standing there, bathed in Christ light. I had no perception of normal reality, but I could feel my body - a very different feeling body that is for sure! There I was, standing on (above) this rock, arms outstretched and energized to a point that I had no idea whether my feet were on the ground or not.

Every cell in my body felt that it had expanded and blown up. Every cell on fire with pure energy. The feeling is indescribable - just total expansion. I remember looking out at my hands because I was sure that my fingers were about to pop under the pressure. I tried to move them, I could not, it was as if they were great big long balloons all pushing against one another. I had total awareness of the energy that made up my aura and it was so powerful that my physical body and it had no separation.

That is why I felt that I was blowing up. I had full and total awareness of all of me - the physical and the energy part of myself - but as one, not two. My being felt so, so big. Of course my logic was trying to confine this expanded state to the part it could accept, the physical, and the only way it could get around this new expanded reality was to give me a perception that my physical body had blown up.

Because my energy field had become so strong and enlarged, the extreme tightness of a balloon that I was feeling was my logic's way of conveying it to my consciousness.

I remember trying to call Zara, who was further down the field, and it took me two or three attempts to get any sound from my voice. As she turned to look at me she dropped to the ground in fright, shielding her eyes with her arm.

"What's wrong, what's happening?" I asked.

"I can't see you," she answered, "You are too bright, you are nothing but light."

She then fell forward burying her face into the grass.

I asked her to come to me and she slowly crawled to my rock on her hands and knees, carefully keeping her eyes shielded.

"Don't be afraid," I said reassuringly, "I will help your eyes to adjust."

There was at this time an amazing thing happening with the weather. Where we were it was a still, perfect day, absolutely silent. But down in the valley below us, a few miles away, and over the mountains beyond, a rain storm with dark clouds and lots of lightening was raging.

I reached down and helped Zara to her feet as I stood behind her. Then asking her to look towards the storm, I stretched out my arms and with what felt like a great shaft energy extending from them, parted the storm clouds and the sun burst through and shone directly on us.

I remember feeling very pleased and said.

"Right on cue," then I told Zara that the Father had a gift for her and that she was to look directly into the sun.

Obviously somewhat afraid, she slowly lifted her head and looked directly into the sun. I moved away from her so my energy would not be influencing hers. She held her focus on the sun for about five minutes, then turning to me smiling she said.

"I can see you now, but you are still brighter than the sun."

I think she then sat down on my rock and I went to her and lay down with my head on her lap.

I must have been there for twenty or thirty minutes just being, allowing, feeling; mind not really thinking. This was way beyond thinking. This was total being. I remember standing up and becoming aware that my arms were outstretched, palms facing up.

As I brought my focus onto my hands I became aware that I had been given the cosmos to hold, it was sitting in my outstretched hands as an all powerful crystal ball, but within it I could make out three of the most exquisite triangular crystals. The power of these crystals was out of this world - like nothing I could have ever imagined. This was my gift, my key and I knew what it meant the Father, the Son and the Holy Spirit. I was complete.

I had a deep conceptual understanding of what had taken place, but it was impossible for my logic to get around the reality of it so soon, so I lay down again, hoping the sacred mountain would take care of me, and I asked my guides to make sure my body would not explode.

It was some time before I started to feel and move my body with some semblance of what I perceived as normal. Normal, no that was gone forever, my body has never been normal since!

So what do you do after this sort of experience? Nothing, yet on the other hand, everything. I needed time to just be, to allow myself time to become the new me and accept my new reality (and what a reality). Whatever was about to happen, I was going to let happen.

I was in heaven - no - I was heaven. I had a knowingness deep within me that I was complete, I finally knew what I was all about, what I was doing here and why, that life would unfold for me despite the human part of myself. I knew I would need some time to integrate all that had happened and also that this would not always be easy, but for now I was going to enjoy the experience and life.

In the months that followed the "experience," my newfound happiness faded somewhat. The reality of life slowly took hold and I found myself once again starting to become reactive. The old me was still patterned in my consciousness, and that pattern was very easy to fall into, especially when I went back to New Zealand.

Old familiar surroundings brought back the aspects that I had despised in myself and had worked hard to change. I soon realized that to fully integrate all that I had experienced was going to take some time and one heck of an effort.

But isn't that what life is all about? It is about being aware of who and what we are and making our choices, and then working at it to make our choices become our reality.

It was exactly as old Bill had said, I had the knowledge and now I needed time to **become** the wisdom.

My awareness had been expanded and my parameters had been reset, but the choice was mine whether I put the effort into becoming the being I knew I was capable of becoming. Did it not say in the Bible that many are called but few are chosen? I think we are all called to wake up to who we are at some time in our lives and it is us who have to make that choice, each one for ourselves.

There is nobody out there waiting to save us, we have to save ourselves. That is our choice, our responsibility to change our consciousness, to become heart centered beings, to let go of the old reactive emotional aspects of ourselves.

This is the great transformational process we have been waiting for. It comes from within us, from our hearts desire - not from anything outside, not from some guru, not from some teaching, not from some experience. These things only help us to reset the parameters of possibility. It is our desire, our will, that finally changes who we are and sets us free.

CHAPTER 17
KEEPING IT ALL TOGETHER

I often chuckle over the memories of some of the things that I went through, that happened to me, and I have changed, changed most everything about myself. Well not quite everything; I still like having fun, in fact having fun ***with*** life is what it is all about.

During the past years, I have lived an international globetrotting life and met some amazing, wonderful people.

Without any planning, I go with the flow from one incredible experience to another. Life on earth can really be everything you ever desired; and you know what, it has nothing to do with anything outside of yourself. The path to enlightenment can only be taken through your cells, that is, the being you are on this planet is the key.

Everybody is searching outside of themselves for their happiness. They are looking for outside experiences to give their life meaning. Life's experiences are only that, experiences, and there is no need to ever take them too seriously. Your experiences are not what it is all about, ***you*** are what it is all about.

There is a part of you, the real you, that exists just outside of normally perceived reality. And that is the key, to move your awareness to include this other part of yourself.

You see, this is the big part of yourself, this is the part that is connected to the rest of the cosmos, connected to God, **is God**. This is the part that gives you fulfilment, happiness, joy, peace, love, self-worth. This is the part of you that God expresses love through, this is the part of you that **experiences** God. This is the part of you that is called heaven, remember, "Thy kingdom come."

The kingdom of heaven. You do not go anywhere to find it, it comes to you, or rather you create it within yourself. That is what every sage, wise one and teacher has been trying to tell us for eons.

When I was a kid at convent school and the Nuns kept on telling us that if we were good we would go to heaven, I could never understand what they meant. Heaven was this place that was always **out there**. . . always separate from us, cloaked in so many rules and regulations, and yet in the next sentence we were told not to judge. Yet to my early Christian teachings, judgments were what heaven and God were all about.

There was something very wrong with this. It is no wonder so many of us in the western world who grow up under the so-called Christian church have difficulty in our adult lives. Well I did, anyhow, all I did was judge myself and everything and everybody around me. Regardless of how much I achieved, I always felt empty inside, so I judged that I had not achieved enough and I worked harder, still felt empty, got reactive, became unbearable to live with, judged myself even more, pushed harder etc.

Familiar?

I think so, and you know what, when everything around us becomes a burden, our success and gains in the material world lose their good feeling. We then sink into a pit of depression and self-worthlessness. And we did not have a clue what it was that was missing. Why? Because we had never been told the truth.

We were taught separateness, that we had been born blackened with sin, that we had to endure suffering, that we had to prove ourselves to God and that we were not complete.

In fact, we were condemned to hell for all eternity if we were not chosen, if we were not good enough.

Yet deep down, driven by a truth that is our soul, we knew there had to be something more, we had to be something more.

And we are, we are everything, there is no separation, there is no original sin, there are no judgments out there, we do not have to be or do anything to get to the kingdom of heaven. God and the kingdom of heaven are not separate from us, they and we are one and the same.

The lie was the separateness, the separateness was the illusion and the illusion manifested as our personal hell.

I have found my way out of this darkness, this personal hell, I have found the light, my light. I have come *Back to Life* by following my ***Journey to Truth***. The path for me was not easy, but sure as God made little apples I learnt some darn good lessons, lessons that to this day I am working on to put into place on a day-to-day basis.

I have at last learned to feel - no, not feel as in "react from my emotions," which most people call feeling, but to feel - as in "feel with the heart" - to lift my awareness and open my heart to all there is around me.

I have been helped to understand and to experience that we can increase our vibration rate so that we can be aware, from a fully conscious state, of a much greater reality than I had ever thought possible, and to become a full partner in this expanded world.

The limitation of my old world was the darkness, being out of the garden of Eden? The expansion of my new world is being in the light (heaven) i.e. enlightenment. That word means "enter the light." And the word light means, **"energy."** Enlightenment therefore means "enter the energy."

And what happens when you put more energy into anything? It starts to vibrate at a higher frequency, and its reality changes. The reality of ice is very different from that of steam, yet they are both the same stuff, H_2O molecules, but vibrating at very different rates. In this sense, steam is enlightened ice. As the vibration rate goes up, gravity has less effect on the molecules, they become lighter - they become enlightened. So enlightenment is all about increasing one's vibration rate or frequency.

This reminds me of the story of Jesus walking out on the water to talk to his mate Peter. Maybe J.C. had the ability to increase his body's vibration rate to a point where the surface tension of the water was greater than the lessened gravitational pull on his highly vibrating body. If that was the case, walking on water would have been fairly easy and normal for him.

What we are talking about here is **Self-mastery,** or the ability to have full control over the frequency that we vibrate at. To vibrate at a higher frequency, we must let more energy in ... enter the energy (light) ... enlightenment. All of a sudden, all the religious connotations fall away and we are left with a very understandable scientific fact ... increase your vibration rate and you will get lighter. Attain the ability to increase it enough, and we would float (rise up) ... ascension?

Were J.C. and the others before him talking about a very straight-forward scientific fact? Two thousand years ago, the people had no concept of energy, there were no words to describe an energy or an electrical process, so the language of the day was used, often in parable form, to describe this process.

I remember reading that it was said back then that God is light, and God is everywhere. Remember what the word light means in English... *Energy.* God is Energy and Energy is everywhere. Is that not the very foundation of our scientific understanding? It was Einstein who said, "everything is energy $(E = MC^2)$" There is nothing in this cosmos that is not energy - nothing.

We humans have a very narrow perception of the energy that is the cosmos. I show it this way in our Academy schools.

Suppose we stretched a piece of string from Seattle all the way across to New York City, what ... a distance of about three and a half thousand miles or so, and imagined that length of string represented all of the frequencies, realities, dimensions and life forms in the cosmos.

Now if we traveled along that piece of string to the middle, somewhere around Kansas City, and placed our little finger on it, the bit that our finger touched would represent our awareness, our total reality, in comparison to what really exists (the rest of the three and a half thousand miles of reality).

Now if everything is energy, and energy is nothing more than a vibration, then we would only be aware of the frequencies that we are compatible to, or vibrating at. To us, nothing outside this range (the bit our finger was touching) would exist. We would have absolutely no perceptional reality of anything else. Everything we perceived would be in the bit that our finger touched on that string.

Now, go slow here, what would happen if we let more energy into **ourselves,** enlightened ourselves a bit? Our vibration rate would go up. What happens when our vibration rate goes up? Our frequency changes, and as our frequency moves **SO WILL OUR PERCEPTIONAL REALITY.** All of a sudden we are aware of not a half an inch of our string reality, but maybe two inches of it.

A minute ago we had no awareness of anything outside of our little half an inch of string and would have sworn our truth on all the bibles in the world. But our truth was based on our perceptional reality, and that was based on the frequency of our vibration.

But now our frequency has changed, our perceptions have changed, our reality has changed and our truth is totally different. What we thought was true and real yesterday is today completely expanded and different.

Since we are now vibrating at a different frequency, everything that exists in that frequency becomes part of our reality, our truth. What was unreal and did not exist yesterday becomes real and exists very much so today.

THIS IS THE PROCESS THAT IS CALLED ENLIGHTENMENT.

And it can be learned - this is what the ancient mystical schools and initiation processes were all about.

This is what I am all about, this is where I have been led to and this is the wisdom that I, along with many others, wish to share with all who seek. This is why we set up the International Academy of Vibrational Medical Science, to show you that you can become all that you ever desired, ever imagined. This is what Jesus was trying to tell us.

The self control and MASTERSHIP of how much energy WE allow in is the key. We cannot be in control of the level of energy we allow in until we have cleared out our emotional traumas, judgments, old belief structures and negative behavior patterns.

When we achieve this level of MASTERSHIP it is signified by the drawing of a circle above our head: The symbol of completion, or MASTERSHIP (the halo in modern times).

When we achieve enlightenment, we transmit only love and honor, we become love and honor. Science tells us that we only use ten percent of our brain, of course, as normal third dimensional beings we are not operating at a high enough frequency to activate the rest of it.

Let more energy in - Enlighten yourself a bit and see what happens - you will be more than amazed. The old mystical schools called this, the highest initiation, Ascension, and for good reason.

From an energy point of view, this will allow us to ascend out of the third dimensional mire of emotional reactivity, pain and disease, into a utopia of harmony, bliss, love and honor. We ascend beyond the death of suffering (hell) and come....Back to Life (Heaven). We will have experienced our **Journey to Truth.**

POSTSCRIPT

As a result of the life-changing process I went through, I finally started to walk my path.

As well as building up a large international clientele with my healing practice over the last years, in 1994 I founded the Geometry of Divinity, Inner Awareness Movement (God I Am), which has now become part of the International Academy of Vibrational Medical Science (IAVMS).

The Academy was established in 1996 by my life-partner Shelley and myself with an international faculty to teach and share with others the most profound truth of their own beingness. The IAVMS has grown to become one of the leading and most sought after self-awareness learning programs in the world. It runs its programs in the U.S., Canada, Switzerland, New Zealand, England and Denmark.

Looking around the world and noting what was on offer, in regards to self-improvement/spiritual/esoteric teaching, I became increasingly alarmed at how these important life skills were being taught. In fact, it was my opinion that religion and some aspects of the so-called new age movement and their general teachings were cloaked in do-gooders' flowery claptrap and mumbo jumbo.

There was no realness; everything was "out there," where-ever that was. The concepts, the understanding of the myths, the real message of those that have walked the path before us had been missed.

The messenger had been made into a god or killed, and the message got bastardized, depending on the cultural and vested interests paramount at the time.

The new age movement is floundering in a hotch potch of misinformation and half-truths, of taking seekers down a path that has very little to do with themselves and everything to do with something outside of themselves. It is becoming a religion all over again. A judgment? Well maybe, but I would rather call it an observation.

To me, spirituality can only be an inner journey, a journey that takes the seeker on a path that cuts through all dogma, all control, all shoulds and should nots. This sets the seekers free to be everything that they are and allows those who truly want and are ready to experience the god presence from within - not from an intellectual or knowledgeable third-dimensional thinking reality, but from actually being that reality. To experience such a change at cellular level we can never go back to our old emotional reactive ways.

The journey is to a knowingness at such a deep level that there would never be any doubt that they and God are one and the same. To realize that the cosmos is our home and there is no separation on any level, that God experiences through our cells.

These bodies of ours are not in isolation from the rest of the cosmos but in fact are an integral part of it. We are connected to everything and everything to us.

Our only limitation is our belief that we are separate. That is the great illusion.

So how do I get this across to people in a way that they can experience a real change, to experience a real shift in their consciousness? That is the hard one; every thinking man and woman since Adam and Eve has tried to crack that. So what would it take? This is where I had come to.

I went back to Ground Zero, the starting point of this whole expansion that is this cosmos to find the common denominator that everything else revolves around. The thing that makes everything tick. And you know what? I did not find God, I found me. And then I found God.

That was the clue I had been looking for. Most every method was trying to teach people that there was this reality out there somewhere, and nobody could find it because they were looking outside of themselves. But how do you look inwards? How do you find yourself? Now that is the real question.

If we have to find ourselves, then surely it would be an advantage to start with what we are made of. So what is that? Flesh and bones. Yes, but what is that made of? Cells, yes and what is that made of? Atoms, and what is that made of? Vibrating frequencies of energy. Right.

So we are energy and that is the basis of all of the known universe, and the basis of all our scientific understanding ($E=MC^2$). Wait a minute you say, am I saying that those on a scientific quest and those on a spiritual quest are heading towards the same goal but from different ends of the field? Darn right, and what's more they are playing on the very same field and if each one of us let go of our judgment and belief structures, we would see that everybody is on the same field and we are all heading towards the same goal.

This is the background on which we base our school, the International Academy of Vibrational Medical Science.

The goal was to cut the floweriness and dogma out of what most would call a spiritual quest, and to share, with those who are ready, a level of mastership and knowing that few have achieved.

We start with energy, energy awareness, and that leads us to self, and self leads to mastership and mastership leads to enlightenment.

This is the mastership school. From small beginnings this school has grown to be recognized as one of the major esoteric and personal growth learning institutions in the Western world.

EPILOGUE

I could write volumes about how you, all of you, can rise above your controls and fears, how you can make life work for you instead of vice versa. I could write volumes about the miracles I see during healings, hundreds of them, until they become expected and normal, which is of course, the case. I could write volumes about how each one of you could stop looking outside yourselves to find the answers that you seek, for you are the answer.

I am able to be with Shelley, the love of my life, because for the first time I am able to have a relationship that is based on honor and not some needy emotional requirement. I have finally found myself, so I can now share myself, all of me, in a perfect dance of bliss, love and honor with another on the same frequency.

It is only now that I realize I am able to have a total relationship on all levels because I am now complete on all levels (well nearly, anyhow). It took me most of my life to get to this point, but from here on out its all up, up and away.

There is no going back this time. Every day I feel more and more blessed, every day I feel more and more expansion, and every day I become more and more of the being I am. But most of all, I am living and loving with a depth and wonderment that is heaven.

My Kingdom has come and so can yours.

The only reason I have shared this story, this true story, of my **Journey to Truth** is so that you may take courage and give to yourselves the honor of walking yours. If I, a farm boy from down under can do it, then so can you.

In one of the seminars and schools that I give around the world, a young man asked,

"If all this is true and we are more than we think we are, then where is this place that called heaven?"

I asked him to stand up and turn around three hundred and sixty degrees. Then I said,

"You have just seen it, but we have messed ourselves up so much that it is unrecognizable."

If we each walked our path with honor and from the heart, then maybe we would recognize it again.

Be blessed, each one of you, for you are the power, for you are the light; take it, it is your right, it is your inheritance.

The choice is yours, you are not a human struggling to find your spirituality, you are a *spirit* having a human experience.

I thank, honor and bless you all for taking the time to share my Journey... I pray that you will be inspired to *be...* your Journey, to *your* Truth.

In Love and Light,
Denie (Heart Eagle) Hiestand

My Vision . . . My Poem . . .
The deep longing to be whole to be completely me,
to feel free, light, alive.
To fill the void within.
God, if only I could feel whole... always an emptiness.
Driven on... until at last.
An awakening, an acceptance, a knowing, an understanding.
No more excuses, no more procrastination.
Time to step out, to be counted, to allow.
I had a vision, a vision of a school, a school for those who really wanted to go beyond.
But how? Me? I am no teacher, yet I could not walk away.
Deep inside, something kept pushing, pushing me towards the vision.
The vision I carried in my heart - in my being.
The drive, to manifest this vision... overpowering.
The fear, that held me back... real.
Am I ready... please not alone... who will help... how will I find them...too frightening.
God forbid I might fail.
Searching always searching, to understand, to know the what ifs, the hows, the whys.
More time alone... deep within... asking... waiting... restless, always restless... the vision, never fading.
They came... the helpers... at first one, then another, and another.
Now it is up to me... to allow... to allow the vision.
So was born. **Geometry of Divinity, Inner Awareness Movement ...** (God I Am)... the school.
To show, to gently show you, that you too are **special,** that you too can be **whole,** that you too can be **free,** that you too can be **love.**
If this is your vision, your dream, your longing, come, and we will gently hold your hand; join in, and we will gently guide you. Enter a new reality, take back your power, become whole, find the you in you and together we will rejoice. The dream, the vision... has manifest.

The Geometry of Divinity, Inner Awareness Movement school is now an integrated part of the
International Academy of Vibrational Medical Science (IAVMS) with Offices in Canada, the U.S., New Zealand and Switzerland.

Head office mailing address is:
International Academy of Vibrational Medical Science,
PMB 654, 15600 NE 8th St., B1,
Bellevue, WA 98008, U.S.A.

International Academy of Vibrational Medicial Science information on following pages.

INTERNATIONAL ACADEMY of
VIBRATIONAL MEDICAL SCIENCE

Canada   New Zealand   Switzerland   U.S.A.

**PMB 654,
15600 NE 8th St. B1.
Bellevue WA. 98008 U.S.A.**

**Phone: 425 785 3468
E-mail: info@vibrationalmedicine.com
www.vibrationalmedicine.com**

The International Academy of Vibrational Medical Science offers experiential in-depth learning intensives at the highest level. These advanced courses include the full spectrum of leading edge discoveries in Vibrational Medicine, Energy Awareness, Emotional/ Mental Mastership, Sexuality, Personal Relationships, Movement & Music, Kinesiology, Nutritional Training and Energy Mastership. The Academy's courses are taught around the world.

Contact the Academy at the above address or e-mail to:
info@vibrationalmedicine.com
Visit the Academy's web site at:
www.vibrationalmedicine.com

INTERNATIONAL ACADEMY of
VIBRATIONAL MEDICAL SCIENCE

*An integrated school of awareness to
rapidly expand your consciousness.*

Statement of Intent:

Dear Seekers,

*We are excited to have created a world class
school of learning that will assist you on your path
of awareness, so you may grow spiritually and
emotionally to achieve everything that you are.*

*The purpose of the school is to assist you in
attaining your own healing and self-mastery, so
you can become that totally powerful, loving and
free being that you are, and with that help
humanity.*

*At the same time, you will be introduced to
one of the most advanced methods of healing
currently available on the planet, that of
Vibrational Medicine.*

*This will take your knowledge from a basic
understanding of the body's electromagnetic
energy circuits, to your connection with the
unseen world beyond, and culminating, if you so
desire, with total mastery of your emotions and
releasing all your limitations.*

*These intensives (trainings) are very powerful
gatherings which seek the unfolding of the highest
in each of us. The message is clear: "The Time is
Now" to fully understand, realize and live the truth
of who you are, without fear, dogma or restriction
of your expression in any way.*

Each intensive will be unique because people come with their own unique desires and levels of willingness to learn, stretch, and go beyond.

The entire focus of the Academy's teachings will be for you to find and express your own Empowerment, Freedom and Truth. You will be introduced to beliefs and understandings from many cultures and societies, ancient and modern, from this earth and beyond, so you can develop your own perceptions, realities and truths.

These trainings are very powerful, life changing, heart opening experiences. This is the Mastership School and has profound effects on all who avail themselves of it.

"Everything is energy. Energy is everything. Once you learn to master energy, you can be the master of everything: Life, Love, Wealth and Health."

Denie Hiestand.

Thus the objectives of the International Academy of Vibrational Medical Science are:

◆   To bring participants to a point of consciousness that will allow them to know and experience their fullest expression of the power, gloriousness and greatness they are.

◆   To bring participants to a point of consciousness that allows them to be free of any dogma, limiting belief structures or inhibitions.

◆ To show women that they are allowed, and in fact, should and can, take back their power and self-worth and that they have a right to be all that they are, including being powerful, outrageous, wild, succulent and free.

◆ To show men that they can honor their maleness, and, at the same time, let go their ego-based domination, control and emotional reactivity. To show them that they can open their hearts, learn to feel, to unconditionally love, to increase their power and self-worth with full expression and honor.

◆ To bring participants to a point of consciousness so that they can live this life without any limitations (mentally, physically, sexually and expressively) and in a state of total joy, bliss and honor. "I am free, free to be, totally me."

◆ To create an awareness and a comprehensive understanding of how to maintain their own and/or their family/clients' health and happiness by using their knowledge of the body's electrical system with a full understanding of Vibrational Medical Science.

A further objective for those who desire to continue their training in the Vibrational Medical Science Practitioner Program, is to ensure participants are highly trained, fully informed, capable and professional practitioners of Vibrational Medicine - the Health Care of the future.

Or to enter the Personal Growth Program to pursue their further development in personal growth, tantra, sexuality, relationships, personal freedoms and expression, to fully live life without limits.

The International Academy of Vibrational Medical Science, so you can be,
                    "Free to Be, Totally Me."

The Academy offers the following course of studies:

Vibrational Medical Science Practitioner Program.
Personal Growth Program.
Master Practitioner Certificate Program.
Vibrational Medical Science Degree Program.

The following is a brief outline of two of the Academy's many courses:

VB001: Energy Awareness
(5 day intensive)

This course focuses on understanding what is energy, energy patterns, flows and meridians. Physicalizing the energy, experiencing it and raising your vibrational frequencies through awareness, music and movement. Greater awareness of yourself in relation to the whole. Honoring yourself and each other. Moving away from judgments of yourself and others. Becoming aware of the energy frequencies that allow past traumas to be held onto.

This course will also start the process that will take you to a new frequency, that of the heart, to remove and transmute all disharmonic frequencies. You will start the learned process of enlightenment. An introduction to some meditation techniques will help center yourself, aid the discovery of your purpose/direction, and enhance the development of self-acceptance and honor. Nature trips are included to heighten your awareness of energy.

The focus is always on increasing your conscious awareness of Energy. This course has the potential to be the most life changing week you will ever experience. Powerful, dynamic and full on, this is the Mastership school.

Suggested reading, "Journey to Truth" by Denie Hiestand.

<u>VB002: Emotional Mental Mastership</u>
(8 day intensive - prerequisite VB001)

Awakening the Body, Heart and Soul to their full potential and becoming aware of the ninety percent of yourself that has no conscious reality. You will dive within, take the plunge, face your fears and overcome them. You will free yourself from the shadows of the past by releasing parental and societal patterns.

You will learn to change the frequency of your cells to detraumatize your body, free your mind and release your soul. You will release the chains and blockages from your second chakra and allow your creative, expressive, energy to flow in all areas without limits. This is Mastership.

Mastership is attained by using that extra part of yourself that you will rediscover. You are complete in every way. By increasing your vibratory rate that completeness becomes your reality.

Become one with yourself and everything around you through the experience of your soul merge. Expand your consciousness so you can live free of any limitations. Learn to truly hear the voices from deep within which are your conscious connections with your higher self (frequencies).

These eight days will be spent looking within and being honest, freeing yourself from your emotions, your sexual blockages, your dogmas and belief structures. Finding and living this newfound part of yourself, you will experience your greatness, your love, your passion, your joy, bliss and honor.

Contact the Academy for a free informative catalog.

Testimonials
Next page.

Testimonials for the IAVMS

"In my recent spiritual work, I encountered a quote: "A psychologist only mends you, he doesn't transform you." As a psychologist, I found this to be all too true. Thus, with great delight, I have encountered Denie Hiestand and his transformational work. The courses offered by the International Academy of Vibrational Science are a must take for those who seek to transform themselves."

Dr. Stephen Vizzard, PhD. Seattle, WA. U.S.A.

"I have learnt more attending the IAVMS schools than I did in all my time at medical school."

Dr. Mary Pellicer, MD.Yakima, WA. U.S.A.

"As a medical doctor and student of Denie's International Academy of Vibrational Medical Science, the Christ force healing energy Denie teaches us to open our hearts to, is truly one of the most extraordinary, powerful, profound experiences of my entire life."

Dr. Linda C. Hole, MD. Spokane, WA. U.S.A.

"Attention, all you mid-life crisis-ing baby booming, health professionals. . . this man can truly lead you into a more satisfying and meaningful life as a healer. I know."

Dr. Frederick Kimball, MD. Everett, WA. U.S.A.

"Reflections: I am sure the workshop will continue to affect me in the coming weeks, like a coil unfolding. You lay groundwork so carefully, I would not hesitate to send any of my clients to your training. Each of you model what self acceptance is. You really gave me food for thought about "self esteem" and "intention," terms bandied about so much among therapy groupies. Your training is very practical and yet jumps to the esoteric so easily. Because of your insistence upon simple function, subjects like kundalini become safe and possible. Shelley and Denie, I hear the sound in your voices that mends my heart. Thank you."

Dr. Roger Ehlert, PhD. Coeur d'Alene, Idaho. U.S.A.

Testimonials for "Journey to Truth"

"Journey to Truth is one man's inspiring and soul bearing story of his journey to truth and healing. More importantly, it is an introduction to the work of Denie Hiestand. As a medical doctor and student of Denie's International Academy of Vibrational Medical Science, the Christ force healing energy Denie teaches us to open our hearts to, is truly one of the most extraordinary, powerful, profound experiences of my entire life."

Dr. Linda C. Hole, MD. Spokane, WA. U.S.A.

"Somewhere in our hearts we each know that something more exists - some path that, once found, will explain, will exhilarate and will heal. Denie's journey takes you there. Journey to Truth irrevocably alters your life. It all becomes clear. A new kind of good is how you'll feel."

Linda Buzzalini, Durango, CO. U.S.A.

"Journey to Truth is an adventure story. It is also a story of spiritual transformation, an exciting account of innumerable precisely sequenced "coincidences" in the life of a charismatic New Zealand farmer, and the journey of a man who simply could not avoid his destiny as a remarkable healer and teacher."

Margaret Pinyan, Sedona, AZ. U.S.A.

"In the words of Francis Bacon... "Some books are to be read in full and digested slowly." This is one whose full import does not hit one until long after they have closed the last pages. I needed to read this book twice with a month in between in order to realize that Journey to Truth *is about being truly human in a way that everyone's being longs to be."*

Cora Goodman, Kamloops, B.C. Canada.

"Yahoo! Finally a new book that will take people beyond the Celestine Prophesy - and it's true! Totally inspirational!"

Rio Zeviar, Fall City, WA. U.S.A.

"The book every woman wants every man to read!"

Jan Turner, Oliver, B.C. Canada.

"Journey to Truth does for men what Shirley McLaine's book Out on a Limb *did for women. Finally we all have permission to feel."*

Denise Lovell, Ashburton. New Zealand.

"Journey to Truth - *a book that gives one hope for humanity*".
Joey Landon, Kelowna, B.C. Canada.

"This year I gave myself the best Christmas present ever! I opened Journey to Truth *at 8:00am on Christmas morning, thinking I would read a little of it before cooking Christmas dinner, and I couldn't put it down until I had finished it completely, at 7:00pm that night!"*
Adell Woodruff, Bellevue, WA. U.S.A.

"I haven't read a book for 20 years and I picked up Journey to Truth *and couldn't put it down!"*
Dennis Manning, Salmon Arm, B.C. Canada.

"I've read a zillion books and it takes a lot to impress me. Journey to Truth *is the first book I have read cover to cover, in one sitting, for eight years - it was that good!"*
Jenni Huskey, Durango, CO. U.S.A.

"I am 84 years old and in all my years of living Journey to Truth *is the book that has had the biggest impact on me. Every man should make this book compulsory reading. It contains all the messages we need for living. I have bought many copies of this book and given them to all my friends as Christmas presents to ensure that they read it."*
Les Grieves, Salmon Arm, B.C. Canada.

"You could call me the world's biggest skeptic. However, Journey to Truth *got to me and changed my perceptions completely."*
Radio John, Invercargill. New Zealand.

"In reality it is a question of consciousness, a slow process to which Denie and Shelley provide stimulus with public presentations, but mostly with lively and invigorating courses and workshops. They provide food for the body, mind and soul."
Peter Baumann, PhD. Basel. Switzerland.

"Every Health Care Professional should do this course! I have just completed my Chinese Medicine Degree and this course was the icing on the cake."
Louis Fassbind, CM. Rigi-Staffel. Switzerland.

"Finally spirituality and science in one. I honor Denie for his integrity, mastery and courage to walk that fine line of the leading edge. I am grateful to have found my connection with my heart. I can now make a real difference. Thank you Denie and Shelley for the blessing you have been to me. Your book, Journey to Truth *really propelled me to do the (IAVMS) courses and the incredible electrical private work on me are the reasons I now can say I came back to life and have simple, grounded tools for raising my vibration and becoming more of who I am. I feel peace, joy, more present and in my essence...."*
Afra Rigollet, Victoria, B.C. Canada.

"I have been a teacher of Transcendental Meditation for 25 years, a Reiki Master, Nutritional Consultant and Massage Therapist. I have also experienced over 700 of a variety of "healing" sessions. I unquestionably rate the Academy's first and second levels as the two most valuable things to be done by any person seeking expanded self awareness and greater happiness in daily life. Rather than addressing individual problems (darkness) and trying to figure out how to get rid of the darkness, Denie and Shelley show you how to simply turn on the light."
Allen Glonek, Fairfield, Iowa. U.S.A.

"In twenty-five years of searching, including trips to India, this course has made it possible for me to move further, faster and safer along my path than anything I have previously experienced. The International Academy of Vibrational Medical Science course as taught/channelled by Denie Hiestand is one, if not the most powerful tool that any of us can avail ourselves with to propel us towards enlightenment."
Elizabeth Taylor, Caenarfon. Wales.

"I have done several seminars including the Barbara Brennan School of Healing and this course (IAVMS) has been the most beneficial to me to date. I found the size of the group provided me with a much safer feeling which helped me to show up more. I was also very impressed with the amount of love and honor which I felt. I would highly recommend this course to anyone who has any interest what so ever - you will not be disappointed."
Jennifer Shen Lee, Seattle. U.S.A.

"I feel Oprah should devote an entire show to Denie and Shelley Hiestand's program "Energy Awareness." Denie was an electrical engineer, then a dairy farmer, and now a most gifted healer. During his life he has kept his eyes and heart wide open to every experience and has combined his knowledge of science (electricity, nutrition) to understand the powerful laws of the universe. His head fought this calling for years but his heart finally won out.

Shelley is a dancer with an intuitive and profound understanding of global music and its affect on our energy centers or chakras and cells. She embodies, and shows us how to embody, increased vibrational frequencies so that we may evolve faster and enjoy life more fully and completely.

Combined, Denie and Shelley have the most profound program which combines Denie's knowledge of the electrical nature of the universe (science) with its physical and spiritual implications for us. All of this knowledge and wisdom comes at a time when the planets are aligning, the electrical forces in our universe are polarizing and we have the best opportunity to evolve faster and higher than ever before.

Before attending this course, I knew much of this information. Hearing it again from Denie reconfirmed everything I had learned. But that was all in my head. The power of this course is that it connects the head with the spirit and with the body. Shelley's dance and movement brings the natural laws of the universe into our bodies and changes us forever. It is the complete package.

During the course, I was able to FEEL the wisdom and knowledge of the universe and become one with it. Since taking the course, my own work has been far more powerful, I find people on the street are drawn to me with twinkling eyes, and at 45 I have more energy and stamina than my teenage children! I approach life with confidence and assurance. Problems become insignificant. Joy is everywhere.

I was a tough sell. I am skeptical of gurus and followers. I am a well educated educator and business person who reads voraciously. I do not waste my time on things that do not matter."

Leslie Robinson, Victoria, B.C. Canada.

"I am so excited about all the wonderful changes that are being maintained by me since school. It is impossible to describe what a difference it is to be able to stay in my heart energy and not let the old junk clog up my life. THANK YOU. THANK YOU. THANK YOU."

Annie Wakelin, Alberta. Canada.

"My true being is expressing love, happiness and peace the entire day. It's like coming out of the darkness, into the light. It is like a fairy tale. I am a successful business woman standing with both feet in my life...very realistic. The difference is that now my work and my business are like play ... it is so beautiful. If people would know what it means to integrate spirituality and physicality, then life would be a dream. When we gain self confidence then love, peace and success is automatically following. This workshop showed me that we have powers but we just don't know how to tap into them. Denie shows us the way."

Maria Schuster, Vancouver Island, B.C. Canada.

"Something has shifted in me. I'm 24 years old and I've been living in fear of always doing the right thing - it's time for me to listen to my heart and do my thing."

Deborah Bear, Nelson, B.C. Canada.

"WOW! Can't hardly believe it - my energy is increasing. I may have to abandon my morning coffee!"

Judy Kubrak, Sidney, B.C. Canada.

"Denie got to me and I opened up and felt energy from plants, trees, rocks and people, saw their auras and much more. I arrived home a new, loving person, resonating on a higher frequency, glowing with total awareness to everything. He has taught me to be a Master of my Being."

Ester Lucas, Invercargill. New Zealand.

"July 13th will always stand out as the most incredible experience I have ever had. There are no words to express the feeling. Thank you Denie and Shelley. When people ask about the group I have a hard time explaining because it was so special and I need to hold it close."

Frances Konrad, Mid-way, B.C. Canada.

"During my life I have always been searching for what I believed to be the path and have tried many different disciplines. I have done what many would describe as dangerous hobbies but through Denie and his school I believe I have found MY path. Part of his school can be more terrifying than anything I have done before but also more satisfying, enlightening, and a beautiful cornucopia of esoteric teachings, and he presents them with an understanding and Mastery. Attending these schools has reaffirmed a belief that life isn't meant to be hard, it's supposed to be fun and it surely can be."

Dale Scott, Fox Glacier. New Zealand.

"I feel as though, at some point between my late teens and early twenties I started to smother the sparks of light that were my life and joy, and without the sparks I got colder and colder until there was ice inside. The sparks are starting to glow now, and the ice is melting. I feel parts glowing with joy now that I had completely forgotten about and there are no words to describe this incredible feeling of coming alive again."

Michelle Parry, Penticton, B.C. Canada.

"I'm just so thrilled with the freedom and confidence boost I am experiencing - I love seeing the effects of it on the people around me.... just an incredibly moving, profound and magical week!"

Jan Robinson, Vernon, B.C. Canada.

"The powerful vibrational energy work of Denie and Shelley Hiestand boosted my positive inner strength high enough to finally give me the courage to overcome a long-standing emotional addiction. I am forever thankful."

Joan Dale, Victoria, B.C. Canada.

"I now have an unlimited amount of energy. My food intake has been cut in half. I am positive and happy. The way Denie and Shelley planned and executed the courses is remarkable. I started to understand on the last day why they did it this way. I have high regards for both of them and this has to be taught to mankind. It is our God given right, as Denie would say, and I would not agree more. The sooner mankind wakes up the better for planet earth! All my love to Denie and Shelley, their work is remarkable."

Tjitske Schuurmans, Victoria, B.C. Canada.

"Whoo! Quite some week. It has been fabulous to take some more time with myself and be inside and see the change within. The peace I've gained is incredible. Shelley, you are an amazing person. I enjoyed your love, laughter and light. Denie, you are the blessing I've been waiting for. My legs feel great and the cells are having a ball."

Anne Pullar, Invercargill. New Zealand.

"What a wild ride over here I'm having!! I realized it's important for me to make changes and so I began the day after I arrived home. Shelley I think of you sometimes as I'm skipping through the woods singing GOD I AM, I AM FREE, FREE TO BE TOTALLY ME! And Denie the meditations are excellent! My husband was so blown away with the changes in me after the IAVMS school he now wants to do it himself. Physically I feel more and more alive, I have reached a point now where I have had no pains whatsoever, and it definitely did not start like that. Very cool. I am hearing, seeing, and feeling everything in a very new way. I am !! I am picking up messages every day which is incredibly helpful to me, and I love the answers and awareness I am receiving. Last night I felt like I stepped off a cliff, and instead of going into fear I thought, well I will either fly or there will be something solid to stand on, faith told me I would fly. I had an amazing day all day, I felt love whizzing out of every cell of my body. I felt like a human energy ball. I also put an ad in the paper for anyone with depression and anxiety to give me a call, I am talking to them about you. So many changes over here like black to white. I have the vision of learning much more of vibrational medicine from you. I am alive and vibrating.

Lorraine King, Victoria, B.C. Canada.

"Denie Hiestand, thank you, I have really enjoyed being in your company, you are a great crazy guy. I also want to say to you: thank you for the greatest gift you could give and have given me, which is your belief in me as a beautiful being. You have told me often and so forcefully that I have finally been able to make a start in believing it myself. Thank you."

Marian de Ruyter, Christchurch. New Zealand.

"No more searching! I have found within me the compass needed to navigate through life with a knowing and awareness of my destination."

Elie St. Laurent, Victoria, B.C., Canada.

"An incredible way to wake up to all that you are! I now see things I had never yet seen, I hear things I had never listened for. I am going beyond every parameter and breaking free of all limitations I have put on myself. I have made a pact with myself that every time I see a heart I will tell myself how much I love "me." Since then the most incredible thing has happened... I see hearts everywhere! Amazing what happens when you raise your vibration! I am fine tuning the instrument that I am so that I may sing "My song" to the world. To Denie and Shelley - two incredible beings, two special friends, my heart thanks you, my soul thanks you. I share with you a quote from the I CHING Harmony Symbol, "Things that accord in tone vibrate together. Things that have affinity in their innermost natures seek one another." I encourage all of you to honor yourselves, to speak your truth and to follow your hearts."

Elaine St. Laurent, Victoria, B.C., Canada.

"The first module was outrageous. I loved the nature walk and seeing the lively energy. Since I have done this module I express myself better and love myself more. Denie and Shelley are fantastic people. I hope more kids my age take the course."

Janelle St. Laurent (age 12), Victoria, B.C., Canada.

"I was crushed when I was 18 in an industrial accident, the doctors told me there was nothing wrong with me, since then I suffered back problems for the next 30 years. Through the natural health industry I found people who put my bone structure back into place but I still had a sciatic nerve knot (about the size of 4 fingers). Because this was not corrected it progressively got worse over the years and then finally shut off the electrical flow to my leg. At that point in time the knee cap starting rotating, leg turned to rubber - massive, massive pain! I couldn't sit for 18 days - had to kneel, lay or stand. Then thanks to Harold Stevens, I was introduced to Denie Hiestand, who worked on my electrical circuitry and for the first time in 18 days I could sit down. Three more treatments thereafter and it was mostly gone. Life is hell without a leg to stand on! This inspired me to attend the seminars taught by the Academy founded by Denie and his partner Shelley which I have thoroughly enjoyed and benefited from."

Frank Reglin, Kelowna, B.C., Canada

Electrical Nutrition

Denie & Shelley Hiestand
ISBN # 0-9684928-1-9, US$14.95

POWERFUL, DYNAMIC AND CONTROVERSIAL

"The only way we can understand ourselves, our world and our universe, is to understand it from an electrical/energy perspective. The only way we can ever hope to understand this body is from an electrical/energy perspective. The only way we can ever alleviate disease is from an electrical/energy perspective. The only way to formulate our supplements and medicine is from an electrical/energy perspective. That is all there is!"

- Electrical Nutrition is a self-help health guide, written in logical, easy-to-understand language.
- Totally new electrical/energy perspective on health, nutrition and well-being. Food for the body, mind and soul.
- Redefines the various causes of disease, and how life's issues, the birthing process, emotions, pharmceutical drugs, immunizations, antibiotics, and food all affect the body's electrical system. The authors address such things as how getting older does not have to be associated with feeling old; moving into mid-life does not necessarily mean a loss of libido; weight gain is not inevitable; how to increase energy levels, stop degeneration and live a full, healthy, abundant life.
- Backed with profound logic, medical references, support from doctors and world class researchers.
- A different level of thinking creates a different level of consciousness. Electrical Nutrition is a different level of thinking.

Testimonials
for Electrical Nutrition.

"Dietetics describes in the old Greek world, 'the wholeness or the naturally correct behaviour of humans.' Electrical Nutrition, *explains itself in the same way. A manual in life philosophy, it also teaches concepts in dietary intake. Nutrition, though decisive, is only a part of it. In reality, it is a question of consciousness, a slow process to which in this work, Denie and Shelley Hiestand provide a much needed, powerful, but logically presented stimulus. It is* Electrical Nutrition *for the body, mind and soul."*

Peter Baumann, PhD. Basel. Switzerland.
Retired Head of Research, Novartis AG, Basel,. CH.

"In my nearly 20 years experience as an MD, Denie's work is truly remarkable. In my younger years, I studied honors physics with a Nobel laureate. Denie's work is likewise genius. Electrical Nutrition *represents a paradigm shift in how we view the human body and dis-ease and is a must for anyone interested in health and healing. I've had the honor and blessing to work clinically with Denie - with patients suffering from chronic pain, fibromyalgia, chronic fatigue, cancer, etc. Denie's clinical results are consistently astounding..."*

Dr Linda C. Hole, MD. Spokane, WA, U.S.A.
Graduate Princeton and Duke Universities

Business Bureau Wholistic Doctor of the Year

American Academy of Pain Management

International Academy of Homeopathy

World QiGong Congress

"Reading Denie and Shelley's book Electrical Nutrition *I am reminded of a favorite quote from Einstein: 'The problems that exist in the world today cannot be solved by the level of thinking that created them.' A different level of thinking produces ideas that make us uncomfortable, that push us out of our status quo stupor.* Electrical Nutrition *comes from a different level of thinking - it may make those of us trained in traditional western medicine very uncomfortable but I consider that a good thing. Like all of Denie and Shelley's work, this book is meant to shake us up, wake us up and get us moving down a different path - the path to an abundant, joy filled and absolutely radiant life.*

Mary Pellicer, MD. Yakima WA. U.S.A.

INTERNATIONAL ACADEMY OF
VIBRATIONAL MEDICAL SCIENCE

PMB 654
15600 NE 8th St., B1
Bellevue, WA 98008
U.S.A.
E-mail: info@vibrationalmedicine.com
Website: www.vibrationalmedicine.com

Registration of Interest Form

Dear Seeker,

It is with heartfelt joy that we invite you to apply to register your interest in the International Academy of Vibrational Medical Science.

Please fill out the form below, copy or cut and return it to **IAVMS Head Office,** PMB 654, 15600 NE 8th St., B1, Bellevue, WA 98008 U.S.A.

Upon receipt of your registration we will send you confirmation of your registration, and all details of the dates, times and place that the school will be in session.

All students must start this program with the first module, Energy Awareness.

We look forward to sharing with you on your path of Expanded Awareness.

May you be blessed to find all that you seek.

INTERNATIONAL ACADEMY OF
VIBRATIONAL MEDICAL SCIENCE

REGISTRATION OF INTEREST DETAILS

NAME: _____

ADDRESS: _____

CITY: _____

STATE: _____

COUNTRY: _____

PHONE: _____

E-MAIL: _____

FAX: _____

MALE/FEMALE: _____ DATE OF BIRTH: _____

SIGNED: _____

.

BOOK ORDERS:

Electrical Nutrition; ISBN # 0-968428-1-9

By Denie & Shelley Hiestand.   **US $14.95**

Journey to Truth; ISBN # 0-9684928-0-0

By Denie Hiestand.   **US $19.95**

All orders plus shipping, handling and taxes.

Credit Card Orders please phone;

1 800 207 2239

or

780 352 9997

if calling outside US or Canada.

All other orders please contact the Publisher
Or send order with check/money order to:

ShellDen Publishing,
PMB 654
15600 NE 8th Street, B1,
Bellevue WA 98008.
U.S.A.

Ph. 425 785 3468
E-mail: info@vibrationalmedicine.com
www.vibrationalmedicine.com

Bulk discounts apply and
Trade orders accepted